Heart Advice
from a Mahamudra Master

Gendun Rinpoche

Heart Advice
from a Mahamudra Master

NORBU EDITIONS

Copyright © 2010 Norbu Verlag

Norbu Editions
An imprint of
Norbu Verlag
Germany
www.norbu-verlag.de

ISBN: 978-3-940269-04-1

Translated from the German by Jochen Kleinschmidt
Book designed and typeset by Gerd Pickshaus

Printed in the United States of America on acid-free paper

To read the instructions of the Buddha
or to offer them to others is spiritual practice.
May the buddhas delight in this gift
and grant their blessings.

May the merit created by this action
join the stream of merit
of all the wholesome deeds performed by beings
in countless realms since beginningless time,
and may all this energy
be dedicated to the awakening of all beings.

Contents

Contents

Introduction

In this book we introduce you to the teachings of Lama Gendun Rinpoche,[1] a master from the *Kagyu* tradition of Tibetan Buddhism. His teachings show us the Buddhist path all the way to complete awakening, starting from the most basic instructions. Lama Gendun, as we simply called him, brought the teachings of the Buddha into our lives – lives that had been molded by Western culture.

He did not only instruct us through his words, he also showed us the path of awakening through his living example. Through his clear words we meet his clear and pure being; his simple teachings have the power to change our lives. When he was teaching, at times he began to speak in verse or even expressed the liberating truth in song. We have included six of his spontaneous songs in this book. In the Tibetan Buddhist tradition it is not uncommon for awakened masters to express the qualities of awakening in such songs or poems. As a spontaneous expression of their liberated mind they invite us to release our own mind into this state of openness.

Gendun Rinpoche's teachings provide us with deep and comprehensive guidance on the path to liberation. As simple as they may

---

1   We have used English phonetics for Tibetan and Sanskrit words in accordance with the scheme generally adopted by the Padmakara Translation Group.

appear, his instructions express a profound view of the Buddhist teachings[2] and can be regarded as representative of the approach of the Kagyu tradition of Tibetan Buddhism. They comprise advice on how to practice in all aspects of our lives – practice that will undoubtedly greatly challenge us but will also bear rich fruit. What that fruit may come to look like can be seen in the life of Gendun Rinpoche which serves as a particularly inspiring example of what a person can achieve.

If we wish to follow this path of awakening, nothing is more beneficial than to personally encounter a master who can explain the path in clear, easily understood words that lay it out step by step. The instructions in this book are the record of such a meeting of a Buddhist meditation master from Tibet with students from the West.

In the Buddhist tradition, the essence of the transmission is embodied in the spiritual master. So we should not only seek the teachings in texts but also engage in a living relationship with such a master. This form of oral transmission from teacher to student has continued without a break from the time of the Buddha, roughly 500 B. C., until today.

Gendun Rinpoche was an heir to this long tradition of transmission of knowledge and spiritual practice. He was one of the outstanding yogis of the generation of practitioners that still grew up in the old Tibet and was able to practice in the caves of the Himalayas. Before he was sent to the West by his teacher, he had meditated in seclusion in Tibet and India for thirty years and attained complete realization, according to statements made by other masters.[3] From 1975 until his death in 1997, he lived in France and taught in many countries.

---

2   His teachings correspond to the sutras and the commentaries of the *"Great Vehicle,"* the *Mahayana*, e. g., the Samadhiraja Sutra and the Uttaratantra Shastra.

3   These masters include the 16th Gyalwa Karmapa, Dudjom Rinpoche and Dilgo Khyentse Rinpoche.

Everything Gendun Rinpoche taught, he had deeply realized himself. As an exemplary monk, perfect *bodhisattva* and realized yogi, in these teachings he addresses people from all walks of life. He stresses the necessity for all practitioners to open their hearts and develop compassion and devotion as well as to practice deep relaxation and letting go of all self-centeredness.

This book, of course, can only reproduce his words and not his surprising, flashing humor, his easy laugh, his inimitably varied tone of voice, his apt facial expressions, the flowing, perfect gestures of his hands and the love that radiated from his eyes. But today, as when he was alive, his words can still help us access the essential core of the teaching of awakening. He only taught what is truly important for us on the path to awakening and enlightenment. His words come straight from the heart, from the rich treasure of his personal experience.

In the following chapters, Gendun Rinpoche explains the basics of Buddhist practice. He talks about how to find our direction or *refuge* and familiarizes us with the ways in which we can generate the mind of awakening *(bodhicitta)*. Only when such a basis has been established will his explanations of the nature of mind and of *Mahamudra* meditation fall on fertile soil. He goes into many of the difficulties that we may encounter on the path, describes the mechanisms of our *afflictive emotions* and details how we can free ourselves from them. Finally, he explains how we can use our life in order to prepare now for death, even though we imagine that it is still far away.

In this way, the reader is guided through a cycle of instructions that Gendun Rinpoche frequently gave to his Western students. We learn how we can develop compassion and devotion and practice deep meditation, following in the footsteps of the great Buddhist masters. We find out how to work with the energies of our mind and how to bring forth the wisdom that will change our lives from the ground up.

Only intensive meditation practice will make it possible for us to penetrate the veils of our ignorance and recognize the nature of mind and of all appearances. When we receive guidance in this through the oral instructions of an experienced master, we quickly and without great difficulties or detours arrive at a personal, direct understanding of the teachings of the Buddha.

This close relationship between teacher and student persists until the student has attained direct and unequivocal insight into the nature of mind. Realized students then become teachers and pass on the instructions. Through this mode of transmission, the original realization of enlightenment that the historical Buddha Shakyamuni experienced underneath the bodhi tree has remained alive until today.

When Gendun Rinpoche taught, his listeners often had the feeling that the historical Buddha was speaking through him. A written compilation of his teachings cannot reproduce more than the external form of this exceedingly vivid transmission. Its full content will disclose itself only through profound contemplation and meditation as well as through contact with a qualified teacher.

We will derive the maximum benefit from this book if we pause again and again to let what we have read affect us deeply and to relate it to our own thoughts and experiences. The true meaning of these instructions, however, will open up to us only through personal meditation practice. Gom, the Tibetan word for meditation, means to practice, to accustom ourselves to a practice or view, to engage with it time and again, until its true meaning is revealed to us.

The present text was compiled from public talks and personal interviews that Gendun Rinpoche gave between 1990 and 1997. One of our objectives was to retain the natural flow of his instructions. Sentences in italics summarize the content of surrounding passages or are characteristic expressions of Gendun Rinpoche. To clarify a subject by looking at it repeatedly from different angles was part of his teaching style, so the occasional repetitions are quite intentional.

The biographical chapter is quite full and detailed, to make this information widely available and prevent it from being lost over the years. Readers who don't already have a connection with Gendun Rinpoche or who are relatively new to Tibetan Buddhism may not find it all of interest. If so, please just skim over any technicalities. However, the basic story of Gendun Rinpoche's tireless practice in Tibet, his almost miraculous escape to India, his devotion to his teacher the *Karmapa*, and how he gave himself wholeheartedly to the task of helping his western students and establishing the *Dharma* in Europe – all this can inspire us in our lives regardless of whether we know much about Tibetan Buddhism or have ever heard of Gendun Rinpoche before.

For the benefit of readers without much experience of Tibetan Buddhism, we have provided a glossary of Dharma terms used in this book. Terms explained in the glossary are italicized when they first occur. You can find more detailed explanations of technical terms in "The Jewel Ornament of Liberation" by *Gampopa*, a text Gendun Rinpoche warmly recommended to all practitioners.

We express our heartfelt thanks to all those who have worked together to produce this "Heart Advice from a Mahamudra Master," in particular Gendun Rinpoche's personal translators.

Lama Sönam Lhündrup
for the Karmapa Translation Committee,
Auvergne, Summer 2010

Note about this translation

Gendun Rinpoche gave his teachings in Tibetan and they were orally translated and then transcribed into French. A set of published compilations of his teachings in French was put together and much enlarged with additional unpublished material and then translated into German by Lama Sönam Lhündrup, one of the senior students of Gendun Rinpoche who has been retreat guide for a number of cycles of the men's three-year retreat at Dhagpo Kundrol Ling.

The present book is a direct translation of this German compilation of Gendun Rinpoche's teachings, entitled "Herzensunterweisungen eines Mahamudra-Meisters" (new edition: Norbu Verlag, Obermoschel 2010). The translator of the English version wishes to thank Vessantara and Vijayamala for their numerous suggestions for improving the quality of this translation and Lama Sönam Lhündrup for checking it to ensure that it closely matches the original version.

Generating the Mind of Awakening

Fundamental Thoughts

When we wish to follow a spiritual path, we need to be clear about why we should walk this path and with what motivation, where it is meant to lead us, and by what means we will get there. The goal and fruition of the Buddhist path is complete liberation from all suffering and the realization of full enlightenment – a happiness that cannot be diminished or exhausted by anything.

Sooner or later, we will all be confronted with death – that is inevitable. However, when we have practiced the teachings of the Buddha during our lifetime, we will be able to face death without fear, with full confidence. We will have reached certainty about what to do and what to avoid at our death and about the mental attitude with which we should die, in order to use our death as an opportunity to liberate ourselves from the cycle of rebirth. The true purpose of our daily practice lies in this preparation for our own death.

It is very important that we follow the spiritual path with the correct motivation. We should not practice with the desire to achieve personal gain or improved conditions in this life. Such a motivation runs counter to the purpose of the Dharma and does not produce any lasting benefit. Similarly, the objective of seeking pleasant circumstances for our next life, for example to be reborn as a wealthy, respected person or to be reborn in the god realm with its illusory enjoyments, is short-sighted. These pleasant circumstances inevitably will come to an end one day.

We have to be clear about the fact that at death we will have to leave behind everything that we have valued and accumulated in this world, our possessions as well as our friends. None of this will accompany us. Because of this, all worldly pleasures, abilities and things can bring us temporary happiness at best, but they cannot be a long-term goal.

> *The path of the Buddha has but one goal: to reach the changeless happiness of perfect awakening and to help all beings attain that same happiness.*

Most people in the West live in a state of great affluence. We possess many material things and enjoy many freedoms. This wealth is indicative of the fact that in the past we have performed many good actions. But our actions were geared toward attaining short-term well-being, not toward attaining enlightenment. Therefore, we should now turn to the other aspect of positive action that consists of the accumulation of merit, a force that eventually leads to full enlightenment. Without the development of this spiritual force, we will gain no lasting benefit from our efforts. In times of well-being and abundant freedom such as these, we should further develop the powers of loving-kindness, compassion and wisdom, so that in more difficult times we can overcome obstacles on the path to liberation.

We have found not only very favorable life circumstances but also access to the Buddha's teachings. This is not so much the result of our actions in this life but more because of our wholesome actions in former lives. It indicates that we have already undertaken some efforts to accumulate merit and to free ourselves from unwholesome habits. We have already developed some insight and wisdom and have repeatedly made wishes to stay in contact with the teachings of the Buddha.

Through the force of our previous actions, not only do we now possess material wealth but we also have access to the spiritual wealth of the path to liberation. We should use this opportunity and from now on devote our entire lives to the practice of Dharma, in order to realize enlightenment as quickly as possible. We should apply all our energy to deepen our understanding of the Dharma with each passing day.

Many people take their present life circumstances for granted and live with a sense that this human life is nothing special. But this impression is false. Our human birth does not come to us automatically. Rather, of all the forms of being in this universe, our human existence is the most difficult to attain.

In addition, there are not many countries in the world in which the Dharma is available, and in the places where the Dharma is being taught, only a few people are interested in it. Among these, only a few actually apply it in practice. Even more rare are those who truly practice it as it is taught. In fact, people who practice the Dharma authentically are as rare as stars in the daytime.

In this life, we have been given an exceedingly rare and precious opportunity. We have encountered the teachings, we have been able to find spiritual friends, and we have the time to practice the Dharma. We can study it, apply it, share our experiences with others and help one another. We have the amazing freedom to do what we really want to do! This extraordinary, precious situation that we enjoy because of our wholesome actions and the kindness of the *Three Jewels* (Buddha, Dharma and *Sangha*) can disappear in no time at all, as it depends on many conditions that may change quickly.

In view of the transitoriness of this precious situation, a feeling of urgency should arise in us, paired with a joyful enthusiasm, in which we say to ourselves: "What could be more important to do in my life than to deepen my understanding of the Dharma and to share it with all beings?" With this joyful aspiration, we vow to use our precious human existence untiringly in the practice of Dharma.

Many of us have encountered the Buddha's teachings and believe them to be true, but in spite of this we do not find the time to put them into practice. The reason for this lies in our clinging to worldly values, owing to our faulty assessment of what is important in life. We are easily seduced by the attractive tokens of affluence that surround us in so many forms and colors, and we do not want to go without them. At times, we even consider our ordinary, sorrowful lives in cyclic existence to be rather pleasant. Above all, we devote ourselves to the material side of our lives, and our labors are of a purely worldly kind.

Even if we have listened to many teachings, because of our nondharmic priorities we find neither the time nor the conditions to really dedicate ourselves to our practice, and eventually we may turn away from the Dharma entirely. Instead of following the example set by realized masters, we are fascinated by personalities who are successful in the world. We waste much time and energy in emulating them and striving to acquire as much wealth, influence and fame as they possess. These desires and longings become the source of great suffering, as our mind is continually stirred up by desire, the main cause of all unhappiness.

As long as we are not aware of impermanence, of the truth of becoming and ceasing, we remain trapped in these worldly desires, and thereby in cyclic existence, and we run after an endless variety of things without recognizing how impermanent and unreal they are. Everything changes from moment to moment, and even if we attain what we covet, we will not be able to hold on to it for long. Our lack of awareness of impermanence always leads to disappointment, as it prompts us to attempt in vain to protect things and situations from inevitable change.

In relating to their life experiences, people act much like children who are fascinated by and attempt to catch a rainbow.

A child will never be able to grab hold of the rainbow it desires, as by nature it is not capable of being seized. We are just as unlikely to be able to capture or hold on to the things of the world, which by their nature are impermanent and fleeting, regardless of how much time and energy we spend trying. Our wishful thinking runs contrary to the changing nature of all things. Unhappiness and suffering arise because of this gap between our wishes and reality.

Dreams are a good example of our clinging to supposed reality. Because we consider the situations experienced in a dream to be real, we react emotionally and allow ourselves to get carried away by them. Pleasant dream experiences make us happy; unpleasant ones we want to get rid of. In this way, we ensnare ourselves in attraction and aversion. We do not recognize that our dream is merely a mental projection, and we consider events to be real that do not possess any reality. This creates tension in our mind and brings about suffering.

In the same way, we also cling to situations in our waking state, because we consider them to be real and permanent, even though by their nature they are unreal and impermanent. Because of our effort to appropriate them and hold on to them, disappointment arises by necessity, and we waste our time needlessly.

As we become aware that everything changes continually and ultimately possesses no true reality, our clinging to things dissolves and the resulting suffering is abated.

We understand then, that all our efforts cannot bring us lasting happiness, as the things we strive after are not at all permanent – they are empty like the sky. We become aware of the fleeting character of existence, and our erroneous assumption that we can possess things permanently and protect them from perishing evaporates.

The old masters of the *Kadampa* lineage meditated on impermanence every day. When they drank their tea, they said to themselves: "It is my good fortune that I can drink my cup of tea today. Who knows whether this will be granted me tomorrow." And every night, before falling asleep, they put their teacup next to themselves and turned it over, in the awareness of their possible death that night. When they woke up next morning, they put their cup upright again and said to themselves: "How lucky I am that I can live another day! Others have died this night. I must make use of this opportunity and without fail act positively today." In this way, they practiced the awareness of impermanence, of the changing nature of all things.

The world in which we live is a projection of our karmic tendencies, the natural consequence of our past actions with body, speech and mind. When we do not understand this conditionality of our world, we live in an illusion of freedom. We live with the sense that we can create our life at will, as though we were in a position to secure happy circumstances for ourselves and to avoid suffering. However, this is not possible, and it will remain pure self-deception, as long as we do not consider the law of *karma*.

Our present life circumstances are the result of our past actions. All joys, all successes and all happy circumstances that we experience have their source in wholesome actions of body, speech and mind that we carried out in this or in previous lives. In the same way, all suffering, all difficulties and all unhappy circumstances are the result of past unwholesome deeds of body, speech and mind.

Within this interplay of forces that influence us in many ways, there remains some small scope for the power of free decision. We can use this space to make better choices in our present actions, words and thoughts and in this way prepare a freer, happier future for ourselves. Gradually, we can free ourselves from our conditioning and prepare the ground for a deeper understanding of reality.

The variety of karmic mixtures of happiness and suffering is as large as the number of beings. Since every individual action has its corresponding individual consequences, what any one of us experiences is a very personal affair. Because of that, different people have very unique, personal experiences, even if they live in very similar external circumstances. Everyone experiences a different world. Only we ourselves experience the consequences of our own actions and perceptions. And only we ourselves are able to influence what experiences we will have in the future.

To know what we have done in previous lives,
we only need to look at our present life. And
to know what our future will look like, we
only need to look at our present actions.

As a natural consequence of our actions, their fruits will ripen without fail, and we cannot prevent this process. Because of that, despite all our efforts, we will never succeed if we attempt to control our present experiences through our present actions. Even though we may wish with all our might to escape from our present problems, we never manage to influence our present situation according to our wishes. This demonstrates that additional forces are at play. These forces are the result of our previous actions whose consequences we cannot escape.

Therefore, instead of exhausting ourselves in trying to change circumstances that can no longer be altered, we should concern ourselves with the future and focus on the fact that it is the qualities of our present actions what determines our future. If we act in a wholesome way now, we plant seeds of happiness that will ripen into favorable, happy circumstances in the future. If we perform unwholesome or harmful actions, we can be sure to later find ourselves in unpleasant realms full of suffering.

For the person who has performed them, their actions
without fail will ripen into happiness or suffering.

The prerequisite for a freer and happier future is to learn from our mistakes of the past and avoid them in the future. Taking this into account, we should resolve under no circumstances to act negatively – be it at the cost of our life. We do not need to undertake anything special for this, such as escaping from ordinary life or mortifying our body – we simply have to control our mind. We change our conduct by changing our intention. Intentions are the motive power behind all actions. That is where we must start and pay attention.

When our self-cherishing and jealous attitude is replaced by an altruistic, benevolent attitude, then peace, happiness and well-being appear automatically. To "give up" *samsara,* which is equivalent to suffering, does not require undertaking any additional thing. It merely involves recognizing the causes of suffering and letting go of them. We must stop getting entangled in harmful emotions, as they are the source of all unwholesome actions and all suffering.

The point is not to change others or the
world but to master our own mind.

When we resolve to develop an altruistic motivation, our behavior of body and speech will change all by itself, as all actions have their origin in the mind. The mind is like a king giving commands that his servants have to carry out. When we have a pure motivation that is directed toward the welfare of others, all our actions will naturally reflect this aspiration, and the more we practice this intention, the more our mind will open. Ever more opportunities will arise for us to act in a wholesome fashion, and the path to awakening will naturally open up for us. Our pure intention will also act to quieten our emotions, because our own happiness is no longer of prime importance to us.

The difficulty in our present situation is our confused, passion-driven relation to the world in which we live. We are not fully aware of the pervasiveness of suffering in this conditioned world; we have adapted ourselves to our situation and may even feel that we are doing rather well. We project our hopes and desires onto the external world and focus our entire energy on attempts to realize these hopes. But we miss the fact that our conceptual base, our view of the world, is full of mistaken assumptions. As long as we do not see the world as it really is, we remain prisoners of our desires and plunge into pain and disappointment time and again, as our hopes are not fulfilled. To try to attain lasting happiness and well-being in a conditioned world that is by nature impermanent and filled with suffering is simply not going to work. Our problem is that this has not become clear to us, and we cling to our hopes and wishes and continue to circle in conditioned existence.

A wise person strives after enlightenment and takes pains to try to recognize and see through the patterns that determine their existence. That is what Buddha Shakyamuni did. He clearly saw that cyclic existence is characterized by endless suffering, and that it contains no possibility of achieving lasting happiness. His exceedingly clear vision of things prompted him to break loose from the fascination that binds ordinary beings to the world and to search for a way that puts an end to all suffering and leads us out of cyclic existence. He did find that way, and by practicing it he attained complete liberation.

In contrast to the Buddha, we ordinary beings have not as yet recognized the shortcomings of cyclic existence and still strive after worldly happiness, after a little more joy and well-being in ordinary life. Of course, everyone strives after happiness, and that is nothing to find fault with. But we should recognize that worldly happiness is superficial and ephemeral and that it carries within itself the seeds of suffering, principally because of our self-centeredness, with its patterns of hope and fear. Cyclic existence is inherently characterized by change and suffering – and wherever there is self-centeredness and attachment to what is transient, there is suffering as well. To recognize this and to look for a reliable refuge is the very first step on the path to liberation from conditioned existence, the dissolution of our attachments.

If we continue to run after transitory joys and allow them to deceive us about the sorrowful nature of existence, then we will forever circle in samsara.

Commonly, we are quite obstinate in denying this truth that was expressed by the Buddha. But, uncomfortable though it may be, it is true: as long as our mind clings to worldly interests, it is not possible to realize the nature of mind and find freedom. We would like to evade this insight into the deceptive nature of our worldly preoccupations: we shirk the confrontation with impermanence and death, evade the present moment and live in the hope of a better future. Meanwhile, with every passing day, our time runs out. With every breath we take, we get closer to death.

Intellectually we may know all this, but our continued attachment to worldly affairs shows that we are not truly conscious of the inexorable impermanence of our existence. We ignore the fact that death can surprise us at any time, and we prefer to believe that we still have enough time for this and that. We continually project our hopes into tomorrow and the day after tomorrow and dream of a better life. We believe that things will look up for us. But we are deceiving ourselves – if we do not do something decisive now, then the future will not be any different.

At death we have to leave everything behind: our possessions, our reputation, everything that was important to us and for which we have labored arduously. Then, only the noble teachings will be of any help to us. We will be in need of the protection of an authentic refuge and will require a lot of positive spiritual power in order to pass through the process of dying in a bearable manner. Because of that, the practice of Dharma is the only truly meaningful thing to do in this life. At the moment of death, the futility of worldly activities becomes abundantly clear. The only thing that will help us then is the force of our wholesome deeds and the degree to which we have truly developed *faith*[4] and have learned to *go for refuge* from the depths of our heart. At the moment of death it will be too late to start trying to practice these things.

As long as we are not aware of impermanence, our mind is incessantly stirred up by thoughts that center around worldly affairs – how to become happy, how to avoid pain – all of which spring from our clinging to the supposed permanence of this life. We should look carefully at this and realize how pointless our clinging to this world is. We should thoroughly examine our priorities: "Why are these things so important to me? Where do these desires come from? What benefit do I actually derive, if I realize them? Where will they lead me?" When we analyze our motives carefully, we will see that in the end pursuing worldly affairs brings nothing but suffering.

When through contemplating karma, impermanence and death we begin to understand our actual situation, a sense of urgency arises in us.

---

4   See the Glossary for the usage of the term *faith* in this book.

Our fear of being handed over to death without preparation and possibly being reborn in a realm full of suffering, together with our compassion for all beings, becomes a powerful incentive for changing our lives and resolving to only engage in wholesome actions from now on. We ask ourselves what we can do to encounter conditions for the practice of Dharma in the future that are as favorable as our conditions at present and how we can purify our karma so that it becomes possible for us to attain deep insight. Having only the Dharma in mind, our mind then becomes calm and clear. No longer is it churned up by worldly affairs, and meditating becomes easy.

When we put the teachings of the Buddha into practice, we gradually find our way out of the cycle of suffering. We cease to perform harmful actions that could become the cause of further suffering, and we learn to engage only in wholesome actions that will eventually ripen into favorable circumstances. In the Dharma we must not restrict ourselves to a mere intellectual understanding. Serious practice is indispensable. To make progress, we must begin to actually practice.

The great practitioners of the past have realized enlightenment quickly because they turned away completely from worldly concerns. The practice of Dharma was the sole important thing in their lives, and they were completely convinced of the futility of worldly concerns. Because of that, some of them realized buddhahood within a single lifetime. They never practiced with the goal of merely attaining calm and peaceful states of mind and feeling better in this life. They were concerned with something much more fundamental: final liberation from cyclic existence. After thorough reflection on the true nature of all experiences in this conditioned world, they became deeply convinced that conditioned existence is inevitably pervaded with suffering, and so they freed themselves from striving after worldly happiness, once and for all. What is beyond this life became more important to them than the concerns of this life. Recognizing the conditioned nature and impermanence of worldly happiness, they made the irrevocable decision to concentrate on what lies beyond all change: the immutable nature of mind, the source of true happiness.

For example, when they saw a bone, they would contemplate as follows: "This bone comes from an impermanent body, with which a being identified that was born into this life out of ignorance and clinging. And anyone who remains ignorant will again grasp at a body following their death, be reborn and die again, and in this way return to the cycle of suffering, again and again."

Reflecting deeply in this way, they were able to free themselves from attachment and desire and through meditation bring about a genuine change in themselves. They did not merely sit there, trying to have peace and a good time, but they truly saw that they were caught in the trap of samsara, in ignorance and constant attachment, and they developed a deep yearning for enlightenment. Because they understood the nature of suffering, they developed inner detachment, a deep renunciation, and so attained liberation from samsara.

We, however, are less thorough, and our approach to the Dharma often reveals great ignorance. We pounce upon the highest teachings on the nature of mind, Mahamudra, and only some time later realize that we should practice the preliminary exercises first. In this regard, we are a bit like children who want to have a beautiful object the moment they see it.

If we truly wish to realize Mahamudra, first of all we must become aware of the rare opportunity that presents itself to us right now: we were born as human beings, we have encountered the Dharma, and we possess all the necessary preconditions for attaining enlightenment. We should not waste this opportunity but realize that any further lingering in cyclic existence is a pure waste of time.

All forms of existence in samsara have countless disadvantages and are pervaded with suffering. We should constantly be conscious of impermanence and death. That will spur us on and generate in us a glimmer of understanding of the urgency of serious practice. In addition, we must make the inevitable, direct connection between actions and their consequences clear to ourselves time and again and focus our attention solely on performing wholesome and useful actions. Through these kinds of contemplations we acquire a basic understanding that is a prerequisite for all subsequent steps on the path to awakening. Were we to skip these steps on the path and concern ourselves solely with the destination itself, we would inevitably fall on our path to the summit.

In order to ensure stability on our path, it is essential that we begin with the foundations and then climb one step after another.

Some practitioners are so much attached to the external forms and methods of the Dharma that they hardly pay attention to its essence, its heart. They rashly plunge into the most varied practices and stop seeing anything else. In their enthusiasm for the outer "packaging" of the Dharma, they miss the true meaning of what is being taught: the significance of going for refuge and reflecting on impermanence and karma, the necessity of developing the correct view, and the deeper meaning of our relation to our teacher. They remain on the surface and entertain themselves with their fascinating spiritual project. By picking from the teachings only what appeals to them and promises to be pleasant, they remain trapped in their samsaric patterns. Their practice will bear no fruit because it does not go to any depth. Everything remains the same with them on the inside; only the external trappings have changed.

We should, therefore, be careful not to get carried away by fascination for the methods of Dharma practice but instead focus on the heart of the teachings, the actual spirit of the Dharma. We must also not get stuck in mere intellectual knowledge. The Dharma must penetrate into our entire being and lead to a profound change in our inner attitude and outlook. The correct application of its methods, in daily meditation and in formal practice, will follow from this more or less automatically.

Going for Refuge and Generating the Mind of Awakening

From a spiritual point of view, our current situation is a turning point, at which we have the options of either going upward or downward. We can decide which direction our life will take at this time. But there are not thousands of possibilities. Basically we have the choice between a path that dissolves all attachments and one on which we continue to follow our self-centered interests. Even though our karmically (see *karma*) conditioned tendencies put certain constraints on us, as human beings we have the freedom to decide whether we wish to turn toward awakening or remain in confusion and sorrow. If we choose the path of awakening, we should make this a conscious decision and stick to it. This is a personal decision that no one else can make for us. Once we have made a clear decision, we will easily be able to overcome all difficulties and make progress.

So that our motivation becomes stronger and our decision irrevocable, we should familiarize ourselves with the teachings. We should understand what awakening into the dimension beyond sorrow means and what benefit arises from a realization like this for ourselves and for others. Understanding this gives a clear direction to our mind and fills us with faith and devotion. Then the path to awakening becomes easy.

Problems will arise for us only if we have not made a definite commitment. Although we may understand that we are at an important turning point and tentatively walk a few steps in the direction of the Dharma, after a while we may say to ourselves: "Back there it wasn't all that bad," and return to worldly pursuits, only to observe a little later: "This is rather painful, Dharma is better after all." If we are torn in this way between worldly concerns and the path of awakening, difficulties will invariably arise. However, as soon as we truly begin to appreciate the value and qualities of awakening and completely orient our mind toward it, we begin to make headway in a completely natural way.

> *To find our way to awakening from a condition of confusion, we not only need to make a clear decision, we also need a spiritual teacher, as well as methods and companions on the path.*

We meet these conditions by engaging in what is called "going for refuge." Going for refuge is an act of inner orientation toward the essence of the path. Every practice of Dharma begins with it. We go for refuge in enlightenment as well as the Dharma and the community of guides that show us the path to liberation. We ask them for blessings, help and protection and at the same time wish that all other beings may receive the same help. Inwardly, we go for refuge for them as well as together with them. With our going for refuge, our altruistic motivation becomes the heart of our practice. But it is not sufficient merely to recite the words of the ritual; our purpose is to generate a deep wish for the liberation and buddhahood of all beings.

Going for refuge requires a longing trust in the Three Jewels: in the Buddha as our aim, i. e., in the extraordinary qualities of awakening, in the teachings of the Dharma as our path, and in the Sangha, the community of all who help and guide us in this endeavor.

On the relative plane, going for refuge protects us from problems that we may encounter here and now in this world. On a higher plane, going for refuge makes it possible for us to free ourselves entirely from conditioned existence through the practice of Dharma. Entering the refuge helps us, bit by bit, to acquire real freedom and put it at the service of others.

A sincere, altruistic motivation of wanting to make swift progress ourselves so that we are better able to help others is a basic prerequisite for entering the path to awakening and ultimately realizing buddhahood. From the depths of our heart we develop the wish to liberate all beings from their suffering, and we put this aspiration into action by studying the Dharma, reflecting on it and practicing it with our body, speech and mind. This is what gives our life its true meaning: to practice the Dharma in order to liberate all beings from their suffering. With this intention alone should we walk our spiritual path.

If we truly wish to help all beings, we must attain enlightenment. Only then are we in a position to lead others in this direction. Fully awakened beings have realized the complete freedom of a buddha – they have dissolved all *obscurations* and developed all enlightened qualities. Buddhas are free of suffering because they do not perceive reality in a dualistic way and are not mired in emotional reaction patterns. That is what is meant by "being free of all obscurations." When all obscurations have been dissolved completely the qualities of buddhahood become apparent.

These qualities are the dynamic expression of awakened awareness, and they spontaneously accomplish the benefit of all beings and manifest in multifarious forms in order to assist them. Therefore, awakening provides the greatest benefit for ourselves, since we gain complete freedom, and at the same time it provides the greatest benefit for all other beings, since awakened awareness spontaneously manifests all the qualities of compassionate action.

In order to attain enlightenment, we need a path that leads us there. This path was shown to us by the Buddha. Motivated by compassion, he taught us a variety of methods for attaining this highest aim, starting from our present situation. Later, his methods and teachings were put down in writing and compiled into collections of texts that contain all the instructions of the Buddha as well as commentaries by later masters. These texts are the foundation of the written transmission which is accompanied and authenticated by an oral transmission.

In this lineage of transmission originating with the Buddha, his methods and instructions are transmitted from the teacher to his students. The students contemplate them and apply them in meditation until they attain the same realization as their master. In this way, not only the words but also the true meaning of the teachings have been kept alive until now, and that is what we encounter today as the Dharma.

The transmission of the Dharma is implemented by the Sangha, the community of all who have received the teachings, understood them and practiced them. These committed practitioners are either master, teacher or friends on the spiritual path, depending on the degree of their realization of the teachings, and in these capacities they are extremely valuable and of great help to us.

Our goal is the realization of the Buddha, our instructions and methods for the path are the Dharma, and collectively our helpers comprise the community of spiritual friends, the Sangha, who keep the teachings alive and continue to transmit them. These three factors are of vital importance for our attaining the goal of awakening. Our ultimate aim is buddhahood, and one might think that the Buddha would be sufficient as a refuge, but Dharma and Sangha are also indispensable for our getting there. Because of that, we go for refuge in all three of these Three Jewels. They are as precious as wish-fulfilling gems and are worthy of receiving our gratitude and deep veneration.

All buddhas and bodhisattvas[5] of the past have followed this path and have taken refuge in the Three Jewels. They have relied on the Sangha and practiced the Dharma and eventually attained realization. None of them have found the path by themselves, without being shown the goal and the methods, even if this happened in former lives. All beings need methods as well as guides and companions on the path, in order to extricate themselves from confusion and be able to realize the wisdom of complete awakening. Therefore, going for refuge in the Three Jewels is indispensable. This is a universal spiritual law.

In going for refuge, we direct the energy of our body, speech and mind toward the practice of Dharma, with the firm intention of carrying out wholesome actions that benefit not only ourselves but all beings in the universe.

> *We go for refuge not only for our own benefit but also in order to gain the ability, as quickly as possible, to lead all beings away from suffering.*

Going for refuge is both a mental attitude of trusting openness toward the goal of awakening and a daily practice through which we find our way into this openness again and again. We imagine that all sentient beings in the universe, human as well as nonhuman, are congregated around us and that we are leading them in going for refuge collectively. Assembled before us in space are all the buddhas and bodhisattvas, together with all the other sources of refuge. We focus all our attention upon them and develop complete confidence in their ability to liberate us from suffering in cyclic existence and protect us from the fear that is caused by this suffering.

---

5 *Bodhisattva* here refers to Dharma practitioners who have vowed to attain buddhahood for the benefit of all beings and who have already attained a stable recognition of the nature of mind.

With this conviction, and accompanied by all beings in the universe, we recite the refuge prayer. We imagine that it fills all of space with its vibration, and that in response to our trust light radiates from the sources of refuge. This light fills us with the blessings of the body, speech and mind of all the buddhas and evokes in us deep devotion toward them. Suffused with devotion and trust, we then commence doing our various practices, which further develops our understanding and appreciation of the refuge.

Buddha, Dharma and Sangha, the Three Jewels, are expressions of enlightenment and embody it at different levels. When we become aware of their qualities and begin to see how precious and indispensable their help is to us, we abandon our pride and our self-centered attitude. We realize that we cannot find the path to awakening on our own, and we entrust ourselves to their blessings.

When we open ourselves to the blessings of the Three Jewels and make the right effort in our practice, then the veils of dualistic views dissipate and the primordial qualities of our mind emerge without any obstruction.

In this opening up our mind becomes filled with peace and joy, and reveals itself in its natural aliveness and clarity. Confidence and insight replace emotional confusion. Undisturbed by our ego's willful exertions, we know exactly what we have to do. If, on the other hand, we pursue our Dharma practice like a personal battle and think: "I must practice. I will win. I must reach enlightenment," then attachment to our ego has taken center stage. We elevate "enlightenment" to an exalted concept and exert ourselves to get closer to this idea, using contrived conceptual crutches of all sorts. Caught in our desire to conform to an idealized image of holiness or enlightenment, we no longer want to listen to anything else.

If we then run into difficulties, we do not question ourselves but insist it is the fault of the lama or that the instructions are flawed. But if everything appears to go well, we become proud and think smugly: "I'm practicing well. I certainly am a genuine practitioner." In reality, we are not making any progress; we are so certain of our own idea of enlightenment that we close ourselves off from true awakening. We become increasingly close-minded, the blessings cannot reach us, and our practice misses its mark completely.

If, on the other hand, we develop an open and receptive attitude of mind and from the depths of our heart devote ourselves to the welfare of all beings, then awakening is not far away. We become more open in all situations; we experience them as a blessing and accept them with an attitude of equanimity. Good fortune or suffering cease to trigger pride or dejection - we experience them as gifts that enable us to dissolve karmically caused obscurations.

When we go for refuge, we relinquish pride and self-centeredness and turn toward something that is more powerful than us: the enlightenment represented by the Three Jewels. At the same time, we also turn toward the spiritual master, our lama, who unites these three aspects within him- or herself. Buddha, Dharma and Sangha are the foundations of the Buddhist path, and our trust in them is the heart of our practice. Without this trust, we would take personally all difficulties that appear in the form of suffering and obstacles and quickly lose our courage. But if we hold fast to our refuge with unshakable trust, then all difficulties transform into aids to our spiritual development.

I myself experienced the power of going for refuge very impressively during my escape from Tibet. Together with a group of companions, I was on my way through the mountains. At the end of a valley, with rock faces on both sides, we encountered Chinese troops who had set up their camp in the bottom of the valley and blocked our way. We were overcome with fear and worried that we would not be able to continue our flight to India. It seemed impossible to get past them, as they were numerous and well armed. We prayed to the Three Jewels and slowly continued on our way, with confidence that they would protect us effectively. We approached the soldiers ever more closely and walked past them in their immediate proximity – so closely in fact that we could hear them talk and smell the smoke of their cigarettes. But nothing happened; they did not appear to notice us.

From then on, we did not have the least amount of fear but great trust and a deep conviction that the Three Jewels truly were with us and provided us with certain protection. In spite of the fact that we were in the immediate proximity of the Chinese, we were able to traverse the mountains and get to India without further difficulties. We owe this to our trust in the refuge. The protection of the Three Jewels is ever present. Every one of us can receive it. It only depends on our trust in them.

To some these thoughts may be very familiar. Others may perhaps find them strange and believe that they are not able or not ready to practice the Dharma in this way. However, that would be a great error, as the minds of all beings already contain the qualities of awakening and they are able to bring them forth with a little bit of effort. Of course, in actual practice there are differences between individual practitioners.

> *We should approach our spiritual work in accordance with our own rhythm, in harmony with ourselves and our own abilities.*

Through our encounter with the Dharma, we develop a new vision of the world and of our task in it. We should integrate this new outlook gently, rather than plunging into it abruptly. We should not force ourselves to do good and make exaggerated demands on ourselves such as, "From now on, I will only live the Dharma," only to torture ourselves with self-criticism when we do not reach our goals.

We need a certain flexibility and tolerance toward ourselves. To be stern with ourselves in this undertaking is completely inappropriate. Rather, we should undertake a gradual transformation of our tendencies, gently and without coercion – without setting goals for ourselves that are way too high and whose non-attainment might lead us to berate ourselves. We must not fall into a state of self-torture in which we continually aim to accomplish the impossible. The Dharma does not demand the impossible, but only that we change our outlook.

The fact that we have become acquainted with the Dharma and perhaps also already met a master shows that a karmic seed is present in us, a potential that we should give room to grow. Most importantly, we should develop trust in the Three Jewels as the means and the goal of our path, because that is how our mind can change and manifest its qualities.

Those whose potential has already ripened greatly and who bring with them a great treasure of wholesome energy will be able to penetrate into the heart of the practice with ease and with unshakable confidence. Others will simply cherish the teachings and be glad that there is such a thing as the Dharma and that it makes spiritual work possible. This joy and the attraction that the Dharma exerts on them ignite in them a spiritual development that gradually guides them toward faith, toward a deeper sense of conviction and toward engaging in practice.

Thus, applying the Dharma is a very personal effort that begins where we stand. It starts with our developing trust in the Three Jewels, going for refuge in them and then arousing the mind of awakening, in intention and in actual application. The obscurations that cover our *buddha nature,* which is the potential for awakening that lies in every one of us, will then gradually dissolve.

Perhaps we cannot imagine that we could ever realize such a seemingly high goal as buddhahood and think it is very far away, perhaps even unattainable. However, when we know the path and the means, buddhahood is not far away. In fact, it is very near, as our mind *is* the awakening, it actually already is Buddha. It is only because of our ignorance, with all its veils, that we are blind to this reality.

Tilopa, one of the great realized beings of India, expressed this in the following way: "Because of ignorance, beings perceive a difference between themselves and enlightenment and search for it outside of themselves. This causes them much anguish and trouble. How unfortunate!"

In order to uncover enlightenment within ourselves, we must orient our entire lives toward the welfare of all beings. Only when we cease to strive after personal gain will we be able to bring our wandering in cyclic existence to an end. Because of that, right at the beginning of the path, we should generate the mind of awakening, the firm intention to direct all of our energy to the goal of freeing all beings from suffering. We should realize that wherever there is space, there are beings, and that all of them are subject to their own karma.

Their karma causes their minds to be disturbed by the various emotions, and this leads them to experience innumerable kinds of suffering in the various realms of existence. All of these beings, in a never-ending succession of lives, have been father and mother to one another innumerable times. And when they were our parents in previous lives, they gave the same attentiveness, tenderness and loving-kindness to us as did our own parents in this lifetime.

> *We can appreciate the kindness that we have already received from all beings in our former lives if we just reflect on the care that our own parents devoted to us.*

Some of us do not know how to properly appreciate the kindness of our parents and think that they brought us into the world purely out of self-interest and that in a sense they are responsible for our present suffering. But this lack of gratitude only indicates that we have not reflected sufficiently on the magnitude of their devotion. When we wandered about in the after-death state and desperately sought shelter in a new body, we found refuge in the womb of our mother. She nourished us during her pregnancy with her energy and gave us birth, often in great pain. We were naked when we were born and brought nothing with us. Without our parents, we would have been helplessly exposed to many dangers. We had no knowledge of this world and were completely dependent on the good will of those who surrounded us.

Only because of the care of our parents did we remain alive. Our mother looked after us, saved us from hunger and cold and washed us. She carried us on her body and clothed us. She tried to anticipate all our needs and comforted us when we cried. Our parents kept us away from fire, from deep water and from precipices. They taught us how to walk and talk and cared for us when we were sick. They looked after us with devotion and at times even took harmful actions upon themselves in order to help us. They bestowed their loving-kindness upon us and taught us how to live in the world so that we can take care of ourselves now. Due to their care, we have become reasonably healthy, self-sufficient adults who are able to communicate with and relate to others.

All beings have been our parents at one time or another in the past, and they are all like us in that they yearn for happiness and want to avoid suffering. But in spite of their great longing for happiness, they do not find it. Trapped in ignorance, they do not recognize that in order to experience happiness they must carry out wholesome actions and in order to avoid suffering they must abandon unwholesome actions. Because the karmic connections between actions and their consequences are not apparent to them, in their search for happiness they continue to perform harmful actions, which only leads to suffering. And because of that, they wander from one life to the next and experience endless and often intense suffering.

When we become aware of their suffering, we develop the outlook of a bodhisattva: the wish to liberate all beings from cyclic existence and consequently from their suffering. We resolve from now on to devote all of our energy to this end. This commitment must not be merely empty talk. Rather, it should be a motivation that changes us to our core, a motivation that completely dissolves our self-cherishing frame of mind. When we truly adopt it, we are no longer the "owners" of our lives. Our lives then no longer serve personal ends but are entirely dedicated to the liberation of all beings.

Once this "aspiring mind of awakening" has been generated unequivocally, as a pure aspiration, it then becomes a matter of actualizing it through wholesome deeds of our body, speech and mind. This implementation of our aspiration in concrete action is called the "engaged mind of awakening" – with full commitment we actually venture out now on the path to awakening. To compare it to a trip to India: our intention to travel there corresponds to the aspiration and the actual journey to the engagement. Once we have committed ourselves to walking this path, we should always cultivate the resolve of all bodhisattvas not to give up halfway but to continue to practice until buddhahood is realized.

This commitment requires courage and strength of mind – it is not appropriate to be timid with regard to possible difficulties and troubles. We should carry on with our practice with perseverance and joy, never doubting our capacity to realize enlightenment and lead all beings to this goal. When this pure motivation of bodhicitta, the mind of awakening, is present in us, then all our actions, including the most ordinary, become means to the attainment of enlightenment.

When we ask ourselves continually how we can help others, we no longer need to worry about our own welfare – it will be taken care of all by itself.

Generating the mind of awakening can be reinforced by formally taking the bodhisattva vow under the direction of a spiritual teacher. When we take this vow, we visualize all buddhas and bodhisattvas in the space in front of us and commit ourselves before them to practice the mind of awakening in all of its aspects. We pledge to follow their example in all situations and circumstances and to make a continual effort to act for the benefit of all beings, until all of them have attained enlightenment. We vow never to abandon this commitment and to do everything in our power to continually expand this attitude of mind. By engaging in a practice that aims to bring about the well-being of others, we will find that our recognition of the true nature of mind increases at the same time. When we fully realize it, we become a buddha who is able to manifest in the most varied forms for the benefit of all beings.

We may perhaps question whether completely disregarding our personal advantage and dedicating ourselves entirely to the well-being of others will really lead to our awakening. However, there is no doubt about it – the Buddha himself set the example when he gave up all forms of self-interest and dedicated himself wholeheartedly to the realization of enlightenment. According to Shantideva, a famous Indian master, the Buddha said: "Childish people only care about their own well-being and forever wander about in cyclic existence. Wise people care about the well-being of others and attain enlightenment."

Wise people do not shrink from problems and from suffering. They take the difficulties of others upon themselves and offer them their own advantages, successes and gain. They abandon unwholesome mental attitudes and through wholesome deeds devote themselves unreservedly to the welfare of others. When we act in this way, we develop ever more loving-kindness and wisdom, until compassion for all beings pervades our entire conduct. That is the sure way toward awakening.

If, however, we mainly think of ourselves first, we remain spiritually immature. We are not even aware of our opportunities to act for the benefit of others, as our main concern is to become more important and influential and to protect our own reputation. We try to attract agreeable situations, to garner success, and to pass difficulties on to others. Being chiefly concerned with our own advantage, we are intent on furthering our own interests, even if that involves causing harm to others. In doing so, we completely lose sight of the mind of awakening and perpetuate cyclic existence and its suffering.

To strengthen the mind of awakening requires great vigilance.

We should be able, at any moment, to be aware of our motivation, asking ourselves: "At this instant, am I motivated by the intention to help others, or am I intent on my own personal gain? Am I engaged in manipulating others, using them for my own interest, or even in harming them?" Unless we honestly examine ourselves in this way, we run the risk of believing that we have a positive attitude of mind, when in reality we are self-centered and have no genuine interest in the welfare of others. To recognize our unwholesome tendencies enables us to counteract them in good time and avoid harmful actions. In this way, our altruistic attitude will gradually be strengthened.

If we want to help others it is important not to retain a self-cherishing frame of mind. Any acting for the benefit of others that is a mere pretense would only strengthen our self-centeredness and perpetuate the cycle of suffering. Therefore, we should track down our egotistical tendencies and gradually rid ourselves of all selfishness. The firm resolve never to harm anyone but instead to do everything possible to help others is the basis of the mind of awakening.

Normally, going for refuge and generating the mind of awakening are explained separately, as though they are two distinct steps. But actually they take place at the same time. While we go for refuge, we are conscious of the fact that all beings are trapped in ignorance and suffering, and we ask ourselves what would provide the best protection for them. The best protection is going for refuge in the Three Jewels, and we therefore naturally arouse bodhicitta, the wish to gain enlightenment as quickly as possible so that we are able to provide this protection for all beings and liberate them.

Going for refuge and generating the mind of awakening belong together since the commitment to act on behalf of all beings is the basis of our path and since from the outset the way our practice will develop depends entirely on our motivation. From this perspective, going for refuge is an expression of the engaged mind of awakening, and it is the first practical step a bodhisattva takes.

Going for refuge can be aimed either at our own welfare or at the welfare of others. Externally, the practices may look alike, but their consequences will be completely different. Let us take the example of two men each of whom plants a fruit tree. They each dig a hole, set a tree in it and nurture it. But one of them plants it in his own garden, thinking: "This is my own land, and when this tree bears fruit, I will enjoy it. The tree and its fruit belong to me." His intent when planting the tree is to become happy himself.

The other man also plants a tree, but he picks a public place for it, thinking: "This land and the tree, too, belong to everyone. May all who pass by enjoy the fruit of the tree and be able to rest in its shade." He views himself as a gardener who acts for the benefit of others. His mind is open and generous, and he has nothing to defend.

The other man, however, out of fear that someone may take his fruit will have to watch it and may even have to set up a fence. And the closer the fruit gets to ripening, the bigger grows his worry. He may even become aggressive, if he suspects that someone may take his fruit. Both men have to nurse their tree so that it thrives, but the mind of the man without personal interest will be considerably lighter and freer. If his tree bears fruit, he will be delighted when many people come and partake of it.

Obviously, the tree planting will have very different consequences in these two cases, since the motivations of the two men were so different from the outset. The same applies to going for refuge and indeed to all Dharma practice. A taking of refuge that is aimed merely at securing personal well-being is an obstacle to the attainment of enlightenment, since it is the motivation that determines the outcome.

When we begin to understand how great are the qualities that reside in Buddha, Dharma and Sangha, a great joy arises in us that is joined with a great longing to follow the way of the Dharma and the example of the Sangha and realize Buddhahood. This joy and aspiration then become the central axis of our lives.

Spiritual development depends on the degree of openness of our mind: bodhisattvas dedicate the fruits of their practice entirely to others. When we sincerely arouse this motivation of the Great Vehicle in us, then our spiritual practice will have immeasurable positive results. This is because when we practice the teachings of the Buddha genuinely for the liberation of all beings an inexhaustible energy and a boundless joy will spring from that activity. This joy is nourished by our faith in the Three Jewels and our compassion for all beings, and it is accompanied by a deep resolve to devote ourselves entirely to our practice. Then our determination is not just empty talk but a genuine power that arises from our joy.

This joy dissolves all despair in our lives. We are deeply happy to have encountered the Dharma, as a result of our previously created good karma and the kindness of our teachers. We have been given refuge, we have gained access to our potential for awakening, and we now have every opportunity to make use of our lives in the best and most meaningful way. Filled with joyful energy, we are able to devote ourselves to the spiritual path without reservations until we have realized the fruition of buddhahood, with all its qualities. We will no longer experience difficulties as a threat to our personal happiness but as a challenge to further growth on the path to happiness for all beings.

To aim at the welfare of all beings gives us the strength to overcome all difficulties.

Again and again, we renew our commitment to attain enlightenment for the benefit of all beings, and we do not allow ourselves to lose courage through self-doubting thoughts such as: "Am I at all capable of attaining this goal?" When we are free of such doubt, we are full of joy, and our practice happens entirely naturally. The more we are permeated with this joy, the more evident it becomes that it springs from the Dharma itself – from the deepest good – and the more it grows, until it becomes limitless. This happiness fills us more and more, and we radiate it ever more strongly.

Our mind becomes light and carefree, and our confidence in the Dharma grows steadily. This inner light removes all obscurations and self-centered tendencies, and we become more sensitive to the suffering of others, without our mind darkening and getting drawn into their suffering. We sense ever more clearly how we can contribute to their well-being. The Dharma gives us courage, and our practice becomes easy. It evolves as if by itself, without any drudgery or need to force it.

*This joy is like a great fire that cannot be
contained – a fire that burns from within
itself and that consumes all obstructions.*

There is no longer any place then for sorrow, inertia or doubt, for any
kind of self-tormenting talk. Our faith grows and produces a clarity whose luminous power removes all self-centered tendencies and
doubts. Devotion to practice becomes natural and a matter of course.
We no longer ask ourselves: "Should I or shouldn't I? Don't I still need
some time for myself?" When such deep conviction and joy are present, then our practice no longer requires any effort. Everything falls
into its rightful place.

Why do we often experience a certain heaviness, a physical sluggish-
ness or a kind of headache that prevents us from practicing the Dharma? Why is it sometimes difficult or even impossible to practice the
Dharma? The practice seems to be difficult to us because we endless-
ly circle around ourselves, due to ignorance, desire and anger. We are
prisoners caught in the net of these emotions; we are tense and continually doubt our capacity for practicing and developing genuine devotion. We think: "I absolutely must be good at this. I must accomplish this work and be a good meditator." We are totally preoccupied
with ourselves and give ourselves so much grief that we become incapable of reciting even a single mantra. The Dharma that is actually
so easy then becomes difficult and almost grows into a burden. This
happens because we are utterly possessed by the desire to do good or
be a good person and succeed in our practice.

This clinging to ourselves is the root of all our problems. We cannot
manage to set ourselves free internally, and we feel pulled in two directions at the same time. On the one hand, we strive after liberation
and wish to release ourselves from clinging to our ego, and on the other hand, we hold on to our worldly involvements with both hands.

This difficulty resolves itself when we abandon all hope of finding our little pocket of happiness in this world. Then things go upward by themselves, like a balloon whose mooring line has been cut. When the ballast has thus been discarded, practice becomes easy, and faith and joy lift us upward.

In order for our balloon of practice to rise, we must cut the ropes that tie us to our self-centeredness and release ourselves into the open space of the refuge.

In our ordinary lives, we expend an enormous effort whenever we truly wish to accomplish something, and we show astounding perseverance, even in the face of great difficulties. When we have got an idea in our head, we know no tiredness and need no breaks. We are incredibly motivated – and all that for worldly goals! On the other hand, where Dharma practice is concerned, we quickly find it too demanding, become dissatisfied or even angry with it, and give up as soon as difficulties appear.

What we are lacking and what we must develop, is a true aspiration toward the Dharma. A sincere motivation like this will release joy and lead to a natural practice, through which more and more confidence, devotion and compassion arise in turn. Then our path becomes very easy. We no longer ask ourselves: "How long should I continue to practice?", since the answer is clear: "Until I reach the end of the path!" Our practice acquires real power – we totally abandon ourselves to it. Our joy becomes so great that in the end there is no-one anymore, no 'I', no subject that carries out the practice. It goes on all by itself. In relaxed self-recognition, our mind experiences complete freedom. This path of true refuge is based on an unselfish motivation, on loving-kindness and compassion.

Loving-kindness and Compassion

The heart of all spiritual practice is the development of loving-kindness and compassion. The extent to which these two capacities have been developed determines the exact way in which an individual follows the spiritual path and is an indication of how much their mind has ripened and opened up.

If, in applying the teachings of the Buddha, we are principally concerned with our own well-being, then this reveals a very limited attitude that is also called the "Small Vehicle." If we have been roused by the experiences of suffering in our lives and have become conscious of the fact that they will not end unless we put the Buddha's teachings into action, then we are a practitioner of small aspiration. We wish to avoid further suffering and set ourselves the happiness of our own liberation as a goal. But we do not care about the liberation of other beings.

When we think of others, as well as of ourselves, we exhibit the aspiration of the "Middle Vehicle." We recognize that we share the wish with all living beings to be free from suffering and in possession of abiding happiness, and in our striving after enlightenment we feel compelled to practice the Buddha's teachings not only for our own benefit but also for the benefit of all beings in the entire universe.

When we do not care about our own desires but dedicate ourselves entirely to attending to the needs of all beings, we practice the aspiration of the "Great Vehicle." We use our body, speech and mind wholeheartedly for the benefit of others and regard all beings as our parents in former lives. All our energy is focused on freeing them from suffering and leading them to buddhahood. This attitude demands great courage and untiring dedication to the welfare of others. If our courage is not sufficiently great and constant, we cannot follow the way of the Great Vehicle.

*Loving-kindness is the wish that all beings
may experience perfect happiness. We express
it in working for the benefit of others at
every place and in every situation.*

Loving-kindness is not merely an intention – it must show itself in action as well. Dharma practice entails training our body, speech and mind in wholesome behavior and applying the power thus gained to helping all beings, so that they may attain enlightenment as swiftly as possible. Our mental attitude of acting for the benefit and well-being of all gradually becomes an all-pervasive life orientation. This loving attitude pours out in our daily behavior and activity. We become an inspiration to others, showing them what to do and what to avoid. With every moment in which we have a pure motivation, our mind clears a little more and our conduct becomes purer. In this way, our bodhisattva activity grows, and step by step all the meditative realizations manifest that result from cultivating loving-kindness and compassion.

*Compassion is the wish that all beings may be free
from suffering and its causes. We express it in working
on ourselves and not carrying out any harmful actions.*

To develop compassion, we must reflect on the fact that due to their ignorance sentient beings have carried out a multitude of self-centered actions in the past that now produce a multitude of sorrowful life circumstances. And the great diversity of their present life situations in turn leads them to experience many varied emotions and actions that become causes for a multitude of different situations in the future. In this way, countless individual life circumstances arise that have one thing in common: they are characterized by the experience of suffering.

When we see the suffering that is being experienced by all forms of being, a limitless feeling of compassion arises in us, a wish that all sentient beings be completely free of all suffering and of all the karmic patterns that forever drive them to engage in new actions that only cause further suffering. Day and night, we pray that we may be able to help them and wish that they may direct their minds in ways that lead to wholesome action, the cause of future happiness.

But the wish to help others in itself is not sufficient. If we truly wish to liberate others from suffering, we must first be free of it ourselves. If we try to lead others to happiness while we are still mired in suffering ourselves, then this will bring no real benefit and ultimately will fail. To be able to help others, we need to have free space internally, and this will only be created if we work with our own difficulties, recognize our own limits and gradually dissolve our self-cherishing.

This kind of work will release more and more good qualities in us. We will no longer perceive our problems as annoyances but as aids that enable us to put ourselves in the shoes of others and directly understand their difficulties. The more difficulties we have experienced ourselves, the more effective we can be in helping others. Viewed from this perspective, it is a downright advantage to have problems. We can show others the way because we know it from our own experience. The practice of compassion begins with working on our own problems.

In order to first put an end to our own suffering, we must abandon unwholesome actions and carry out wholesome actions. At the same time, we should encourage others to give up actions that lead to suffering and help them use all situations for cultivating wholesome attitudes and actions. When we apply our energies in this way, we will free ourselves from suffering and develop the necessary power to assist countless beings.

Our benevolent orientation should extend to all sentient beings, whoever and wherever they may be, without any exception and with completely equal regard for them all. We should not entertain any preferences or aversions, whatever the qualities or faults of individual beings may be. We should neither give certain individuals preferential treatment and regard them as friends because we find them to be agreeable nor should we reject others and treat them as enemies or strangers because we dislike them or do not know them. We should not carelessly pass over anyone and should also include those we do not know personally or whose fate does not touch us. Our feeling of compassion should embrace all beings with benevolence, down to the very last and the very smallest.

True compassion is very different from worldly love or sentimental attachment. All beings have such feelings of affection but they remain exclusive; they extend only to their close relatives. Even the most dangerous predators feel love and compassion for their young but this is mostly an expression of their attachment. Driven by this self-centered love, they fight, hunt and kill other beings, in order to protect and feed their offspring. They are indifferent to the suffering of their prey and their enemies. Their loving care for their young has nothing to do with the impartial loving-kindness and universal compassion of a bodhisattva.

To love and protect family and friends and to wish the best for them is relatively easy but it is rarely more than a form of possessive thinking that excludes others. Those who we consider as belonging to us are supported and defended. We love them as long as they meet our expectations but when they contradict us or go their own ways, we get angry with them or turn away from them and perhaps even despise them. This common love is contaminated with desire and partiality. We must not confuse it with the outlook of a bodhisattva.

*Bodhisattvas free themselves from worldly
attachments and abandon all partiality.*

They do not regard the beings whom they help as their property
and expect no thanks. Their readiness to help springs from their full
awareness of the suffering of all beings and from the deep wish to
show them the way toward awakening. They do not make threats such
as: "If you don't do what I want, I'm not willing to help you, even if
you get into the greatest difficulties."

The loving-kindness and compassion of a bodhisattva embrace all
beings equally, without making distinctions between the like-mind-
ed and the dissenting, between friends and strangers. They know no
barriers or boundaries. Their compassion is not limited to any particular person or group but embraces all and everything. If we want to
generate such universal compassion, we must give up all judgments.

Our loving-kindness and compassion often remain superficial –
we do not truly open ourselves to the suffering of others but judge
all situations from our own perspective. We assume that our limited
perception is valid. Without much thinking, we kill bothersome insects that crawl across our table or buzz around us while we eat. We
want to be rid of them and claim that insects do not feel anything.
But we do not know what they experience internally.

If we were able to perceive the world from the perspective of an
ant, presumably it would suddenly appear to us to be a very dangerous place. People would be as tall as mountains, and these mountains
would move unpredictably and could squash us suddenly. We would
have to be constantly on our guard. To experience the world of an ant,
with the many sorrows that it involves, would arouse deep compassion in us and a genuine interest to work for their well-being. If we
want to act altruistically, we need to become conscious of the suffer-

ing of others in a way that gets under our skin. Then loving-kindness and compassion go beyond being mere intellectual pastimes.

Even with human beings, we often lack the necessary ability to empathize. We may believe that we feel compassion because we ourselves become very unhappy and suffer, too, when we see those nearest to us suffering. But this supposed compassion may be mere attachment and identification. We only suffer with them because we experience them as extensions of ourselves and project our own feeling of suffering onto them. We identify with them so strongly that we feel personally affected or even assailed by their suffering. Such commiseration has nothing to do with the compassion of a bodhisattva.

Common pity is very limited because it is directed at something that we can see, imagine or feel concretely. In addition, it is often marred by traces of condescension: we may look down upon others and give them our attention with a feeling of superiority. That would be pure pride. The external world then serves as a stage that can mirror back to us an attractive picture of ourselves, as a person full of empathy.

In contrast, the compassion of a bodhisattva is a broad, all-encompassing intention that arises from our becoming aware of the sorrowful nature of conditioned existence. Independent of any specific external situations, this compassion radiates into the entire universe from the depths of our heart and embraces even beings whom we have never seen and perhaps cannot even imagine.

In our efforts to help others, obstacles and difficulties may arise. It may be that we simply cannot help someone because we do not as yet possess sufficient experience and wisdom. Instead of getting discouraged by this, we should do the best we can with our present capabilities and make wishing prayers to acquire greater ability to help later. If someone rejects our help, we should not turn away from them in disappointment, or even get angry at them, but accept that there are situations in which we cannot help directly. Here, too, we make wishing prayers that help will become available later. By virtue of making these wishing prayers, we always find our way back to the intention of a bodhisattva and in this way are able to transform even difficult situations into opportunities for progress on the path to awakening.

Compassion arises from our awareness of the suffering of others – and if we look closely, we really will only see suffering everywhere. We will realize that even those who live in favorable circumstances and outwardly appear happy are still suffering. We should not be deceived by appearances: there is suffering even where there is no hunger or thirst, no war and no material worries.

If we look more deeply we will see boundless suffering.

If we want to be able to help others, it is absolutely necessary for us to see this suffering. Hence, we must look behind the scenes with a loving, compassionate and yet clear and penetrating gaze. When, free from personal interests and fascination, we observe the lives of others, we can see their fears and their never-ending suffering, which is a little different for everyone. We can observe many varieties of suffering and at the same time recognize a common basis that applies to all beings. This common basis is omnipresent ignorance, and it expresses itself in a constant alternation between hope and fear. Rather than rendering us sad or depressed, seeing this should generate ever more energy in us to work for the liberation of all beings and to give the key to it to as many of them as possible.

We observe how beings search for happiness and in the process create only more suffering because they are blinded by ignorance. It becomes unbearable for us to watch this. We would like to flee to some place where we can forget what we have seen, live out our small, personal happiness and rest a little – but that does not work anymore. We will not succeed in forgetting the suffering we saw. We cannot stop thinking about it, and we realize that only the Dharma can lead beings to liberation. It becomes an urgent necessity for us to practice the teachings, so that we may be able to help others as much and as quickly as possible.

By thinking of the suffering of all beings, we practice the mind of awakening, until in all situations their welfare automatically becomes more important to us than our own. Whenever favorable circumstances, joy and happiness arise for us, we immediately dedicate them to the benefit of all beings, and in this way orient our mind toward the greatest possible benefit for all. And every time we encounter harmful situations and difficulties, we immediately take them upon ourselves, for the benefit of all beings. With this intention, we act as bodhisattvas who continuously practice the exchange of self and other. This attitude of giving all benefit to others and taking all difficulties and all loss upon ourselves is a wholesome counterweight to our habitual tendency to look out for our own benefit above all else.

To generate the mind of awakening amounts to a radical transformation of our way of thinking.

We start putting the well-being of others above our own and stop being concerned with our own ego-centered interests. This aspiration plants in us the seed of the mind of awakening, and all situations and encounters become opportunities that allow it to grow further. In order to keep this new outlook alive in us and to strengthen it, we continually return to the motivation that lies at its root.

Every morning, we set aside a moment of recollection in which we give our day a clear direction and dedicate it to this practice for the benefit of others. If we do not do this one day, then not for several days and finally not for weeks, this mindset will be lost, until with time we forget it completely. We need this daily recollection in which we consciously dwell on the qualities of the refuge and the mind of awakening and refresh our motivation. Then we will be able to utilize the entire day for our inner transformation and live in the light of the Dharma.

Sincerity – Looking Inward

Before we can begin to help others in concrete ways, we must make an effort to become aware of the state of our own mind. Ordinarily, our attention is exclusively directed outwards. We continually observe, judge and criticize our fellow humans. It is indeed much easier to observe the external world than to observe ourselves, as long as we have not cultivated the habit of looking inward.

> *It is essential that we develop the attitude of looking inward so that we do not act unconsciously.*

As long as we do not succeed in becoming conscious of our thoughts, we remain ignorant of the true state of our mind. We imagine that we are nice people full of good qualities, with a clear mind and an unselfish attitude. But we have never looked inward to find out how we really are and what actually motivates us.

Without our being conscious of it, our afflictive emotions distort and cloud our perception. We project our own faults onto others and do not trust them. In our eyes, one person displays repulsive behavior; in another person we suspect base motives; a third person has wrong opinions, and so on. We believe that others think bad thoughts, we are suspicious and adopt a negative view of our circumstances, and all this produces annoyance, anger, jealousy or aversion in us. Since we do not really see ourselves and look at others through the spectacles of our own faults, our mind gets carried away with emotions, and as a result of this emotional confusion, we encounter a plethora of difficulties that recur continually.

Our emotional entanglements are driven by the five poisons that rule our mind: pride, jealousy, desire, ignorance[6] and hatred. Not being aware that they all originate in our own mind, we project them onto our surroundings and develop a view of others that is completely colored by our emotions. To us, the emotions appear to come from anywhere but ourselves!

We continually project our problems outwards and impute our own neurotic attitudes to others. For example, when we are under the influence of jealousy, we see jealousy everywhere around us, as though we were wearing spectacles of jealousy. We are completely convinced that others are jealous of us and interpret their actions with that bias. And that may possibly even feed our pride, as we may come to the conclusion: "If others are jealous of me, then that can only be because I am so wonderful. I simply am better than them."

We hardly ever question ourselves. We do not see when anger rules our mind but are completely convinced that it is others who are aggressive. Because of this, our relations with other people are riddled with conflict, and our emotions grow ever stronger. This leads to a feeling of chronic unease and to the accumulation of more and more negative karma.

In general, we are very astute when we want to ferret out the faults of others and judge the external world. We would be better off applying these analytical skills to ourselves to find out where we are in error and stray from the path to awakening. We should use our gift of observation to track down any unwholesome and possibly even malicious tendencies in which we ourselves are stuck. If we do this, then

---

6 The emotion corresponding to ignorance is fear, which includes the inclination to turn our attention away from something troublesome and the desire to stay in states of lesser awareness.

we can work on our own previously unconscious tendencies step by step and gradually change our behavior.

We do not lack the necessary perspicacity but only the willingness to apply it to ourselves. Most of the time, we feel ill at ease when we have to look at ourselves objectively, and we try to avoid looking inward. The only thing that helps here is to bravely override our own inclinations and continually commit ourselves to doing away with our faults.

The world is our mirror. If it appears to be full of aggression, then that means that we ourselves are full of aggression. If it smiles at us, then that shows that we ourselves are friendly. As long as we do not understand this, we will constantly be concerned with the outside world. We will project our own thoughts onto others and think: "Ah, surely they are thinking this and that now. One can clearly see this."

> *Our picture of others is nothing but a mirror of ourselves.*

When we look inside, we are usually content with discovering a few qualities that float on the surface. From that we conclude that on the whole we are fairly passable. Since we do not look more deeply, the unconscious projections of our own neurotic tendencies onto others continue unabated. We direct our gaze outward and discern even the smallest faults in others but think that everything is quite all right with ourselves: "I may have one or two minor shortcomings but I don't have any real faults."

If, however, we honestly look at what really motivates us and how much suffering we have already caused others, then we realize how great the negative potential is that we carry inside of us. We realize that we are incapable of carrying out even a single action that is not motivated by ego-clinging. A process of becoming more conscious is gradually taking place in us, and we are developing the sincere desire to change ourselves.

The ability to look inward and become conscious of our own attitudes of mind is called the "eye of wisdom."

With the eye of wisdom we discover a lot of anger in us, any amount of jealousy, resentment, ignorance, desire – mountains of emotions whose existence we would never have suspected in ourselves. When we see the extent of our own emotional blindness, then the confusion of others appears to us as much less grave. We recognize that most of the faults that we perceive in others are only the mirror of our own negativity, the reflection of our own disturbed feelings. And in direct proportion to this recognition, our own high opinion of ourselves collapses, like a house of cards. Our pride decreases, and along with this other afflictive emotions also calm down. Mental quiet and stability arise in our mind. At the same time, we relieve the world around us of the burden of our own negative judgments.

To think that we possess many good qualities is a sign of blindness and pride. On the other hand, it is a genuine quality for us to perceive the many flaws we have. We are able to see ourselves more clearly than before, and that will enable us to work on our faults and eradicate them. Our situation can be compared to that of a person walking down the street with a spot of dirt on their face. As long as they do not see the blemish, they are convinced of their own attractiveness and do not suspect in the least that something might not be quite right with them. Only when they pass by a mirror can they discover the spot and wash away the dirt. In the same way, we cannot free ourselves of our own negativity as long as we do not notice it. However, as soon as we perceive it, the wish and the ability arise to dissolve it.

*Only when we become aware of our own flaws
is it possible for us to become a buddha.*

On the path to buddhahood, we need this inwardly directed attentiveness, an increasingly acute perception of our own flaws that we
then set out to dissolve through our practice. Whatever we do and
wherever we are, whether we meditate, work or rest, through this
mindfulness all our actions become steps on the path to awakening.
With continued practice, the genuine purity of a clear mind free of
faults will begin to manifest – not an imagined purity that is based
on pride and ignorance.

*Through our looking inward, we realize that the root
of all happiness and unhappiness lies within ourselves.*

For example, if we feel discomfort when we see others being happy or
joyful, or if in meeting others we feel ill at ease or find ourselves having reservations about them, then these are signs of envy and jealousy. Without having noticed it, we are in competition with others. We
ask ourselves who is happier, who has more success, who meditates
better, who has more insight. We compare their happiness with ours
and begrudge the fact that they are well, or better off than we are.

   Our own happiness is more important to us than theirs – and that
is proof of our own self-cherishing tendencies and of an absence of
the mind of awakening in ourselves. A true bodhisattva does not
make any distinctions between themselves and others. When others,
as a result of their previous wholesome actions, experience happiness
and joy, a bodhisattva feels unreserved sympathetic joy, without the
slightest trace of anger or jealousy, since the happiness of others is
exactly what they most desire.

Even though all our behavior is determined by these feelings, it is not at all easy for us to become conscious of them, as they may be quite subtle and have become so much a part of ourselves. If we only look superficially, we do not find anything and think we are not at all envious or jealous. If we investigate more deeply, we gradually become aware that envy, jealousy and pride are indeed present in us.

When we practice the Dharma, pride may express itself, among other things, in our wish to receive recognition from our teacher. When our teacher does not pay attention to us, our pride is hurt. We react by being irritated and jealous and by criticizing the other practitioners. When we praise our own teacher to the skies, it is often only to emphasize our own importance. When, in our study of Dharma, it is important to us to receive admiration for our knowledge and we feel superior to others, then again pride is involved. If we were not full of pride, we would be glad when somebody else was able to explain the Dharma well, and we would wish to learn from them.

Pride, jealousy, resentment, anger, and all the other afflictive emotions are nourished through our habit of constantly judging our surroundings: "I like this, I don't like that. This is good, that is bad. This is right, that is wrong." We do not notice how subjective our judgments are. Self-righteously we hold on to them as self-evident truths that no one may question, and we get angry when others do not share our opinions. If instead we were to look inward and cease to judge the world according to our own standards, then we could gradually allow the source of all these emotions to run dry.

The first step is to acknowledge: "The world is simply different from the way I would like it to be; many people think in ways that are different from mine. If this bothers me, then it is because it puts my own point of view in question, doesn't fulfill my hopes, or arouses fear in me. Instead of getting upset about this, I should keep to the point of view of the Dharma." But to be able to do that, we must first become aware of our own faults and admit to ourselves that we indeed harbor a great deal of negativity. When we develop mindfulness and compassion, we gradually recognize our own unwholesome attitudes and become able to free ourselves from them. Most important for this is the desire to truly change ourselves. We must become our own teachers and look inside ourselves. With a little bit of intelligence and looking in the mirror of sincerity, we will see for ourselves what we have to work on.

In the Dharma, we are concerned with only one enemy: the negativity that rules us internally. There are no external enemies that have to be fought. When we conquer our inner enemy of self-centered emotions, we simultaneously defeat all external enemies, since none of them are equal in strength to the inner enemy. Where do our enemies come from? They all come from the root of our self-cherishing.

As long as there is the thought of an 'I', there will also be enemies.

If we cease clinging to a sense of self, then there is no longer anyone to be harmed by an enemy, and consequently there is no longer any need to fight. Ordinarily, we feel safe once we have locked the door on our external enemies. But it is only our sense of self that is seemingly safe. And when what we call our self feels safe, we are in fact in the gravest danger, as we are then ruled by an increasing clinging to self, and that should be cause for real concern. The biggest enemy is inside, in our own house! If we throw out this enemy, then we are simultaneously freed from all other enemies.

Using Difficulties

If we do not work on our ego-clinging, then in a situation in which someone angrily rejects our help, we may lose our good intentions and perhaps get angry ourselves and think: "I've had enough of this! If this person doesn't want my help, they won't get any help from me whatsoever!" If we were to do this, we would violate our bodhisattva vow to support all beings. To avoid such a transgression, we must develop an attitude free of all self-interest. We offer our help without stipulating any conditions and without discriminating between those who are grateful to us and those who reject us. Regardless of how challenging the reactions of others may be, we should always treat them with that same attitude. Thus, we must practice patience, so that we do not abandon the mind of awakening in a fit of anger. Patience is essential if we want to help others. Where else could we practice patience better than in difficult situations?

The qualities of a bodhisattva are born in the fire of difficulties.

Only by living through difficulties do we develop patience and perseverance. We should consider challenging situations as a test of progress in our spiritual development. When we adopt this outlook, we no longer have problems with criticism and personal attacks; we simply regard them as tests that give us an indication how deeply rooted our commitment to compassionate action actually is. They tell us whether we are still attached to attaining personal peace or are truly determined to act solely for the benefit of others.

When someone hates us, attacks us or tries to harm us, we practice patience. We begin by clarifying the causes of the situation: through harmful actions in the past and through the consequent suffering that we have created for this person and others, we ourselves have set into motion karmic forces that are the actual cause of the present conflict. Our adversary is not the causative agent here but merely a participant in this situation that is unpleasant for both of us, and it is not right for us to put the blame on them. We ourselves have to repay a karmic debt. This understanding will help us accept the situation. We have to pay our karmic bill, and we learn from this for the future.

Karma ripens at the moment when we encounter a particular problematic situation, and it is purified at the moment when we fully accept the situation. We ought to be glad that we have the opportunity to purify our karma now, as this saves us from the misfortune of it ripening at a later time, under circumstances that potentially are much more difficult for us. In addition, we develop compassion for our supposed adversary and pray that the karmic consequences of their anger will not result in additional suffering for them but instead ripen upon us.

We should guard against dividing our fellow human beings into friends and foes. To regard people who are close to us as friends quickly leads to regarding those less close to us as potential enemies. When we identify with our friends, then instinctively aversion arises toward those who harm or attack them. Because of this identification, we carry out many unwholesome actions to protect our friends and defeat their supposed enemies. Only when we do not get entangled in attachments, can we develop an impartial equanimity and learn to regard all beings as equals.

It will be impossible for us to attain enlightenment as long as we categorize those who make trouble for us as real enemies. We actually need such "enemies," obstacles and problems – otherwise we would never have the opportunity to practice patience, and without patience our meditation experience cannot deepen.

From a spiritual point of view, those whom we ordinarily regard as our enemies are actually our best friends.

To regard ourselves and all beings as of equal importance allows us to develop genuine patience. If we do this, then our mind will no longer be churned up by attachment and aversion but will rest in perfect equanimity, a state of spontaneous ease, lightness and happiness. Possessing such even-temperedness is a sign that the mind of awakening has truly arisen in us. Whenever we have difficulty maintaining this attitude, we should consider the person who evokes anger in us to be our spiritual teacher. They help us purify our karma and make us notice the extent to which we still lack patience. We should be grateful for this, because without the valuable hints that we receive through them we would never be able to produce the qualities that are essential on the path to buddhahood.

All wholesome qualities grow in us as a result of encountering difficulties.

Without challenges and provocations, it would be impossible for us to develop patience. And without beings who are experiencing suffering, we would not be able to develop compassion. Likewise, without lack and poverty there would be no scope for practicing generosity, and without desire and attachment there would be no need for developing discipline.

The crucial point in dealing with difficulties is to not solidify them. Whether we encounter illnesses, obstacles or emotions, we are always inclined to think of them as real. We become fixated on our problems and begin to attribute great importance to them so that eventually they appear to be gigantic and take over our entire consciousness. Holding on to suffering in this way only intensifies our pain and despondency. Rather than solidifying our problems, we should remind ourselves that we are presently experiencing karma that at some point will be exhausted. The troublesome situation is only temporary and possesses no absolute, permanent reality. It is merely a manifestation in our mind that, like everything else, is dreamlike and impermanent.

The practice of Dharma accelerates the ripening of our karmic seeds. It is due to the kindness of the Three Jewels and the purifying power of compassion and devotion that our karma, which ultimately we cannot escape, ripens in this very lifetime. At present, we are in conditions that allow us to come to terms with difficulties much more easily than if we had to face them later, in other realms of existence, and without the support of the Dharma. We should dissolve the karmic potential for great suffering that lies dormant in us as quickly as possible now, before it grows any further.

Figuratively speaking, we should uproot the tree of suffering immediately, before it becomes so big that it is only possible to do so with an inconceivable effort. We ought to be glad that we are able to tackle this purification now and thereby release additional qualities in us that will benefit other beings. When we confront our difficulties head-on, with joyful energy, we will overcome them and leave the limitations of self-centeredness behind us.

Also, we will be able to accept difficulties more easily when we consider how minor our present suffering is by comparison with the suffering that we might have to endure in less favorable realms of existence, if our karma is not purified already in this life. Despite its apparent intensity, the suffering in the human realm is like a simple nick in the finger compared to the unceasing tortures and agonies that beings have to endure in the hells of panic and hatred.

If we adopt this perspective and accept our present suffering calmly or even joyfully, then we can dissolve all our accumulated negative karma little by little. We know we are on the right path if we feel grateful when we experience the ripening of difficult karma. Our problems are then transformed into challenges to work more deeply on ourselves and unfold our dormant qualities.

Difficulties are a challenge to our intelligence and creativity.

They enable us to grow and make progress in our practice. Viewed in this way, it is extremely useful for us to be attacked by someone – in fact it is the best thing that could happen to us! If we only rest in peace and quiet, we cannot see what it is that we still have to develop. We may think that we are calm and compassionate, but we will only discover how it really stands with us when we get into difficulties. Tilopa said that difficult situations show us what our practice is really worth more than meditation sessions do.

Pride can easily creep in, and we may regard ourselves as highly realized practitioners. But the moment a small conflict arises, we feel miserable and become aggressive. Then the truth about ourselves comes to light. In fact, it would be a good thing if every day we were to experience a small conflict that brings us down to earth.

When difficulties arise on the path, we should recall our refuge vow: "My body, my speech and my mind no longer belong to me – in going for refuge I have vowed to dedicate them to the liberation of all beings." Then we no longer feel personally attacked, since we are working for the benefit of all beings rather than our own. Difficult circumstances and suffering will stimulate us to develop further spiritual power and dedicate ourselves even more to the liberation of all beings.

We should avoid aggravating our physical or psychological suffering even more through strong attachment. When we become fixated on our suffering, our mind tenses up and our pain gets even worse. We soon forget what it is like to be free from suffering and become ever more susceptible to it. Eventually, out of pure habit, we even keep it going ourselves. To find our way out of this vicious circle, we should direct our attention to the suffering of others and realize that all beings in the universe have to endure similar and often harder trials than we do. Then we generate the wish that all of them may be free from suffering. We can also imagine that we take their suffering and despair into our own painful experience and by doing this open the path to happiness for them. May they all find true happiness! If we practice in this way, we will never really suffer anymore, as we are ready to accept suffering with joy, transform it and use it as a means of helping others.

When we suffer, typically we immediately look for someone whom we can hold responsible and blame for the situation. And the more we think about what they supposedly have done, the bigger our anger gets, which tenses us up even more, until we suffer much more than is commensurate with the original karmic situation. Instead of looking for guilty parties, we should recall that suffering is not an extremely serious thing. It is merely a playing out of karmic forces that are impermanent, like everything else. Suffering does not last forever.

It does not help at all for us to revolt against suffering. We only need to wait until our karma is exhausted. We can detach ourselves inwardly from its manifestations, in the knowledge that they will subside by themselves once the karmic forces have been exhausted. Suffering manifests as an expression of the resolution of our karmic debts, and when these debts have been discharged, it will disappear by itself. Thus, the best way to awakening is to simply accept our suffering as an inheritance from our past and to live in the present in such a way that the future will look better.

Dissolving Harmful Patterns

In order to attain enlightenment and be capable of actually doing something for others, we must first be free of the ballast of previous harmful actions and purify the consequences of these actions. The first step in this is to openly admit our harmful behavior patterns and tendencies to ourselves and to all the buddhas. In this confession, first of all we must become conscious of all the harmful, self-centered actions we have performed. As far as we can, we should look back in time, all the way back to our earliest childhood, and carefully investigate which unwholesome actions we have engaged in. We should bring back into consciousness even seemingly slight offenses and self-centered attitudes. Only then will it become clear to us how much of our life we have already spent engaging in harmful actions.

Of course, we can only recollect actions from this life, but we can infer from them that we have acted in similar ways in previous lives. Clearly, we have a lot of negative karma to purify. If we do not look thoroughly enough, we may persuade ourselves that we have never done anything really bad and believe that it is not really necessary to confess anything.

In a further step, we must consider the consequences of these harmful actions and deeply regret them. It should become clear to us how urgent it is to purify them: we are in danger of being reborn in some realm of existence characterized by great suffering, and other beings will continue to have to suffer from our self-cherishing tendencies. Therefore, we should make every effort to dissolve these actions before they ripen into new suffering for ourselves and others.

The best antidote to our harmful tendencies is the meditation on *Vajrasattva,* who represents the original purity of our mind, or on *Avalokiteshvara* (Chenrezi), the Bodhisattva of Great Compassion. We openly confess all our harmful actions and tendencies while visualizing one of these buddhas above the crown of our head. We imagine that light radiates from his body, melting into us and cleansing us of our negative karma. When we have deep faith in the purifying power of their enlightened compassion, then this purification takes place in actual fact. It is important for us to apply antidotes, which also include going for refuge and generating the mind of awakening, so that the power of positive aspiration is strengthened in us with lasting effect.

We seal our confession, repentance and purification of harmful actions with the promise to no longer perform such acts in the future. If we keep that promise, we can be sure that all of the harmful actions that we have accumulated since beginningless time will be completely purified.

Any confession of our unwholesome actions remains incomplete without an inner commitment to no longer perform them in the future.

For a complete and final purification of all unwholesome actions two things are necessary: the firm resolve to stop engaging in such actions and an unshakable faith that buddha mind has the power to dissolve our negative karma and awaken the buddha nature in us. We should be aware, however, that a complete purification must involve not only our mind but also our body and speech.

There are many means by which the negative karma accumulated in the body can be purified. For example, on a practical level, we could help others through physical actions. Also, we could express our veneration of the Three Jewels and our request for purification by circumambulating symbols of awakening such as *stupas* or sites of spiritual practice and present offerings at such places. These physical acts help build up positive power in us and dissolve our obscurations, and they enable our mind to develop devotion, openness and trust. In principle, every physical action can be used for inner transformation when it is carried out with the right mental attitude.

Performing these pure, physical actions should not generate pride or self-satisfaction in us but rather lead to greater humility, to a feeling of connectedness with others. We should value all beings equally, including those that often seem insignificant in our eyes such as insects. They too have the buddha nature. They are future buddhas and as such should be respected and protected. Humility and a deep appreciation of all beings should be the guidelines on our path.

For the purpose of purification on the physical level, we can also make prostrations to the Three Jewels. We let go of ourselves and our pride, bow in humility and recognize the greatness of the path of awakening. As a support for this inner attitude, we can make these prostrations in front of a Buddha statue or similar symbols that remind us of the qualities of awakening while we are saying the refuge prayer.

More advanced methods for purifying the body are meditations in which we identify our own form with a pure, enlightened form, or buddha aspect, the so-called *yidam*. Meditation on a yidam has nothing to do with worship of a deity for whose mercy we are pleading. Rather, it helps us understand the true nature of physical manifestation whose wisdom dimension we ordinarily do not perceive. Thus, yidam practice is also a method of meditating on the awakened aspect of our own physical being. When we view our body as consisting only of bones, flesh and blood, we do not recognize that it embodies awakened wisdom. When we complete the purification of the body and dissolve all forms of identification with it, then we actualize its fundamental nature, the illusory *body of emanation*, called *nirmanakaya* in Sanskrit.

Our speech as well must be included in the purification process. Normally, we only use words to give expression to our self-centered tendencies, without recognizing that speech also has a wisdom aspect. Under the influence of ignorance and emotions, we have used this wonderful instrument, our speech, only for self-centered purposes. Out of pride, we have used it to hurt others and manipulate them; we have talked badly about them and argued with them. In doing this, we may have caused great suffering. For the sake of our own personal advantage, we have lied and made insincere, inappropriate use of our speech. But by using it consciously, we can purify our speech and use it in accordance with its higher purpose, that of supporting others on the path to liberation.

But here, too, we have to watch that pride does not spoil our efforts. To develop our quality of speech entails being full of respect and compassion in all conversation, motivated only by the wish to help others. We will then talk in a manner that is clear, conciliatory, friendly and reassuring to others. However, we should also bring wisdom to bear on our effort to engage in truthful speech. For example, it could be painful and ultimately pointless to tell someone a truth to which they are not receptive. If we want to help, we must use discernment in knowing how and when we could and should say something. If we act according to these principles, we can gradually purify all obscurations of speech that we have created by engaging in unwholesome speech.

In order to draw closer to the pure dimension of the speech of the buddhas, we can recite the texts of awakened masters or say mantras or prayers which are the expression of pure speech and of the truth of awakening. Gradually then, we will discover that speech has a sacred quality. An example of such sacred speech is the mantra. A *mantra* is a sacred phrase that supports and protects the mind. By reciting it we impart openness and compassion to our mind and ultimately enable it to attain realization. With the dissolution of the obscurations of our speech, we discover the deep reality of awakened speech which is called the *body of enjoyment,* or *sambhogakaya* in Sanskrit, the expression of the wealth of awakened qualities.

The principal purification that we have to accomplish though is that of our mind, since the impulses for our behavior with body and speech arise there. At the root of all self-centered action lies fundamental ignorance: the division of reality into 'I' and 'other(s)'. Because we are ignorant of the nature of mind and of appearances, the idea of an 'I' arises in our mind, of an individual who is set apart from everything else. As a consequence of our identification with this isolated 'I', feelings of attachment and aversion arise in us. The 'I' wants to have the best for itself and avoid everything that is unpleasant for itself. Our attempts to satisfy the needs of this 'I' inevitably lead to conflict with others, because the question arises of who has the right to partake of the pleasant things: if it is not I, then it will be others.

When we live with the conviction that we have a greater entitlement to everything than others, then our pride inevitably increases. And when we cannot get something or see that others have more of it or more success than we do, disappointment, jealousy and anger raise their ugly heads. In this way, the entire palette of afflictive emotions appears as a consequence of our attachment to the idea of an 'I'. They completely take over our mind and form the personality, the personal structure of our mind. We have functioned in this way since beginningless time. Our mind has always been trying to get the best for itself and pass problems on to others.

When we make an effort to counteract our habitual tendencies that time and again prompt us to engage in harmful actions, we discover that pride is our main problem. The Tibetan word for pride (ngagyal) means "I-king" or "kingdom of the self." We have performed countless harmful actions to satisfy this proud king. Much suffering has been created because we have been so convinced of our own importance. The antidote to pride is to become aware of our own faults and to appreciate the qualities of others as well as the qualities of the refuge. We must learn to hold others in high regard and become modest and humble ourselves.

To the extent to which our mental obscurations dissolve, we become capable of letting our mind rest in itself. This continues the purification of the mind at a deeper level, as our mind frees itself increasingly of self-centered patterns. In our meditation on the true nature of all things, ignorance and self-centeredness dissolve, and we understand that we and all other beings are not separate and are of equal value. The one, indivisible expanse of mind reveals itself, which is also called the *body of truth,* or *dharmakaya* in Sanskrit.

Our mind arrives at its own primordial reality, the "one taste" of all phenomena, the true nature of itself and of all appearances. In this reality, there are no longer any preferences. However, this condition of equality, of one taste of all appearances, is by no means a state of indifference, as it is totally suffused with compassion and loving-kindness. This is the dimension of the unity of compassion and emptiness. The ultimate purification of our mind is accomplished when time and again we enter into this dimension.

Through this process of purification of our body, speech and mind and the accumulation of merit on these three levels, our karmic obscurations gradually dissolve, and we recognize our buddha nature, which has been the true nature of our body, speech and mind since beginningless time. Only through this very personal work of karmic purification are we able to uncover our true qualities, attain enlightenment and carry out enlightened activities for the benefit of all beings.

Building Positive Power

We should always accompany the purification of our harmful tendencies with the performance of wholesome deeds, as these will strengthen the awakened attitude of mind in us and build a solid basis of merit. By *"merit"* we mean the dynamic power or force that we generate through our wholesome actions and that is directed toward awakening, a power that enables us to move forward with the requisite energy and overcome obstacles. Two things are needed to build up this power: we must purify our existing harmful tendencies, and through our actions we must create favorable conditions for our own inner development.

The former leads to the latter: in the process of purification, we realize to what extent unwholesome actions constrict our mind and lead to suffering. Realizing this, we resolve to practice wholesome forms of behavior that allow us to develop inner freedom and build up positive power. In other words, we remove everything in us that burdens us and leads to suffering, and we cultivate whatever contributes to true happiness and liberation. Purification joined with the building up of positive power enables us to make swift progress on the path to awakening.

To the extent to which wholesome energy increases in our stream of being, the mind of awakening also grows in us.

By carrying out wholesome actions with our body, speech and mind we build up positive power which at the same time purifies the karmic traces of unwholesome actions we have performed on these three levels in the past. Particularly suitable for this are the many ways of the practice of generosity: we can give others our friendliness and loving-kindness, stand by them in times of difficulty, take care of them, and give them joy. We may also be able to inspire them to practice the Dharma and engage in positive actions – even if it is only by encouraging them to recite OM MANI PEME HUNG, the mantra of Avalokiteshvara, the Bodhisattva of Great Compassion.

In addition to the common practice of generosity, we can also make offerings to the Three Jewels. When we do this, the point is not to satisfy the wishes of the buddhas or to earn their grace – such ideas stem from a dualistic view. Rather, making offerings is a means of purifying our deeply rooted tendency to cling to the beauty of things, to pleasant sights, sounds and smells, to pleasures of the palate, as well as to property, to our body, and the like. Because of all these attachments we have carried out many unwholesome actions, and in order to dissolve our proclivity for such actions and release our clinging we now make offerings.

Through this giving we counteract our tendency to always act for our own benefit, because the symbolic offerings that we present to the Three Jewels do not serve to satisfy this 'I' that is the source of all our problems. We need to rid ourselves of the illusion of 'I' and of our tendency to always want to have good things for ourselves, and by making these offerings, we recollect the qualities of awakening represented by the Buddha, the Dharma and the Sangha.

Generosity is an attitude toward life – as is miserliness.

All our actions are inspired by one or the other of these two attitudes. A miser perennially wishes to have more and will act accordingly. In addition, they are chronically afraid of losing something. By contrast, a person who is motivated by generosity lives in a steady stream of giving. This giving becomes a way of life that embraces all aspects of their existence, and they do not limit their offerings to the traditional ones. We can regard everything as an offering, and there are no limits to what we can offer mentally. When we make generosity a way of life, we will no longer know miserliness. We will give without reservation, and through that we will experience complete freedom.

When we offer material gifts, we let go of our clinging to sensory pleasures. But we should not limit ourselves merely to offering material gifts such as a flower, a candle or some incense, because the positive force that is generated by external offerings will always be limited. Rather, we should consider material gifts to be a support for mental offerings that are limitless in number, quality and variety.

For example, we may offer a flower to the Three Jewels, but we do not confine ourselves to this material offering. In our mind we can multiply the flower without limit, filling the entire universe with millions or billions of flowers. The important thing here is our mental attitude. It renders a limited offering limitless and transforms it into something wonderful.

For example, when we offer a bowl of water to the Three Jewels, thinking, "I'm making an effort here, I'm offering some water in a pretty bowl," then the offering is very limited, as our mind confines itself to what is immediately visible. If, however, we offer the bowl of water with the thought that the water stands for life itself, for all the water that exists in the entire universe and that supports all beings, then this small amount of water becomes the symbolic representation of an enormous offering gift. Our mental attitude has made the gift limitless. This expansion of a limited material gift through our wishes and through the mental imagery that accompanies it is called a "mental offering."

In our mind we can offer everything that exists in the universe: the possessions, goods and riches of all beings. We can offer everything, without leaving out anything and without thinking that there are things we could not offer to the Three Jewels. Since our purpose is to purify our clinging to the idea of a self, we should hold back absolutely nothing but give everything that we are attached to.

In addition, in our mind we can offer all sorts of things that belong to no one and of which all partake equally, such as the plants, the earth, the seas, the wind, mountains, sun and moon, the planets, the entire universe. We offer all these things, along with our own body, speech and mind and dedicate them all toward awakening. Not holding on to a single wish for our own satisfaction, we put everything at the service of the Three Jewels and the welfare of all beings. In this way, practicing generosity greatly opens our mind.

Generosity becomes limitless if we not only set no limits to the gifts of the offering but also make them with the intention of boundlessly benefiting all beings without exception. Such generosity purifies countless harmful actions of ours in the past and contributes to the immense accumulation of positive power that we need on the path to awakening. Limited gifts generate only limited merit that cannot begin to offset the huge mountain of unwholesome actions that we have accumulated since beginningless time.

Another source of spiritual merit is our feeling of sympathetic joy over all the good that is being brought about by other beings. When we practice sympathetic joy as soon as we see someone carrying out a good, wholesome deed, then we generate the same positive power as the person in whose deed we are rejoicing. If, on the other hand, we are envious of or angry at people who do good, then we will never succeed in building up any positive power.

When we meet people who are happy about something they have experienced, received or developed in themselves, and our first reaction is to feel happy with them and for them, then this is a sign that we have generated the mind of awakening. If, on the other hand, in our encounter with them we feel dissatisfied or irritated, then this indicates that our basic attitude is still one of self-centeredness. And if we even regard them as annoying or as a source of difficulties for us, then this is a clear indication of our attachment to self and shows that we have not even begun to generate the mind of awakening.

Exchanging Self and Others

One indication that we have genuinely developed the attitude of a bodhisattva is that we desire good things for others when usually we would only be concerned for our own welfare and that we take upon ourselves the difficulties of others that usually we would wish to avoid. We do not try to acquire the best for ourselves and put others at a disadvantage. Our normal way of thinking, characterized by self-cherishing, has been turned into its opposite, the cherishing of others. We have learned that those who cause us difficulties are our best friends, as they help us develop patience. We joyfully take the suffering of others upon ourselves and continually make wishing prayers such as the following:

May the suffering of all beings be purified by my taking it fully upon myself as my own.

When we live with this attitude continuously, we are able to retain a positive and cheerful spirit even in painful situations. Nothing then will trigger a feeling of aversion; nothing will become the source of further suffering. This attitude brings an end to all suffering. By giving up our self-centered attitude and assuming the altruistic attitude of the mind of awakening, we are no longer fixated on the symptom, but instead treat the true cause of all suffering. And when this root cause of all suffering has been removed, its effects also come to an end.

Without self-centeredness we would experience no suffering. As a consequence of our desire to protect our sense of self, we have performed a lot of unwholesome, self-centered actions in the past, and these actions now ripen in the form of painful experiences. In this way, our suffering becomes a catalyst on the path: it wakes us up and shows us where self-centered action leads us. It deters us from continuing to act in the same way. Our experience of suffering is an inexhaustible source of precious instructions and pushes us forward on the path. If we adopt such a perspective, we will be able to face suffering with an open, cheerful attitude of mind.

This transformation of our attitude is central to all the methods that we can employ to make use of difficulties on our path. Normally, we consider ourselves to be all-important, and as a consequence we are in continual conflict with others. If we cease to regard ourselves as the center of the world, our entire life is transformed, and we no longer have any cause for anger. Then our actions are automatically imbued with the wish to help others. At such a moment, the mind of awakening is naturally present. We only have to give up our attachment to our own supposed importance. Seen from that angle, generating the mind of awakening is not as difficult as it may at first seem.

As our self-cherishing tendencies are purified, our perception broadens to include all the beings around us. We become increasingly aware of their manifold suffering and recognize the causes of their problems more clearly. Reflecting on the fact that they all have been our parents in past lives, the desire arises in us to help them. The more steadfast we are in keeping this aspiration in our mind, the more our natural qualities of loving-kindness and compassion will manifest. To develop this inner attitude and awareness we need a practice.

The exchange of self and others, in the form of giving and taking *(tonglen)*, is particularly well suited for this. It is important that we engage in this practice formally, in addition to focusing on loving and compassionate action in our daily lives. It will help us develop an expansive view of problems and of our relationships with other people, as well as an appreciation of the emptiness of all appearances. This meditation has several steps, and it uses the breath as a support.

First, we allow our mind to relax completely and find its way to a deep quiet in which it does not hold on to anything. We rest in the awareness that everything that appears is our own mind – we regard appearances as not separate from us. In this way, we rest with a completely quiet, peaceful mind. Then, in a natural, unforced manner, we turn our attention to the movement of our breath, without trying to influence it or do anything with it. We follow the movement of the breath until we become clearly aware of it. Then we begin with the exchange.

While breathing out, we imagine that white light radiates from our heart and fills all the beings who are the objects of our practice. This light represents all our good qualities, the favorable circumstances that we enjoy, all the positive energy that we have accumulated since beginningless time, as well as everything that might give joy to these beings. While breathing out, we give all of this to them and imagine that they are completely pervaded by it.

We then imagine that this positive power, derived from our wholesome deeds, dissolves the suffering, illnesses and obstacles of all the beings that fill the universe, just as the rays of the sun dissolve the morning mist. All these beings begin to feel happiness and a sense of great relief and are soon beaming with joy. They become filled with a sense of well-being, positive power and all the qualities they need to attain liberation.

While breathing in, we imagine that we take dense black smoke into our heart that stands for the suffering, illnesses, difficulties and obstacles of all beings. Their sorrow melts into our heart, into the openness of our non-attached mind.[7] We imagine that by doing this we free all these beings from all their suffering, their negativities and its causes, and we generate great joy at being able to bring this about. While breathing in and out naturally, we continue with this exchange until we have the feeling that we have taken on all the difficulties of all beings and have given them everything that is beneficial to them.

Finally, in as relaxed a manner as possible, we rest our mind in its natural dimension, in the ultimate reality of Mahamudra, in which there is no longer any separation between self and other, between meditator and object of meditation. We dwell in a state beyond all reference points, letting go completely into the condition of original openness.

At the conclusion of this meditation, it is important to meditate in complete openness or emptiness, because otherwise we run the risk of

---

7 Occasionally, Gendun Rinpoche mentioned that in the tonglen practice we could visualize the openness of our own mind as a luminous sphere or as Buddha Shakyamuni or as Avalokiteshvara, the Bodhisattva of Great Compassion, residing in our heart. However, the practice can also be done without this additional visualization.

holding on to the idea of truly existing suffering. In order to dissolve this and other fixations, at the end of the meditation we rest in emptiness. Moreover, when we do this, our fear of becoming weighed down or contaminated by the suffering of others dissolves. Our awareness of emptiness is the best protection against any such fears.

Now for some more detail on the practice. We begin tonglen with "taking" first from ourselves, by visualizing our own suffering streaming into our heart and allowing it to dissolve there. Only then do we turn to the exchange with others. First, we visualize those we like and who are close to us, and then we expand the practice to include those toward whom we have felt indifferent until now. We try to feel their suffering and sense what they need. Then we widen the scope of our loving-kindness and compassion to include those whom we previously experienced as being difficult or unpleasant. Nobody is excluded from this compassionate action of ours. In fact, we should extend special consideration to those who have particularly great difficulties, as they need our attention the most. In this way, we gradually expand the scope of the exchange until eventually it includes all beings in the universe.

When this meditation is done with the right motivation, our ability to carry it over into our daily lives will gradually increase and our new inner attitude will begin to shine through our entire behavior. The exchange of self and others truly is the root of the tree of enlightenment. From this root grows the trunk of ceaseless wholesome action with body, speech and mind. The more spiritual merit we accumulate through these actions, the stronger the trunk grows, and from this strong trunk the leaves, blossoms and fruits of the highest realization will inevitably emerge. In this way, the mind of awakening produces the fruit of perfect realization of the truth body, the dharmakaya.

However, until now we have rarely if ever acted selflessly on behalf of others. Above all, we have been interested in our own personal well-being, constantly asking the questions: "How can *I* be happier? How can *I* avoid problems? How can *I* achieve more recognition? Who will love *me*?" Everywhere, there is this *I*, *me* and *mine*. And when we actually do something for others, our self-cherishing mind swiftly tries to appropriate the fruits of what at the outset may indeed have been a pure action. Whenever we notice this, we should immediately practice exchanging self and others: dedicating to others everything that is good and taking upon ourselves everything that we ordinarily prefer to shift onto them.

This work requires us to be attentive, to recognize our ego-centered tendencies and be genuinely willing to transform them. As soon as we find ourselves wishing to have something pleasant for ourselves, we apply the exchange with others and change our intentions, actions and words. Instead of holding on to our own good fortune, our perceived rights and advantages, we take suffering, disadvantages and defeat upon ourselves. We welcome difficulties, and we give to others everything that is pleasant, easy and beautiful.

As a result of practicing this new attitude, more and more clarity will manifest in our mind. This transformation will take place quite naturally, and we will begin spontaneously to act altruistically. But this spontaneity is the fruit of steady labor, of a continual effort to bring about this transformation. When we work on ourselves in this way, we gradually become able to genuinely help others. And the more we practice in this way, the better we understand our mind and the more our desire grows to practice the Dharma, so that we may more quickly develop the ability to free all beings from suffering.

Advice for Meditators

Allow your mind to settle
in a state that is relaxed
and free of constraint.

In this state look at
the movement of thoughts,
and rest in this, relaxed.
Through this, stability will come.

Free of attachment to stillness
and without fear of moving thoughts,
be aware that there is no difference
between stillness and movement –
mind arises from mind.

Remain in this state, just as it is,
relaxed, without grasping, without clinging.
In this – reality as it is –
the true nature of your mind, wisdom,
appears as a bright openness.

You will be mute with amazement,
and a natural silence will arise.
Don't grasp at this silence as some thing –
remain natural, relaxed and free.

Without grasping at or rejecting
what arises in the mind,
simply remain ...

Gendun Rinpoche

Teacher and Student

We all possess the buddha nature. It is only on its basis that we are able to work on ourselves. If we want to gain access to this buddha nature, we need a teacher – either a spiritual master or simply a spiritual friend who shows us the way and accompanies us on it. If we want our practice to attain some depth and bear fruit, it is important that we follow a teacher on whom we can rely totally. They teach us what to do and what to avoid, what is helpful and what is not, and how to progress on the path to awakening.

If the joint work of teacher and student is to bear fruit, both must bring to it the necessary prerequisites. This work can be compared to the casting of a statue. In casting a statue, it is most important that the mold as well as the material used be free of flaws. If the mold is without faults, then the statue cast in it may also be free of fault. But if we take material that is brittle or impure, then even with a perfect mold an accurate reproduction is not possible. And vice versa, if the mold has faults, then even with the best material a flawless statue cannot be cast. For a perfect transmission to be possible, master as well as student must be faultless: the master like a mold without defects and the pupil like fine, pliable metal that is free of impurities.

In the Kagyu lineage, there have been many instances of perfect teachers coming together with outstanding students. An impressive example of this is Tilopa and *Naropa*: Tilopa was a perfect master and Naropa a perfect student. On one occasion, when Naropa asked his master for teachings, the latter replied: "If I had a student who was truly ready, he would jump into the water for them." Naropa did not hesitate for a second and jumped into the water. On another occasion, Tilopa said to him: "If I had a student who was truly ready, he would jump into the fire for them," and Naropa instantly jumped into the fire. Because of his total devotion, the transmission of blessings and realization was able to take place in a perfect manner.

If this example appears a little extreme to you, consider the case of *Marpa* and his pupil *Milarepa*. Milarepa carried out even the most difficult tasks without hesitation or aversion. Everything that Marpa ordered him to do – for the sake of his pupil and the transmission from master to disciple – he did without questioning. From such examples, we can get a sense of what master and student would be like in the ideal case and be inspired by them.

What are the characteristics of an authentic teacher? In their outward behavior, they should be moderate and disciplined. They should never entice their students into harmful behavior or endanger their future development. Through their words and deeds, they should inspire others to more and more extensive ethical behavior, doing wholesome deeds and avoiding unwholesome deeds. They should have walked the path of the Dharma to its completion and through untiring practice have attained all realizations. Their mind should be free of self-interest and filled with boundless loving-kindness and compassion for all beings. Another mark of an authentic master is a complete absence of pride. They have no self-centered or worldly interests but only desire to bring all beings to spiritual maturity and enable them to free themselves from their conditioning and the resulting suffering.

In the Tibetan tradition, a capable teacher is called a "lama." The lama is the root of all realization and blessings. He or she becomes the central reference point of our spiritual path, and is inspiration, source of instructions, shining example, and a support in difficulties, all at the same time. As the student's practice progresses and their trust in their teacher deepens, a very close relationship develops between lama and student.

Who is a suitable student? A suitable student should have much loving-kindness and compassion and practice the Dharma with the intention of realizing buddhahood for the benefit of all beings. Their ego-centered tendencies should gradually decrease because they practice a selfless attitude of mind. Trust in and devotion to the Three Jewels and, in particular, the lama, should grow in them, and their pride and self-will should abate. The student should have a balanced mind, should not be thrown by either praise or blame and should maintain equanimity under all circumstances, not allowing changing events to disturb their equilibrium.

Before teacher and student enter into a deeper spiritual connection, they must examine one another.

The student should check whether the teacher lives in accordance with the teachings of the Buddha and whether his or her actions and inner attitudes are clear and transparent. We should not get involved with a teacher whose external demeanor is without blame and who appears to be full of qualities but whose inner attitude shows many faults. A master should express the essence of the teachings of the Buddha in their entire thinking and acting. If emotions rule their mind, then they are not a suitable teacher. A teacher should not be hypocritical, and they should not have to hide anything. Conversely, they should not have a pure attitude that remains only internal and does not show in their external behavior.

In order to be able to show the way to others, the teacher should have received the complete transmission of the Buddha's teachings and be experienced in meditation. In addition, they should have received the oral instructions that are part of the transmission and be able to transmit them further. Finally, we must check whether the teacher truly is a source of inspiration. For that, they must have received the full blessings of the lineage and kept their sacred commitments completely pure. Only then can they transmit the blessings of the lineage to others. Such a teacher is capable of motivating students to attain the same experiences and realization that they attained. Not only are they able to explain the Dharma in a way adapted to the needs of the student, but they have practiced all instructions themselves and attained authentic realization from them, before they transmit them further.

The teacher observes the qualities of the student. A student may initially display much trust and devotion, but if this is merely attachment and not genuine trust, then there is the danger that it may vanish as soon as the relationship with the teacher involves more obligations. Someone who has no stable and resilient feeling of trust in the teacher should not be accepted as a student.

The teacher also cannot accept any student who is not sufficiently steadfast in their behavior or cannot control their actions because of the presence of strong emotions. The student must be capable of practicing the Dharma with perseverance and courage, and they should have a sufficient basis of compassion and loving-kindness. In their actions of body, speech and mind, they should be disciplined and respectful.

Before we request instructions or an empowerment from a lama, we should ascertain that they are an authentic teacher in whom we can have trust. Once such a connection has been created, it is no longer appropriate to criticize the teacher in any form or pass judgment on them. We must then have complete trust in them.

No particular form or ritual is needed to establish a relationship between a teacher and a student. It is not necessary to ask the mas-

ter: "Would you accept me as a student?" and get a confirmation such as: "You are my student now." The connection is established without any formality, based on the shared wish for joint work. The teacher offers their attention, their support and their compassion, and the student brings with them their trust and readiness to engage in this work.

It is exceedingly rare that a perfect master and a perfect student meet. But when the student possesses great devotion and a pure view, then it is not so grave a detriment if their master has few outstanding qualities. If they view the teacher with great trust as a buddha, then they can receive the full blessings of the awakened mind, even when the teacher is only an ordinary person. In such a case, the teacher is merely a link in the chain of transmission of blessings, and it is the devotion of the student that accomplishes everything.

More problematic is the converse case, when the master is fully realized but the student possesses not a hint of any good qualities. In such a case, the teacher cannot accomplish much, as the student regards them as only an ordinary being. The student's mistaken view renders them blind to the teacher's awakened nature, and they may even project their own faults onto the master.

In the more common situation of a realized master encountering an unexceptional student, the master will not turn them down, but help them develop the qualities that are needed for the path. In such a case, the student treads the path principally by virtue of the capabilities of the master – it is as if the master took the student by the hand. If the master is not that accomplished but the student has many genuine qualities, then the latter does the larger share of the work, while revering the master with faith and devotion as an awakened being.

Of course, the best situation exists when a student with many good qualities encounters a fully realized teacher. But if they cannot find such a master, they must be content with a less perfect teacher. For beginners, it is not necessary anyway to have a realized bodhisattva as a teacher. It is perfectly all right if the first teacher on our spiritual path is an ordinary spiritual friend. When we put their instructions into practice and slowly make progress, with our growing experience and spiritual power we will automatically encounter ever more qualified teachers whose capacities correspond to our prevailing state of development and who can help us along.

The invisible bond that connects master and student has two ends. At the master's end is compassion, loving-kindness and support, and at the student's is devotion, trust and joyful perseverance.

The bond with the master is the guarantee of the student's progress.

This bond can be damaged from both ends. If the master lacks compassion, patience and interest in the welfare of their student, then the connection will be weakened or even broken. Similarly, a student who abandons their devotion and trust will damage this spiritual bond *(samaya)* that is vital for the practice and eventually will lose it entirely. They remove themselves from the spiritual activity of the master, and the joint work of master and student is thus disrupted. If this break occurs because of harmful attitudes, then both suffer.

If the teacher abandons their compassion or their interest in the student, then they will experience the karmic consequences of that action. If the break is initiated by the student, then he or she has to bear the consequences. If, on the other hand, their joint work proceeds positively, then as a result of the student's trust and devotion the latter will be pulled forward by the spiritual development of the master, and both develop further at the same time.

Wherever there is faith and trust, there is also blessing.

Faith in the Three Jewels and devotion to the lama are crucial for the development of the student. When we direct a prayer to our master, we do not turn to their person but rather to the awakened mind that they embody. The communication from student to lama takes place from mind to mind. When, full of devotion and trust, we beseech our lama to grant us their blessings, we can do so in very simple language, in our own words. When we sincerely wish to receive our lama's blessings, our heart opens. Through this opening of our heart, our mind will meet with the lama's awakened mind in a completely natural way. Then all words are superfluous.

The physical presence of the teacher is not essential. When our heart is open and we possess great faith, then it is sufficient that we sit down and call the lama in our mind – and behold, the lama is there! This is possible even if we have met them only once or see them only very rarely. The lama is in the mind – that is where we meet the lama and receive their blessings. We only use the lama in human form as a bridge, in order to develop faith and dissolve our veils of ignorance. Through this faith we find our way to the awakened mind. Faith is indeed the key to receiving blessings.

I will tell a little story pertinent to this. An old woman in Tibet had a son who used to travel to India in order to trade there. She begged him to bring back an object for her that had been blessed by the Buddha himself, something that had come into contact with him in one way or another. The son promised to do so but he was so preoccupied with business during his travels that he completely forgot about the gift promised to his mother. He only remembered it as he was already approaching his home village. Since she had already asked him for it several times and since he did not want to disappoint her again, he strained to think of a way of making up for his forgetfulness.

Shortly before he got to his house, he came across the bleached skeleton of a dog. That gave him an idea: he broke a tooth from the dog's jaw, wrapped it in the finest silk and presented it to his mother as a relic of the Buddha, as one of his teeth. His mother was delighted and did not doubt the authenticity of the tooth in the least. She put it on her altar, and during the last years of her life used it as a support for her devotional prayers and offerings. She received not only consolation and courage from this dog's tooth but also the blessings of the awakened mind. In fact, she received it in such great measure that at her death she displayed all the signs of realization and left behind a great number of relic pearls *(ringsel)* in her cremation ashes.

Faith and devotion to the Buddha made this possible – when these are present, the blessings flow. Faith and devotion *are* the master. The master embodies the awakened mind – he or she is not merely what we see as their external form. If they were merely their external, physical form, then we would have to remain in their presence forever!

When we do not have faith and are not receptive to the mind of awakening that dwells in the lama, we may sit at their feet our entire lives, without actually meeting them for even an instant. We meet the person, sure enough, but never the lama. On the other hand, we may live very far away from our teacher and yet, in our mind, be inseparably united with their mind through our faith and devotion.

If we feel separated from our lama, then this shows that we see them as an ordinary person. In actual fact, however, it is the heart of devotion that is the real lama, and from the moment this certainty dawns in us, the lama will always be present. Then even their death cannot separate us from them, as the awakened mind is beyond death and dying. Our prayers will continue to reach them, and their blessings can still lead us onward.

The true lama is deathless – they are beyond life and death.

Only in the mind of the student who has lost their trust and devotion does the master actually die. As long as trust is present and the student is open to the lama's inspiration, the lama is alive and their blessings remain undiminished.

The great realized being Milarepa explained this to his students shortly before his death: when he died, they should not be sad and think he had become inaccessible. His mind was like the expanse of space – omnipresent and limitless. For anyone who directed their devotion toward him, he would be present at any time and they could obtain any blessings they wished for.

Guru Rinpoche also told his students on numerous occasions that he would be wherever they called on him. If they imagined him to be above the crown of their head, in front of themselves or resting in their heart, then he would actually be there. Devotion to the teacher and faith in their awakened mind are the heart of our relationship with the master.

> *The lama is wherever there is a student*
> *who is filled with faith and devotion.*

We need not doubt that this is actually so, as the lama cannot be equated with an ordinary being. Thus, it is said that the degree of trust and devotion that the student displays are of prime importance for their realization. If they possess excellent devotion, then their realization will be excellent. With middling devotion, it will be middling, and with ordinary devotion, it will be ordinary. Without devotion, there will be no realization at all – this would be like attempting to plant something in dry, rocky soil.

If we lack faith, we may fare like the monk who served the Buddha for eighteen years, without ever noticing anything extraordinary in the Awakened One. He thought of him as an ordinary practitioner with some faults. When more and more students congregated around the Buddha, this monk was seized with aversion, envy and anger. This anger eventually led to his rebirth in one of the hell realms. Thus, physical proximity to a buddha is no guarantee of successful practice.

In the instructions on practice, we often hear that we should visualize our "root lama," and many people ask who their root lama is. We should know that it is always the student who chooses the teacher. It is inconceivable that a lama would say to someone: "I am your teacher, and you must become my student."

If the teacher were to choose their students, the teacher would be following his or her personal preferences. A relationship with a student should not be established in that way. The choice lies in the hands of the student. They choose as their root lama the teacher to whom they feel themselves naturally drawn and in whom they have the greatest trust. That particular lama is the one who accords with their present karma. Once the bond has been established, teacher and student devote themselves to advancing on the path to awakening.

The bond with the lama can become very close, but we must guard ourselves against developing a narrow-minded attachment that leads to regarding our lama as the sole savior of this world. When we have formed a close bond to a good teacher, it is only natural that we do not seek elsewhere for additional instructions, since our teacher gives us everything we need for the deepening of our practice. This can lead to great closeness and familiarity.

However, that closeness must never lead to rejection or disparagement of other teachers. Everyone who transmits the true, profound teachings should be deeply respected, even if we personally decide to follow a different teacher. Possibly, we have already received instructions and *empowerments* from many lamas. Through this, connections have been forged that we simply cannot ignore. But when we pray to our lama, we turn our mind principally to *one* teacher who we then consider to be the union of all of the lamas with whom we have a connection.

In times of lack of direct contact with a teacher, association with other Dharma practitioners can provide much support on our path. They have a good influence on us, we motivate each other in our practice, and their advice will help us make decisions in important matters that allow us to progress further in the direction of inner opening and awakening.

We need not worry about ever being separated from the compassion and blessings of our lama: the awakened mind and its spontaneous altruistic activity are omnipresent and pervade everything. As soon as we open ourselves, trust and devotion will arise that will enable us to receive blessings, and we can develop this receptive mind not only in our relationship with our teacher but also in all our daily activities.

The master gives us the gift of the teachings, and his or her mind is open. Now, it is up to the student to develop faith and gain access to this openness. For this purpose, there is the practice of guru yoga in which we unite our mind with that of our teacher. As a result of the blessings that we receive in this way, we can recognize the true dimension of our mind and realize Mahamudra, the ultimate reality.

For the realization of Mahamudra the blessings of the master are essential.

The extent to which a transmission of blessings takes place very much depends on the view of the student. If they view the teacher to whom they pray as a buddha, then they will receive the blessings of a buddha. If they view him as a bodhisattva, they will receive the blessings of a bodhisattva. If they view him as a great yogi, they will receive the corresponding blessings. And if they view their teacher as merely an ordinary human being with some spiritual experience, then they will only receive the blessings commensurate with that view.

If a student has a pure view and sees great qualities in their lama, then every time they turn to him or her in their prayer, the blessings of all the buddhas and bodhisattvas will blend with their teacher. In this way, through their devotion to their teacher, the student can obtain the blessings of all the buddhas. In short, the trust of the student determines the extent and depth of the blessings that they receive.

Guru yoga, the union of our mind with the awakened mind of the master, is one of the most effective methods for bringing forth our buddha nature. When we pray to the lama in a heartfelt way and full of devotion, his or her blessings and realization will blend with our mind and ripen our mind stream. For a seed to germinate, the seedling to grow, and for the plant to eventually produce flowers, not only the seed and soil are needed but also the warmth of the sun and rain falling from the clouds. It is the same with our mind. It is not sufficient to possess the seed of the buddha nature, we also need the warmth of trust and devotion as well as the rain of blessings from the lama for this seed to grow in us.

It is said that the lama is the source and root of all blessings. Through the lama all Dharma teachings become comprehensible and active in our mind stream. It is also said that awakening is impossible without the blessings of the lama. All buddhas of the past have walked the path of devotion in order to realize enlightenment. However, in this connection, "lama" does not stand for a person of flesh and blood but for the body of truth (dharmakaya), the dimension of perfect, timeless awareness. The lama is the pure aspect of our mind, and the outer lama serves above all as a support for us, so that we can realize this pure aspect of ourselves. In reality, the lama is the primordial buddha *Vajradhara*, the truth body itself, the essence of the realization of all the buddhas.

The blessings of this realization have been transmitted from one awakened master to the next in an unbroken chain down the centuries to the present time. All teachers and students of this lineage have kept their spiritual bonds and commitments in a completely pure way. Every one of these masters has transmitted the entirety of the instructions of the lineage and its inherent blessings to his principal students. Nothing has been lost – just as though water had been poured from one vase into another, without retaining or spilling a single drop. Every one of these teachers realized the primordial awareness and was able to pass on the realization of the truth body to their students. And every one of these students, because of their total faith in the lama, was able to open themselves completely to timeless awareness.

The lama is the door to the dimension of timeless awareness. When we pray to the lama with devotion, the door will open and the blessings of the dharmakaya will flow into our mind. Only in this way are the blessings transmitted. If we sit in the dark, while there is light next door, it will not become light where we sit unless we open the door. It is the same with the lama: as long as we do not turn to him with faith, his blessings and realization will not reach us.

Just as we need a mirror to see our face, we need a teacher in order the see the nature of mind.

Our trust and devotion should be free of vacillation, not clear and strong at one time and then again clouded by doubts. Frequently, our devotion feels artificial at first, but the more we pray and ask for the blessings of the lama, the more natural it becomes. Eventually, we do not even have to think of developing devotion or do anything special, but we feel united with the lama all the time. Then, trust and devotion have become something completely natural.

We do not pray in order to obtain something that we feel we absolutely must have, but to beseech the lama that our karmic obscurations may dissolve and that we may obtain direct insight into the nature of mind. Our prayer and the blessings of the lama and the Three Jewels are as inseparable as fire and warmth. Whenever we kindle the fire of prayer, the warmth of blessings will spread. Blessings are the natural result of prayer and not something that is given to us by some special power or a supernatural being.

Praying is really something very simple. In praying, we unite our mind with the awakened mind that we call "lama" or "teacher." Our own mind, the mind of the lama and the dimension of timeless awareness are one and the same thing. They all are the true nature of mind. To allow our own mind to rest in this state of complete simplicity, free from all complications and imagining, is natural prayer – it is the highest kind of practice.

The mind cannot be sought
by the mind.
The mind as such does not exist.
Its nature is empty –
empty and limitless,
it illuminates everything.

Be the great meditator
who practices non-meditation:
rest undistractedly in Great Bliss,
in which clarity and emptiness
are no longer separated.

Gendun Rinpoche

Investigating the Nature of Mind

When we start meditating, we first need to understand what the mind is. To meditate without having acquired a clear theoretical understanding of what mind really is, will not lead to liberation from suffering. We would risk going astray in our practice and missing the goal, the recognition of the nature of mind.

*To attain enlightenment we need to unite
correct view and correct meditation.*

The union of these two aspects of our practice is essential for the path. The traditional teachings say that knowledge without practice is like dying of thirst on the shore of a lake and that meditation without correct view is like a blind person going astray in the desert. Since our mind is the base of all of our experience, of delusion as well as of liberation, it is important that we acquire a clear understanding of it.

In everyday language, we designate that which carries out all thinking, remembering and investigating by the word "mind." We say that the mind is that which thinks – and sometimes this entity is active, sometimes it is quiet, sometimes happy, then again sad, sometimes gentle and at other times quite forceful. All this is the mind – but does this mind really exist? As much as we search for it, we cannot

find anything of which we could say: "This is the mind." It cannot
be seen anywhere; it is not a perceptible object. It does appear to exist, and yet it cannot be taken hold of.

But we also cannot send away this mind that cannot be grasped; it
does not even stay quiet when we want to shut it down. It cannot be
mixed with anything else, nor can it be broken down into individual
parts. No picture or example perfectly applies to the mind; no definition captures all its aspects. And yet none of the examples that we
may choose to describe the mind is entirely inapplicable to it, as it is
not inconsistent with any of them.

> *The mind cannot be defined. It eludes
> all analysis and description.*

We cannot say that the mind exists, as even a buddha cannot find it.
But we also cannot say that the mind does not exist, since it is the
source of all appearances, of samsara as well as nirvana. At best we
can say that it is beyond all conception, that it is reality itself, the nature of everything living and non-living. It is beyond all thoughts and
perceptions; it is intangible and indescribable. When we see it, nothing is seen – it has neither color nor form nor attributes. When we
recognize it, nothing is recognized, since it is not an object of cog-
nition. When we realize it, nothing is realized, since there is no-one
who could realize anything. In short, we cannot find anything that
could be defined as the mind.

The mind has no legs and yet it can go anywhere. It has no eyes and
yet it can see everything. It has no body and yet it can perform all
sorts of actions. It is beyond all philosophical notions such as "existing" or "not existing" or "both existing and not existing" or "neither
of these two." It is beyond thought and cannot be grasped by thought.
Therefore, it is said of the mind that it is the "great middle" beyond
all fixed, extreme views, beyond all conceptual reference points.

When we assert that the mind or some essence of mind exists, we fall into the view of eternalism which posits the actual, permanent existence of the mind. When we say that the mind or some essence of mind does not exist, we fall into the other extreme, the view of nihilism, which totally denies the existence of the mind. Similarly, when we assert that "the mind is beyond the notions of existing and non-existing" or "the mind is both existing and non-existing," we again fall into the error of believing in a permanent existence of the mind, since we essentially affirm the fact that the mind is there. If we think, as a fourth possibility, that the mind must be none of all the above, we deny its existence and again fall into the extreme of nihilism.

The Buddhist "Middle Way" is based on the understanding that none of these intellectual positions nor any combination of them can capture the nature of the mind, because it eludes being grasped by the intellect. And we should not hold on to this middle view either, as something truly existing, or as a new and final position. Intellectual considerations such as these can help us avoid falling into erroneous views, but eventually we have to leave them behind in order to realize the nature of mind.

The ultimate reality of the mind is entirely beyond all imagination, conceptualization or definition. In order to realize it, we must enter the path of meditation. The nature of mind is not to be found in a specific location, and yet we must follow a path in order to recognize it. However, to get to this realization, we must not make an object or a goal out of the mind and its nature.

The mind has no origin, it abides nowhere, and it has no end, no death, as it is not an object with a definable existence. It is not an appearance that arises and then passes away, in dependence on causes and conditions. Rather, it is the true nature of all appearances. There is no place or time of which one could say: "The mind arises here, this is the moment of its birth." Because of that, we say that the mind is unborn. Since it cannot be located in time and space, we say that it abides nowhere. And since it is unborn, it is also deathless because there cannot be an end to an unborn mind.

Even though the mind neither exists nor is nonexistent, we can say that it is spontaneous, unconditioned, eternal, unvarying, indestructible, primordially pure and complete. Its indestructible aspect is also called the body of truth, body of ultimate reality, indestructible body, or buddha nature.

In order to realize Mahamudra, the "Great Seal" of the nature of all things, we need to have a clear idea of the nature of mind that will guide us in our meditation. For that we must develop wisdom. The attainment of the goal of our practice is also called "perfection of wisdom," or "prajnaparamita" in Sanskrit. This wisdom is already naturally inherent in our mind. It is able to recognize itself directly in perfect non-duality, without any distortion through the intellect. And it perfects itself in the deep understanding of the ultimate nature of the mind.

When we speak of the mind, it almost sounds as though this mind is a concrete thing that could be described and named. However, when we look directly at what we call mind, we cannot find it anywhere. If we assume that the mind dwells in a specific place, then we ought to be able to ascribe a particular form to it, because something that exists at a specific place and not elsewhere, has to have a delimited form. But what form or shape does the mind have? When something has a form, it ought also to have a color. So what color does the mind have?

When we ask ourselves these questions, we will come to the conclusion that we cannot say anything definite about this supposed something that we call mind. But neither can we assert that the mind is nothing, or that it does not exist. If this were the case, then the body ought to be able to act even without the mind. Could our body do anything without the mind? Could the sense organs such as the eyes and ears see and hear, if there were no mind? Could a corpse, a body without a mind, see and hear? We should ask ourselves such questions if we are inclined to the belief that the mind does not exist. We could also go one step further and look directly at the mind that thinks it does not exist.

If, on the other hand, we are still convinced that the mind exists, even though we have found neither its form nor its color, we should direct our attention toward that which is conscious of the mind. Is it the body that is conscious of the mind or is it the mind that is conscious of itself?

The mind does not have any material existence, it has neither form nor color, and yet it is able to know and experience everything and be conscious of the most varied perceptions. Because of our mind, we know of the past, the present, and the future and experience happiness and sorrow, bondage and liberation. But it cannot be caught hold of itself. If the mind cannot be grasped by the intellect, how then can we recognize it?

> *The only possibility we have of recognizing the nature of mind is in deep meditation that leads to direct, non-conceptual insight into the nature of all things.*

Only through meditation can we clarify our questions regarding the existence or nonexistence of the mind. Meditation will make it possible for us to leave behind all ideas about what the mind is and what it is not. For this reason, meditation is the heart of spiritual practice.

This mind that cannot be grasped through concepts generates a continuous activity in the form of innumerable thoughts, perceptions and emotions. The forces that are responsible for their appearance are the specific karmic tendencies that are active in our mind, and these in turn have come into being because of attachment. Ultimately, attachment, or clinging, is the cause of everything that appears in our minds.

When we observe the stream of our thoughts attentively, we can see how one thought emerges after another, without our having control over this process. Every individual thought appears abruptly, as if on its own, even without our consciously willing to think something definite. It is not we who decide which thoughts emerge but our karmic tendencies, our karma.

Thoughts are individual movements in the mind – and thinking is a stream of reactions to these involuntary mental movements that is based on grasping. Whether it is with attachment or aversion, our reacting at thoughts leads us to link a succession of additional thoughts to them, and through this process complicated whirlpools are generated in our mind. Our habit of grasping at thoughts disrupts the unhindered arising of mental movements that we could leave as they are without reacting to them.

However, instead of allowing thoughts to dissolve of their own accord, we immediately attach a succession of concepts or ideas to these movements in the mind, such as memories of the past, considerations of the present or speculations about the future. In this way, we become entangled in attachment and aversion, which leads to strain and all the other harmful emotional states. If much grasping and attachment are present in our mind, then this mental whirling will be very strong.

When we give up our attachment to thoughts, our churned-up mind will calm down of its own accord, as it ceases holding on to thoughts. Thoughts continue to appear but the chains of thoughts that ordinarily follow in their wake no longer occur. When there is a movement in the mind, it dissolves at once. The mind perceives the movement just as it is, without turning it into an object of attachment. It does not react to or intervene in the movement, and so the movement can pass without hindrance.

We might ask ourselves now: "Why don't these thoughts simply stop?"

*Thinking has no end because we believe
that external objects possess an independent
existence that is separate from us.*

Because of ignorance, we take appearances, which after all are nothing but projections of our own minds, to be concrete things that exist independently of our mind. And as long as we hold on to the idea of an independent existence of objects, we will be caught in chains of thoughts. We create a connection between ourselves and the object – which we think exists independently – that ties us to it, as if with a rope – and that brings us under its influence.

Our fixation on the object leads to a dependence on it that causes many additional thoughts and emotional fluctuations in our mind. When we relax our mind, we sever this rope that ties us to the objects of the phenomenal world, and then a soothing calm arises in which our mind is no longer stirred up by multifarious thoughts about objects of attachment.

Most of the thoughts that make it so difficult to calm our mind revolve around worldly affairs and desires, about how to achieve happiness and how to avoid suffering. They arise from our attachment to this life and from our lack of awareness of impermanence and death. We do not want to see what really happens in our own mind, and we are convinced that our agitation is caused by other people or external situations. We think it is because of them that our mind is stirred up by pride, anger, and the like.

However, once we understand that all our thoughts and emotions come from inside us and do not originate from external causes, we cease to lay the responsibility on others, and our mind will no longer be shaken by emotional reactions. The moment we become aware that everything arises from within the mind itself, our attachment to the idea of an objective world that exists separately from us dissolves. Through this insight we become free and cease to suffer.

There is suffering only as long as we live in duality.

The world in which we find ourselves is a projection of our mind. Our previous actions have created tendencies in our mind that cause it to project a particular kind of world. But this world does not exist in reality. It is nothing but an insubstantial manifestation; it is empty – without self-nature. There is nothing in it that lasts. It is without substance, empty of any self-existing being through which it could be defined.

The cause of the emergence of the world and of our belief in its concrete existence is our lack of awareness, our ignorance. What we experience as a solid world is in reality nothing but a series of perceptions. All these perceptions, experiences, or events, as well as the perceived objects, arise in dependence on a multiplicity of factors. Everything is conditioned; everything arises in interdependence. Nothing in this world has an independent existence; everything depends on interactions.

Our experience of the world can be compared to a dream. In a dream, the mind is able to create visions of the most varied worlds, but they do not possess any real existence. If the dream takes a pleasant course, we are content and happy and would like to continue dreaming. Unpleasant dreams, however, trigger aversion or fear, and we would like to terminate them. While we are dreaming we believe that the dream events are real, and so we are happy or tense, depending on what appears in the mind. When we wake up, it becomes clear to us that we were only dreaming; none of this really happened. Therefore, there was not the least reason to be happy or unhappy. Exactly the same applies to our experiences in the waking state.

All the thoughts and sensations we identify with have as little reality as dream experiences.

Our belief in the reality of appearances that in fact are empty and illusory causes us to become attached to them. This belief is the source of all delusion, and the interplay between perceiving subject and perceived object keeps up the deception. When we awaken to the true nature of appearances, we realize that we have allowed ourselves to get carried away with emotional reactions that were triggered by completely illusory events. Viewed from the highest perspective, experiences in the dream and the waking state are equally empty, without any true reality. They are nothing but a projection of the habits and patterns of our mind.

Many people cannot let go of their dream experiences because they believe that dreams have a deeper meaning and contain hints for their daily lives. However, if after waking up we hold on to the supposed reality of the dream, we get even more deeply drawn into the delusion. If our dream was pleasant, we take it as a good sign and, full of expectation, try to bring about the situations or experiences that it augured.

If, on the other hand, we had an unpleasant or frightening dream, then we view it as a bad sign and are possibly worried. We see indications of future difficulties in our bad dreams, and we do everything we can to evade the threatening events or to prevent them, as though the dream scenario were likely to repeat itself during the day. And why all this? Because we believe in the reality of something that is nothing but a deceptive appearance in our mind.

Believing our experiences to be utterly real, we cling to them and as a consequence experience suffering. However, if in all situations we cultivate an awareness of the illusory dimension of our experience, as if we had woken up from a dream, we will recognize the empty nature of all phenomena, and the delusion will come to an end.

As long as their minds are caught in delusion and ignorance, the beings in the various *realms of existence* will experience suffering of limitless intensity and duration. The recognition, however, that mind and phenomena in reality are without substance, empty, illusory, and thus beyond suffering, leads to the perfect, unsurpassed joy of awakening. As long as we do not recognize this dimension of the emptiness of all phenomena, their illusory nature, we are caught in suffering.

We may believe that this illusion will dissolve all by itself but that is not the case. As long as the causes are present, the corresponding results will follow. As long as there is delusion, the same process will repeat itself in countless lifetimes, which is why we speak of the "cycle of suffering," or samsara.

When we hear about the immense suffering of beings, their omnipresent delusion and ignorance and their endless wandering in samsara, we may become discouraged or depressed and believe that it would be impossible for us to end this suffering and attain enlightenment. We may think that ordinary people like us could never reach the goal of awakening. But there is no good reason to think in this way and be discouraged. On the contrary:

> *We should not consider ourselves incapable of realizing buddhahood, as the buddha nature is already present in each of us.*

The buddha nature is the true, innermost nature of our mind. It is neither external to us nor far distant from us. Awakening is not an unattainable goal or something that lies in the far distant future. When we know how we should practice, we can get there very quickly, since we do not have to produce enlightenment. It is already present in us now and only waits to be discovered, through our seeing the nature of our mind. However, in order to get there we need a method. This method is the path taught by the Buddha. When we follow it, our buddha nature will reveal itself.

The buddha nature is the dimension of the omnipresent, true nature of all phenomena in samsara and *nirvana*. It pervades all things and sentient beings and is present in the mind of everyone as their potential for future awakening. There is no difference between the latent potential and full enlightenment, with regard to their nature and quality – they are indistinguishable and inseparable.

Although the buddha nature is present in us, we do not see it, because it is covered with obscurations that stand in the way of our mind recognizing its true nature. These obscurations are the result of all the self-centered actions that we have performed with our body, speech and mind since beginningless time. The actual cause of all obscurations is ignorance, the clinging to a presumed 'I'. Because of our clinging to this 'I', we carry out actions that produce karmic forces in the form of self-centered thoughts, feelings and imaginings that conceal the true nature of our mind.

These obscurations separate us from the wisdom qualities of our mind, as they bring about a dualistic perception of reality and deeply-rooted, reflexive patterns of thinking and acting. We can remove them by giving up self-centered reaction patterns, ceasing to accumulate further negative karma and orienting our body, speech and mind entirely toward wholesome action. When all obscurations have dissolved, our buddha nature is revealed, and we see what we truly are: buddhas.

If we dissolve the obscurations now, we will soon realize buddhahood. If we postpone this work, enlightenment will only be attained later, provided we again find suitable conditions for working with our mind. The decision lies with us – our buddha nature accompanies us all the time. When we become aware of the existence of our buddha nature, the desire arises in us to realize it. However, it will not reveal itself to us if we do not know the path that leads to the dissolution of the obscurations and we do not actually enter on this path, or if we abandon it after practicing it for some time because we lack perseverance.

Evidently, in our past lives we have not followed the right path or we have not persevered, or else we would already have attained enlightenment. Now that we know the path to complete awakening, it is important that we follow it to the end, without deviating from it. If we do this, then it is completely certain that our buddha nature will reveal itself, as it has always been there – there is nothing to find or generate that has not been there all along. We only have to decide to walk this path and not deviate from it. Then the goal is not difficult to attain. If we do not venture out and actually set out on this path, but instead leave it at mere intellectual knowledge of the buddha nature, then buddhahood will not reveal itself to us.

The buddha nature is just like butter that is already present in milk as a potential: when we beat cream in the right way, we obtain butter. But if we do not do anything and merely sit there and look at the milk, then at best the milk becomes sour but it will not become butter. The person who knows how this works will beat the milk and with some effort obtain butter from it. Similarly, we must put out effort in order to produce an enlightened body, enlightened speech and enlightened mind. If we wish to attain enlightenment, we must do something.

The veils that cover our buddha nature are based on ignorance. They appear as the three emotional reaction patterns of attachment, aversion and indifference, or put differently, desire, anger and stupidity. These three basic patterns, the common denominator of which is self-centeredness, cloud our perception. They influence all the actions we carry out on the three planes of body, speech and mind and thus become causes for the accumulation of karma. Actions that are clouded by these emotional reaction patterns cause our obscurations to increase and thereby hinder the recognition of our true nature.

All sentient beings in the universe bear the buddha nature within themselves, and even though at the moment they are still ordinary beings, without a doubt they will be buddhas one day, if they practice the Dharma. The reality of buddha nature – the ground of everything, the heart of perfect awakening – is unbounded by space and time. It is omnipresent, like space, and pervades all sentient beings, without any difference in quality or quantity.

If we wish to uncover our buddha nature and develop the correct view that is necessary for correct meditation, we need to familiarize ourselves with the two planes of reality, the relative and the ultimate, and recognize their inseparability. The relative plane of reality is the world as it appears to us. But in this manifestation on the relative plane, the ultimate reality, the empty nature of all manifestation, is present at the same time. The Tibetan word for "world" (jigten) means "destructible basis." The material world is considered to be a basis that inevitably is subject to destruction, because it is conditioned. The world is transitory: it arises, exists for some time, and then ceases. It has no lasting existence – that is its ultimate reality, its emptiness. It is empty of anything that lasts. The fact that it is visible nonetheless and does manifest is its relative reality.

In this relative reality, everything changes from moment to moment. The mind expresses itself unceasingly and spontaneously in a never-ending multiplicity of appearances, but these are not real in an ultimate sense, as everything changes continually and nothing endures. Idea follows idea, one movement of the mind follows another, appearances change incessantly. For that reason, on close inspection, we can see that appearances are not real – they are empty of any true reality. And yet manifestation goes on, as it is the expression of the empty nature and spontaneous luminosity of the mind.

*Appearances are manifest as well as empty – they
are the unity of manifestation and emptiness.*

By relative reality we denote the manifesting aspect of appearances
and by ultimate reality the aspect of the illusory, transitory nature
of all manifestation, its being empty of anything lasting. All appearances, whether in the external world or within ourselves, are the inseparable unity of these two planes of reality.

Generally speaking, we can classify all phenomena and sentient beings according to their participation in one or the other of two kinds
of experience of being: the cycle of conditioned existence fraught
with suffering, samsara, or the dimension of liberation beyond suffering, nirvana. The essence of samsara is delusion, and its distinctive
mark is suffering, whereas the essence of nirvana is awareness and its
mark is true happiness beyond all suffering.

But the true nature of samsara as well as of nirvana is emptiness, as
neither possesses any true, independent existence. They are "empty"
of any essence – nonetheless they manifest. By emptiness of samsara
we mean that the entire living and non-living phenomenal world is
nothing but the unity of appearance and emptiness, emptiness and
form. The goal of spiritual practice is the recognition of this reality.

The recognition of the empty nature of all things corresponds to
the realization of the truth body, dharmakaya. We recognize all appearances on the relative plane as the manifestation of the luminosity of the dharmakaya – they are empty but nonetheless they appear. With this recognition, we experience everything as the unity
of bliss and emptiness, because our belief in the concrete existence
of things has dissolved and we no longer fall prey to attachment and
suffering. Since we no longer succumb to the deception, we recognize suffering as being empty, without true existence. And that is

nirvana, the dimension beyond all suffering, the end of the cycle of death and rebirth.

Whether we succumb to cyclic existence full of suffering, samsara, or experience the dimension free of suffering, nirvana, depends on the presence or absence of this delusion. When our perception is impaired or distorted through ignorance, i. e., through the dualistic delusion, we wander in samsara.

When we become aware of the nature of delusion, the veils of dualistic attachment dissolve, and we arrive at the awakened dimension, the knowledge of the empty nature of all appearances.

We meditate until we recognize that appearances and mind are inseparable. Then it becomes clear to us that it would be senseless or even harmful to block the appearances and perceptions that arise in our mind, since that would entail suppressing the natural movement of the mind. Similarly, we do not need to artificially generate an experience of emptiness, since we can simply rest in the awareness of the unity of appearances and emptiness, by recognizing appearances as projections of our mind.

In this way, we see that we ourselves, the subject that perceives something, are not different from the object that is perceived. In this state of understanding and openness our meditation truly becomes authentic. However, if we are content to merely contemplate an object and call that meditation, then we will never overcome the duality of meditator and meditation. All objects of perception are nothing but manifestations of mind; they are not external objects but mind itself.

Recognizing this pacifies the play of our emotional reactions, because then there is no longer any separation between our mind and its creations, between subject and object. Everything that we experience is the expression of our own mind. Mind and manifestation are one and the same; they are not separated in the least. Just as the mind is not an object that could be described or delimited, so the appearances that the mind projects are also beyond all imagination and description.

> *Meditating means becoming aware*
> *of the true nature of all appearances.*

Since manifestations and mind are inseparable, when we meditate we must not attempt to block appearances – thoughts, images and the like – and generate an artificial "emptiness" in ourselves. We should simply allow our mind to rest in the now, the present moment, in its ordinary consciousness, free from any attempt to influence it. In order to get there, it is sufficient that we relax and let go of all attachment.

Being perfectly aware of even the smallest details and without interfering with the movements of our mind in the least, we rest in the awareness that mind and appearances are mutually dependent and inseparable. Our mind relaxes in the immediacy of the moment. In this way, our meditation progresses from the level of mental calm to intuitive insight and Mahamudra.

Happiness

Happiness cannot be found
through great effort and will,
but is already there, perfect and complete,
in relaxation and letting go.

Do not worry, there is nothing to do.
Whatever appears in mind has no importance,
since it has no reality.
Do not hold on to it, and do not judge.

Let the play happen by itself,
arising and passing,
without changing anything –
everything vanishes and reappears, without end.

Only your searching for happiness
prevents you from seeing it,
just like a rainbow that you chase
without ever reaching it.

Although happiness does not exist,
it has always been there
and accompanies you
in every moment.

Do not believe that good
or bad experiences are real.
They are like rainbows.
Wanting to grasp the ungraspable,
you exhaust yourself in vain.

As soon as you relax this grasping,
space is there – open, inviting and joyful.
Make use of it.
All is yours already.

Do not search any further.
Do not enter the impenetrable jungle
to search for the elephant
that is already quietly at home.

Nothing to do,
nothing to force,
nothing to wish for –
and everything happens by itself.

Gendun Rinpoche

The Path of Meditation

The Three Seals

Every Dharma practice, regardless of whether it is done by a beginner or by an advanced practitioner, should include the "Three Seals": going for refuge, developing awareness, and dedicating the merit. The inclusion of these Three Seals ensures that the practice leads to awakening. They guarantee purity of action and should always be present, even when we recite only a single mantra such as OM MANI PEME HUNG. They are the hallmark of every authentic Dharma practice.

The first seal consists of going for refuge in the Three Jewels and generating the mind of awakening. By developing this highest motivation, we orient our practice towards awakening.

The second seal, the development of awareness, is concerned with the main phase of the practice in which we train in the various methods of the Dharma. For example, we carry out wholesome actions, dissolve our ego-centered tendencies, purify the consequences of unwholesome actions, or apply ourselves to the development of wisdom by practicing the creation and completion stages of meditation and developing mental calm and intuitive insight. All of these practices serve to develop awareness. In order to deepen this further and strengthen our awareness of the true nature of mind, we should always conclude our actions with a moment of resting our mind beyond all reference points.

The third seal is the dedication. At the end of each practice session, we share the spiritual merit that we created with our practice with all sentient beings and wish that all of them, ourselves included, thereby quickly attain complete awakening. By dedicating our wholesome actions to the awakening of all, we channel their power to a clearly defined goal – a goal that is beyond subject/object divisions.

This act of dedicating the merit transforms even ordinary good deeds into a force that leads to awakening. When we do this, we also rest for a moment, in a completely natural way, in the recognition of the empty nature of all phenomena. Thus, in this highest way, we offer everything good and insightful that arose during our practice session, without clinging to the supposed reality of whatever may have transpired.

We seal our meditation by resting in an openness that is free of ego attachment, with the understanding that subject, object and action are all mind and ultimately are not different from one another. Through this openness, in which we let go of everything, the wholesome power of our actions is able to expand infinitely. Thus we avoid our wholesome actions merely leading to temporary well-being and remaining transitory and limited in their effects.

This resting in the ultimate reality is also called the "seal of the reality of appearances." When our actions are stamped with this seal of total non-identification, they cease to be our own. They become true and pure actions, regardless of how limited and imperfect they may have been at the outset.

Through the dedication, the power of wholesome actions is freed from the realm of ego-attachment – it becomes an energy that serves the awakening of all beings. Moreover, it is protected from being extinguished by an instant of strong emotion in our mind. There is a saying: "All the positive energy accumulated in an eon can be destroyed in a single instant of deep hatred." Therefore, as a protection against our own negativity, we dedicate all our wholesome actions, thereby "disowning" them – they no longer belong to us.

In addition, we may also dedicate the merit of the wholesome actions of all beings, in their entirety. When we do this, we link everything wholesome that was generated through our own actions to the powerful stream of everything wholesome that was generated in the past and will be generated in the future through the actions of all buddhas and bodhisattvas and all other beings. When we thus add the collective power of all wholesome actions to the power of our own actions, which may only have been slight, great joy arises in our mind, and this joy has an amplifying effect on our dedication of merit.

Moreover, the dedication of merit is an important aid against jealousy, envy, and our own chronic habit of comparing ourselves with others. Such tendencies may express themselves in the ambition to do these practices better than anyone else, or in the supposedly humble but nevertheless self-centered thought that others are much better at carrying out these actions than we are. When we rejoice at all wholesome deeds, irrespective of who performs them, this will do away with all such comparisons.

The practice of dedication connects our personal actions with the spontaneous dimension in which all qualities become limitless and a wellspring for the happiness of all beings.

Resting in the empty openness of our mind also dissolves hope, fear and all other emotional disturbances that might arise because of ignorance.

What Does Meditation Mean?

The basis of meditation is wholesome conduct – to develop mindfulness in all actions of body, speech and mind.

To be mindful means to be constantly careful not to harm others but to contribute to their highest welfare. Through such mindfulness, the altruistic attitude will expand in our mind more and more and become an all-encompassing way of living. Our egoism will decrease while our selfless interest in others increases and loving-kindness and compassion become a natural part of us. We will no longer think of ourselves alone. That is true mastery of meditation. In this meditation, we practice turning our mind toward others.

Meditation means resolutely looking at our self-centered patterns and working at dissolving them.

The true sign of progress in meditation is that our interest in the well-being of others grows and that it becomes ever easier for us to correct our own faults. When our self-centered, ill-disposed attitude dissolves, the result is that our goodness increases, life becomes easier for us, and our actions automatically bring about the welfare of others and our own happiness at the same time.

Meditation includes reflecting on the teachings, with the goal of understanding the true nature of mind, even if only intellectually at first. In this preparation, we undertake an analysis of subject and object, mind and appearances, at the relative level. This is deliberate, preliminary work that may appear somewhat artificial. On the basis of this intellectual, analytical understanding, meditation then leads us to the space beyond subject and object, in which the mind recognizes itself directly and in which an immediate, direct certainty arises, beyond all analysis. The analytical reflections that we have used to find our way to the correct meditation will have to be abandoned at this point, or else no true, spontaneous meditation will arise.

Only a completely natural meditation that is free of all ideas will lead to liberation.

Meditation does not mean producing any special state of mind, such as putting ourselves into a trance, a state of blissful contentment or any other artificial state. It does not entail evoking any special experiences, having visions, seeing particular forms and colors. Meditation means becoming aware of the fact that for an inconceivable length of time our mind has been prisoner of its attachment to experiences. It means seeing that this condition produces suffering, imprisons the mind and sets artificial limits to it. In meditation, we allow our mind to relax and free itself from this confinement. To be relaxed does not involve letting oneself go loose physically or being inattentive. What is meant here is a relaxation of the mind, in which both body and mind are fully present and awake.

Our narrow, limited states of mind are the consequence of self-centered actions that we carried out in our former lives and of the resultant karmic tendencies. Because of these habits, which have become compulsive, we barely have control over our lives – we suffer even when we do not want to. In many respects, we are the plaything of our karma, with rather limited opportunities for influencing anything. Through meditation we gradually cast off our mental narrowness and compulsiveness. We begin to dissolve our karmic tendencies and become increasingly able to influence our future, until eventually we master our lives with complete freedom of decision.

Generally speaking, we are trapped in reactive patterns of liking and not liking, wanting and not wanting. We live hoping that our wishes will be fulfilled and fearing that unpleasant things may happen. The resulting feelings of dissatisfaction and tension and all of our problems spring from our own compulsive mind and do not, as we commonly think, arise from other people or external pressures. They come from our unquenchable thirst for confirmation of our ego and fulfillment in external things, from the wish to attain something that cannot be attained. This strenuous search for a happiness external to us is the actual cause of our suffering and of our being trapped in a cycle of sorrowful existences that repeat themselves forever.

> *With the aid of meditation, we free ourselves from hoping for happiness and from attachment and tension. Meditation opens up to us the natural spaciousness and boundless joy that is inherent in our buddha nature.*

In this spaciousness, free from attachment and free from all suffering, our mind comes to rest. Our compulsive thought activity is not, as is commonly assumed, aroused by external conditions or contact with external objects, but is maintained by our patterns of attachment, rejection and indifference. Our thoughts and feelings appear as a result of our own tendencies. We project our own inner feeling states outside and then perceive them as the external world. When we learn in meditation to keep our mind free of attachment, no longer fixating on anything or constricting it with preconceived ideas, it relaxes totally and comes to rest. Then there is no longer any cause for the arising of thoughts and feelings.

> *When clinging to an 'I' ceases, projections also cease.*

Without this sense of 'I', the subject, there is no world of external phenomena that appears separate from it, no objects that appear to exist independent of the projecting mind. When we recognize this, our clinging to the supposed reality of appearances dissolves and our mind stops getting tangled up in reactions to its own projections. It becomes quiet and free of emotional turmoil. True mental calm arises.

Ordinarily, the mind with which we identify as our 'I', incessantly grasps at objects and becomes attached to the various situations we experience. In meditation, we give up this grasping and attachment. We release the mind from its fetters, allowing all fixation and distraction to dissolve by itself. In this process of letting go, the mind naturally frees itself of all tensions and attachments that constrict it and keep it trapped. We settle in an ever deepening relaxation, opening up totally. Whatever appears in our mind, we leave to itself, not holding onto or rejecting anything.

Meditation means allowing the mind to rest in the present moment – without rejecting anything, without creating anything artificially, and without manipulating what is there in any given moment.

In one of his instructions on the nature of mind, the great realized being Saraha said: "When we relax this mind of ours that is caught in attachment, without any doubt it will liberate itself." It is merely a matter of allowing our mind to settle in its natural state in which ordinary consciousness rests in the present moment, free from clinging or rejecting, without any artificiality. Then an ever deepening relaxation develops – and that is what leads to liberation. When we succeed in meditating without any manipulation, all of our tensions subside and the mind unties itself. Our open, clear and alive consciousness settles in itself undistractedly, without the slightest trace of dullness.

To take an example, after we have poured a cup of tea, at first the tea is still in motion. But when we leave the cup alone, the tea will gradually settle. The same thing happens when we leave our mind alone:

it comes to rest in a state of natural relaxation that deepens progressively. Not to allow our mind to rest in this relaxed, calm state would be like constantly stirring the teacup.

Meditation consists in becoming conscious of the movements that occur in our mind and allowing our thoughts to freely arise and return to where they came from. This is a natural process that we simply allow to happen; we merely give room to this natural openness and spontaneity of the mind. In doing this, we open ourselves to the recognition that the entire play of manifestation, everything that appears in our mind, is without reality. This leads to a relaxation of our mind and through that to a natural relaxation of our body. This does not mean, however, that our body goes into a slump. Rather, it maintains its erect, open and supple posture, free of all tension.

We have a tendency to shackle our body and mind with thoughts and plans and to maintain this lock with constant tension. In reaction, our mind becomes either wild or dull. In meditation, we loosen these fetters and allow ourselves to open up in a natural way. Through this our mind recovers its spaciousness and eventually its dimension of wisdom. Free at last from compulsion and tension, we cease to suffer. To no longer experience suffering means experiencing total joy – and that is awakening!

> *Opening and letting go is not difficult. It is much more difficult to forever hold on and struggle. In fact, letting go is the easiest thing in the world. There is nothing at all to do in letting go.*

Letting go is a precondition for deep meditation. We must let go of samsara, of our patterns of attachment that cause us to suffer. The difficulty with this is that these patterns are very tenacious, because we have nurtured them for so long and have strengthened them through so many deeds. But now we have the possibility to free ourselves from the fascination and the habits that bind us to the world of our attachments. To do this, we must develop true renunciation – and do it not merely with words.

Renunciation means detaching ourselves from our emotional entanglement in worldly affairs. Renunciation is the basis of all meditation. To develop renunciation, we first contemplate how precious and impermanent this life is. Then we think of the fact that all suffering and all happiness is dependent on our karma, on our actions. We take a close look at the consequences of all the actions that we have carried out previously and consider what the consequences of our present actions will be in the future. We reflect on how we ourselves have been responsible for creating the causes of our attachments and of our imprisonment in samsara.

> *When we admit to ourselves how senseless and ultimately harmful all actions are that we carry out based on our attachments, we will be in a position to free ourselves from them.*

Until now, we have acted in a worldly manner, because we were under the influence of ignorance, but now we can reorient our lives towards awakening, thanks to our access to the teachings of the Buddha. At the same time, we see that all sentient beings are under the influence of ignorance and because of that act in harmful ways and experience immense suffering. Most of these beings have no contact at all with such instructions and, therefore, no possibility of recognizing their ignorance and freeing themselves from it. All of this arouses our compassion, strengthens our renunciation and opens us up even more to engaging in selfless practice for the highest benefit of all beings.

Our renunciation deepens further when genuine devotion arises in us. This devotion connects us with the blessings of the lama and

The Path of Meditation

of the lineage of transmission and makes it easier for us to let go of our limitations and attachments. By practicing the instructions of our teacher, we deepen our confidence in the Dharma and convince ourselves of the truth of the teachings. When we possess such confidence and conviction, it becomes easy for us to let go of our clinging to cyclic existence and free ourselves from our fascination with it.

> *When we free ourselves from clinging and develop compassion and faith, then through a natural renunciation our mind comes to rest all by itself.*

The path of meditation that leads to the recognition of the nature of mind can be divided into two phases: the development of *mental calm* and the cultivation of *intuitive insight*. Through the practice of mental calm, we first stabilize body and mind. This stability develops to the point at which we can apply the methods of the meditation of intuitive insight. As our meditation progresses, we become more and more familiar with deep relaxation which leads us effortlessly to corresponding meditation experiences and eventually to liberation. Relaxation is a precondition for every meditation, regardless of which practice we do.

As a first step on the path of meditation, we must learn to collect our mind. We do this by orienting it toward the awakening of all beings, an inner attitude that combines renunciation, loving-kindness and compassion. In addition, the correct body posture and a specific reference point for our meditation will make it much easier for us to collect ourselves mentally.

The Sitting Posture

If we find it difficult to sit on the floor, because of limited mobility or for reasons of age, we may also meditate sitting on a chair. The future buddha Maitreya is depicted in this fashion. Our back should be straight and our spinal column extended "like an arrow" – and that also applies when we sit on a chair. This posture lifts and stretches the upper torso and reduces the pressure on the inner organs in the abdominal cavity. With a straight back, the mind is clearer, too. Therefore, we should be careful not to slump and not to lean forward or backward or to the side.

The position of our head is also important. It should not be inclined toward the front, the back, the left or right. Rather, it should be kept upright, as an extension of the spinal column. Our chin should be horizontal and put a slight pressure on the throat. Our eyes should simply rest, without being focused on any particular place. We should neither close them nor keep them wide open; they should be half open and relaxed.

The direction of our gaze depends on the kind of meditation that we practice. For the development of mental calm, we direct our gaze downward; in the phase of intuitive insight, we direct it straight ahead; and in Mahamudra practice, we gaze slightly upward, to connect our mind with space.

It is very important that we train ourselves in the correct posture, in particular of the back and the eyes, because then it becomes easy to keep our mind awake and develop experiences and realization. When we slump, our chest cavity becomes constricted, and our mind becomes heavy and dull. We begin to lose clarity and sink into a sleepy, semi-conscious state of mind.

When we hold ourselves erect, our subtle energies can circulate freely and our mind becomes clear.

These are the most important points that we should observe in order to influence the mind favorably by way of the body. Those who are young and supple may wish to practice the seven-point posture of Vairocana which is very useful and beneficial for meditation.

The first point of this posture consists of crossing the legs in the "vajra posture." We bend the left leg and place the left foot on the right thigh. Then we bend the right leg and place the right foot on the left thigh. The soles of both feet face upward.

Second, we place our hands in the groins of the upper thighs, with the palms facing upward. The thumb touches the base of the ring finger. Then we completely extend our arms until the inner arm points forward and the upper arm touches the thorax. The elbow joint exerts a slight pressure on the ribs. Through the pressure on these points in the groin area, on the ring finger and on the side of the thorax, certain subtle energy channels are affected that are connected with the emotions. The pressure exerted on these points interrupts the circulation of certain emotional energies.

Third, the spinal column should be "straight like an arrow." Not only should we sit erect but our posture also involves opening the upper part of the thorax, without stretching it forward, and slightly tilting the upper part of the pelvis forward, without creating a hollow back. Due to this correction, the upper part of the body is completely erect, and at the same time the natural curvature of the spinal column is maintained.

Fourth, the shoulders are raised "like the wings of a vulture." Through the position of the arms, the shoulders are slightly lifted but they are not pushed forward or backward. The raised and straight posture of the shoulders removes the pressure that normally is exerted on the inner organs that are crowded together in the abdominal cavity. This posture contributes to our being able to maintain a clear and vivid consciousness in which the mind is neither excited nor dull.

Fifth, the neck should be "bent like a hook." However, this does not mean that we should literally hold our neck in the shape of a hook and tilt our head backward or bend it forward toward our chest. Our head is kept perfectly upright but our chin is slightly pulled backward horizontally and thereby presses slightly on the larynx. This posture blocks the circulation of emotional energies in the two energy channels located at the right and left side of the neck.

Sixth, our eyes should be kept half open and our gaze should be directed downward. Traditionally, it is said that we should look at a point that is four fingers' width distant from the point of the nose, but this should not be taken literally. We do not need to squint; rather, we direct our gaze downward along the extension of the nose, without moving our eyes or our eyelids. It is said that a peaceful gaze is the entrance gate to mental stability.

Seventh, the tongue should rest in its natural position in the palate. It should not be forcefully pressed against it. The mouth, too, remains totally relaxed. It is opened barely noticeably so that a small stream of air can pass. The point here is not to assume any artificial position but to find our way back into a natural posture.

These are the seven points of the ideal meditation posture that contributes greatly to opening our mind. In addition, we can help our mind rest in calmness by collecting it with the aid of a specific reference point. Once we have developed a certain level of skill in this, we can move on to meditation without an object. The reference point that we choose for our meditation can be an ordinary, "impure" object or a spiritual, "pure" object.

Regardless of what we use as an object, we allow our mind to rest on it and practice in this way until the experiences of bliss, clarity and non-conceptuality arise. When we rest in these experiences of deep mental calm, the second phase of meditation, intuitive insight, will unfold, and eventually we will encounter the nature of mind.

Meditation with a Reference Point

Sitting in the erect posture that was described above, we take some time at first to settle into our meditation. We let go of all attachment and aversion to our surroundings and rest in equanimity. We allow our mind to relax and settle in its natural state.

Then we turn our attention to the object that we have chosen as the reference point for our meditation. Preferably, it should be small, and in order to find the proper distance, we can place it on a small table in front of us. It could be a flower, a glass of water, a stone or any other ordinary object. We look at it undistractedly, not turning our gaze to anything else.

It is important not to fix our gaze on the object tensely and with much effort. If we strain our mind, we may get an impression of stability at the beginning, a feeling that fewer thoughts arise. But this impression passes quickly, and then frustration and anger appear. Our mind should settle on the object in a natural way – we should simply be conscious of the object as a whole, without being concerned with details of its form, color or other characteristics.

When we allow our mind to relax in this way, it will become quiet after some time, and a feeling of clarity, openness and spaciousness will arise. For beginners it is advisable to meditate with the help of such a support until the mind is undistracted and able to rest on the object without any effort. In this way, mental quiet arises.

After some time, we may get the feeling that the size, form or color of the object is changing. It is also possible that our eyes begin to tire, itch or tear, and that we do not see the object anymore. These are signs of fatigue. When they appear, we should turn away from the object for a few moments and allow our gaze and our mind to open to the expanse of space. During our meditation session, we should alternate between phases of intentional collection on the object and relaxation into the expanse of space. If we subject ourselves to excessive discipline, then our mind becomes increasingly tense and blocked.

*Beginners should perform brief meditation
sessions that are limited to a few minutes at a time
but repeat these sessions as often as possible.*

As we get accustomed to this practice, our sessions can gradually be extended. If we attempt to meditate for long periods right at the beginning, our mind will easily become impatient or rebellious. We may lose our joy in meditating and equate meditation with strain and restriction. It is advisable, therefore, to finish the session when our mind is still happy and relaxed and not carry on until it gets to be too much and our mind shuts itself off.

Instead of an ordinary object, we can also use a spiritual, pure object as an aid for collecting our mind such as, for example, the body of the Buddha. We imagine that the Buddha appears before us in space, or if that turns out to be too difficult, we can direct our attention to a statue of the Buddha placed in front of us.

Before his last birth in the human realm, Buddha Shakyamuni had already worked for the benefit of all beings in the universe over inconceivably many lifetimes. While he was doing this, he accumulated great merit and developed deep awareness and thereby purified all the obscurations of his mind. According to tradition, before he manifested as the historical Buddha, he had assumed birth five hundred times in impure realms of existence, in order to help the beings living there, and five hundred times in pure realms, in order to help the realized beings dwelling in those realms. Through these actions he became a perfect buddha. When we visualize him in his human form, we visualize him as a radiant, luminous being, with all of the physical characteristics and signs that symbolize perfect awakening.

An awakened being, such as the Buddha, is capable of showing all beings the way and leading them to perfect awakening. His actions for the benefit of others are without limit. We ordinary humans with limited, impure perception find it difficult to imagine what a buddha really is. For this reason, we choose the form of the historical Buddha Shakyamuni as a support for our meditation. However, we should be fully aware that the Buddha is anything but an ordinary person.

For this meditation we sit down comfortably, upright and relaxed. We let go of all attachment and aversion and rest in equanimity, in the awareness of the moment, in physical and mental relaxation. Then we contemplate the Buddha in front of us, in the form of a statue or a picture, or as a visualized form created in our own imagination.

We first direct our attention to the Buddha's throne. It is adorned with precious jewels and supported by eight snow lions. Its seat is covered with silken cloths and cushions on which a white lotus is resting, with a flat moon disk on top. The Buddha is sitting on the moon disk, with his legs crossed in the vajra posture. We imagine him not having a body of flesh and blood but possessing a wisdom body.

We meditate on the Buddha as a transparent being of light, a rainbow-like, illusory manifestation – the unity of form and emptiness.

If this is too difficult for us, we can also visualize the Buddha possessing a human body that radiates light. His right hand touches the ground, and his left hand is placed in his lap in the gesture of meditation. He is looking at us and all other sentient beings with boundless loving-kindness and compassion. His mind is resting in a meditative awareness that is free of all delusion and knows all beings down to the most intimate detail. His gentle smile evinces the benevolent attention that he is paying to all beings.

Once we have developed a clear picture of the Buddha in front of us, we think of his great kindness and of our good fortune at being able to be in his presence. We imagine that he addresses us and explains the Dharma to us. We are grateful for this extraordinary opportunity and remind ourselves that this situation is the result of the accumulation of wholesome deeds and the purification of our mind stream over countless lifetimes – we now reap the fruits of our efforts in past lives. We are very happy.

Full of joy, we look at the Buddha, note all of the wonderful signs of his body, and imagine that light rays emanate from him that fill our body and mind. They remove our physical and mental limitations and all the obscurations that have accumulated because of our self-centeredness. They dissolve the dualistic attachment that separates us from everything else. We imagine that we not separated from the Buddha and allow our mind to become completely one with him.

In this state we remain as long as we can. When we notice our mind becoming dull or unclear, we direct our attention to the upper part of the Buddha's body, to the crown of his head or his face. Through this, our dullness and mental heaviness dissolve. On the other hand, if our mind is restless and many thoughts arise, we direct our attention downward, to his feet and legs or to the throne and the lotus. This serves to soothe our mental excitement. If we feel neither sleepy nor restless, we remain in the union of our mind with that of the Buddha. We contemplate the entire form of his body or place our attention on the area of his heart.

If we become easily distracted while we are looking at the Buddha and experience some difficulty in settling into recollection, we can let our gaze wander downward on his body, from above to below, again and again, and point by point recollect the characteristics of his external appearance, in a completely relaxed fashion, without any effort. This will help our mind to gradually calm down.

If, after some time, we do not see the form of the Buddha distinctly anymore, or if our eyes become tired, we need a break and we can let go of our contemplation for a few minutes. We direct our gaze upward and relax it in the expanse of space. When our mind livens up again, we continue with the practice.

During the entire meditation session, it is important to cultivate the joyful certainty of the presence of the Buddha and confidence in the power of his blessings.

At the end of every session, we imagine that light rays emanate from the Buddha's forehead, throat and heart (the centers of body, speech and mind, respectively) that merge with our respective centers. Through this, our body, speech and mind are blessed and all our obscurations and negativities are purified. Finally, the Buddha completely dissolves into light which blends with us, so that there is no longer any difference between him and us – as though water has been poured into water. We then allow our mind to rest in its natural dimension, free, relaxed and without any artificiality.

This practice is very useful, as it enables us not only to develop mental stability but also opens us to receive the blessings of the Buddha. Through this, we purify our karma and set the stage for meditative experiences and realization to arise.

Another reference point that we may choose to collect our mind is the breath. When we meditate on the breath, we follow the natural, steady, inward and outward movement of the breath, without trying to influence it in any way. We put our body and mind under no strain but remain completely relaxed and are simply aware of the inward and outward movement of the breath, without following any thoughts. We allow our mind to join with the movement of the breath until it is completely merged with it. As an aid, we can count the breaths, for example to twenty-one, and try not to let anything distract us from that. Then it is good to make a short pause. Once we are continuously aware of the breath in a relaxed manner, we can meditate for longer periods, without counting the breaths, but simply being attentive to it.

*To be attentive to the object does not mean
to concentrate on it with all our might.*

We should not say to ourselves: "Under no circumstances will I lose my attention on the breath. I must concentrate on it with all my might." Thoughts like this only feed our restlessness and disturb our meditation and the natural movement of our breath. If we run a commentary on our meditation, we create a distance that prevents us from merging with it. We should simply be aware of our breath without any great strain – and to accomplish that, gentle, regular practice is the most important thing we can do. The ensuing stability will help us penetrate more deeply into meditation.

Being in the Present

In our meditation we allow the stream of thoughts to flow by naturally, without grasping at them or judging them. When we are free of attachment, can any thoughts remain at all? Can the mind be restless when we hold on to nothing? Surely not. But ordinarily we hold on to every thought and judge it to be "good" or "bad," with the accompanying feelings of liking or disliking. This triggers an entire chain of thoughts that continue to agitate the mind. If we were free of attachment, we would not attribute good or bad properties to any thought upon its arising, causing us to want to hold on to it or push it away. To us, the thought would merely be a movement created by the non-attached mind. Our attachment, however, interferes with these playful, natural dynamics.

During our meditation it is important not to think of things we have done in the past. Normally, we grasp at such memories and spin them out further. For example, if the memory of a good deed or a success comes up, we think: "How was it again? I did this and then that. And everybody commented on how wonderful it was and how well I'd done..." We then get carried away on a wave of happy memories, and our mind becomes clouded with self-satisfaction. And the longer we think about how wonderful we are, the prouder we become.

If, on the other hand, we remember a failure, a loss or a mistake we made, we become depressed and get tangled up in self-doubt, sorrow or regret. And immediately, we also think of the future: "I should do this and that, so that this does not happen again...", or with a happy memory: "I should do this and that, so that this continues..." We make plans to reach certain goals and wish that events will take a certain course. This creates tension: when we talk ourselves into believing that we will manage to influence the course of events according to our wishes, we become filled with hope, and when we doubt that things will in fact go our way, we get worried. Our hope for success and our fear of failure put our mind under strain and pressure, and it gets more and more tangled up in a web of concerns and speculations.

All this mental activity happens in the present, which thereby becomes a firework display of thoughts: "In the past, I did this, in the future, I'll do that", and so on forever. Hope and fear cause unceasing stress. On the erroneous assumption that our impressions and thoughts are real and permanent, we become more and more attached to them and move far away from the awareness of the present moment.

*In meditation we let go of all preoccupation
with past, present and future.*

The past is irrevocably gone and will not come back. Consequently, it is pointless to hang on to things of the past and mentally chew them over again and again. To dig them up again changes nothing of what has been, but only serves to agitate us. With this reflection, we let go of everything past and do not go back to it again.

Similarly, we should not waste our time daydreaming about the future. The future has not arrived yet, and it makes little sense to rack our brains over something that is not yet here. Moreover, we will hardly be able to influence the future with our speculations and calculations. Thinking about projects and ambitious plans during the meditation session is a pure waste of time, as the future will not suit itself to our wishes. It is determined chiefly by actions that we have carried out in the past.

This will quickly become clear to us, if we attempt to stop the course of events and bring about circumstances that are not already nascent in the situation as karmic potentialities. If we try such a thing, we will soon have to admit to ourselves that even with great effort we are not able to steer events in a completely different direction. Whether and how a situation occurs, does not depend primarily on our own intentions and concerns, but mainly on what we and others involved in the situation have done in the past, i. e., what forces we have already set in motion.

*To try to predict or predetermine events is a
futile undertaking. Also, it is no use worrying
about the future – the future comes all by itself.*

In meditation, we simply allow our mind to rest in the present moment, to be present in the ungraspable now that is neither the past nor the future. This present moment cannot be grasped by the intellect. It is not an object of intellectual understanding and cannot be described. Trying to hint at it, we may say that it is the awareness of the direct experience of the present – beyond time and space. It is the eternity of the non-temporal, and it cannot be experienced in any other way than in the awareness of immediate, non-dual presence.

The present moment is simply the way it is. If we rest in it, then things appear by themselves and also dissolve by themselves again. There is no longer any interference, pressure, clinging or rejecting, only the play of thoughts that come and go without any hindrance. When we let go of our attachment to thoughts, then they simply appear and disappear, without a chain of thoughts latching on to them. Thought waves arise and disappear. Since there is no interference, the thought dissolves by itself.

> *Thoughts do not have any autonomous nature. They are like clouds in the sky – without origin and without destination.*

Clouds neither originate from a definite location nor do they go to a definite place – they do not exist in any lasting way. They are the result of the evaporation and condensation of water, are subject to impermanence and change continually, until they finally dissolve. Thoughts are similar. They are the creation of the mind and ultimately have no reality, no lasting existence. When we do not hold on to them, they vanish like clouds, and we recognize them as the natural play of the mind. All confusion regarding their supposed reality dissolves, and we open ourselves to the experience of spontaneous ease.

We speak of the three times – past, present and future – as an expression of the insight that nothing lasts but everything is characterized by impermanence. Our impression of time passing is brought about by the continual movement of our mind, with its incessantly changing world of experiences. Intellectually, this is easy for us to understand, but we find it difficult to apply this insight to our daily lives, in which we often have the tendency to want to stop time and prevent certain situations from developing.

It is precisely our wish to want to halt the continual change of things that causes us to suffer. When we deeply accept becoming and ceasing as something inevitable, then there is no longer any cause for suffering. If we live impermanence and deeply understand it, then it becomes a friend who helps us settle in the dimension of the present moment and experience the unity of mind and its projections.

If our mind did not project appearances, would there be past, present and future? Surely not. There would be no feeling of time passing, as the impression of time is solely caused by the changing projections of our mind. If we wish to achieve certainty about this, we must look directly into our mind in meditation again and again; words and intellectual understanding are not adequate for this. Only through repeated investigation of our own mind can we truly grasp that the world that surrounds us is nothing but a projection of our mind – its dynamic expression, its luminosity.

Our mind is a succession of moments of awareness – and these moments of present awareness cannot be extended. We cannot say: "Thoughts, please stop for a moment, so that I may look at you and understand you." Trying to stop the movements of our mind, in order to look at a thought or insight more carefully, blocks the natural, spontaneous dynamics of the mind. There is no point in trying to seize an insight so that we can look at it closely. In true insight, there is nothing that could be looked at or understood.

As long as we cherish the desire to understand something, to define and explain it, we miss the real point of our practice and continue in our ordinary mental fixation. If we wish to appropriate an insight, there needs to be someone who wants to understand something – and immediately we recreate the 'I', the thinker. In reality, there is nobody who understands and no object that is to be understood – there simply is only seeing. As soon as we cling to an 'I', there is no more seeing.

If we are dissatisfied with the prospect of not being able to understand, that is because we wish to have something for ourselves. We hope to be able to control and master things. But in truth we cannot control or understand anything. If we wish to arrive at a true understanding, we must let go of all personal desire. We should search for the thinker who wants to understand and control. Then we will see that we cannot find them, since they do not exist as such. If there is no thinker, then it is only natural that there is no understanding of thought processes and the mind.

Thinker and thoughts are empty, without true existence. This fundamental emptiness is the truth body. The luminosity, or dynamics, of this empty mind, its capacity to create thoughts, is the enjoyment body. The manifold expression of the mind, its capacity to assume a myriad of forms in continual change, is the emanation body.

> *When we allow our mind to engage in its*
> *natural, spontaneous activity, we will recognize*
> *its three fundamental qualities: emptiness,*
> *luminosity and unobstructed manifestation.*

We will not, as we may have feared, find ourselves in an empty, blank state. Rather, we will discover that our thoughts are the treasure of the three bodies of enlightenment, the inexhaustible source of a wealth of qualities.

What can we do to gain insight into the nature of mind? We should meditate and allow our mind to rest in the awareness of the present moment. The true nature of mind is nothing other than this moment of open awareness. In this sense of presence, there is nothing that could be grasped by thought, described or seen. This does not mean, however, that there is nothing at all, but only that no awareness as such is seen. When we rest in this immediate awareness that is the nature of mind, we understand that all appearances are created through the habitual tendencies of our confused mind.

The goal of Mahamudra meditation is to see directly the nature of this confusion. This happens when the mind merges with the awareness of the present moment which is its basic nature. In that moment, it is freed of all the negativity and obscurations of all our lifetimes. To penetrate to this experience, we must meditate again and again, over a long period of time, and use all situations for the meditation on the true nature of mind. If we do this, one day we will attain realization and with it complete certainty. We will see directly what the mind is and how it works. From that day on, all our doubts will have been resolved completely.

In Mahamudra meditation, we simply allow body and mind to relax and rest in openness. To relax completely does not mean to slump in a lazy way. Rather, it entails maintaining a clear, vivid awareness that perceives all impulses of the mind to hold on to something and lets go of them immediately. Without getting annoyed about our attachment, we simply perceive it and allow it to free itself. Attachment is the sole thing we must abandon, and that is why the teachings speak so insistently of the need for complete relaxation of the mind.

In the view of Mahamudra, in which we make no distinction between good thoughts and bad thoughts but allow all appearances equally to dissolve in their true nature, there is one danger. We may regard ourselves as great yogis and think that with this view that is as expansive as the sky, we no longer need to pay attention to the small details of life and of our actions. This erroneous view is rooted in a pride that is as big as a mountain. To think that everything in its nature is emptiness and, therefore, it is no longer necessary to perform wholesome actions and to avoid unwholesome ones, leads to arrogant, inconsiderate behavior. A "great yogi" of that persuasion would entangle themselves more and more in worldly thinking and acting. Their disturbing emotions would increase, and they would move further and further away from awakening.

In order not to fall into this error, we should cultivate the flawless behavior of a bodhisattva and constantly check whether our body, speech and mind conform to the teachings of the Buddha. Even with the very expansive view of Mahamudra, a view that is as all-embracing as the universe, we have to be very sensitive and exact in our actions. As soon as we have developed the correct view and actually apply it in practice, we are able to recognize the ultimate reality in ourselves, without having to undertake any great effort to accomplish this. The recognition of the nature of mind is the only thing that we actually need – it has the power to liberate us from everything and to liberate all beings in the universe, too.

All phenomena of the external world are only the manifestations of the luminosity of our own mind and ultimately have no reality. When we allow our mind to rest in the recognition that everything that it experiences is its own projection, the separation between subject and object comes to an end. Then there is no longer anyone who grasps at something and nothing that is being grasped at – subject and object are recognized to be unreal.

In order to experience this, we allow our mind to remain in its ordinary consciousness, the awareness of the present moment, which is the deep, unchanging nature of mind itself and which is also called "timeless awareness." That is the natural insight that arises spontaneously when in every moment we look directly at the true nature of mind.

In seeing the nature of mind, there is nothing to "see" since it is not an object of perception. We see it without seeing anything. We know it without knowing anything.

The mind recognizes itself spontaneously, in a way beyond all duality. The path that leads to this is the awareness of the present moment, free of all interference. It is an error to think that the ultimate truth is difficult to recognize. The meditation on the nature of mind is actually very easy, as we do not have to go anywhere to find this nature. No work needs to be done to produce it; no effort is required to find it. It is sufficient for us to sit down, allow our mind to rest in itself and directly look at the one who thinks that it is difficult to find the nature of mind. In that moment, we discover it directly, as it is very close and always within easy reach.

It would be absurd to worry that we might not succeed in discovering the nature of mind, as it is already present in us. It is sufficient to look into ourselves. When our mind directs its gaze upon itself, it finds itself and understands that the seeker and the sought are not two different things. At the moment, we cannot see the nature of our mind because we do not know *how* we must look. The problem is not that we do not possess the capacity for doing this but that we do not look in the right way.

To become capable of recognizing the nature of mind in the way described, we have to work at relaxing deeply and letting go of all wanting, so that the natural state of mind can reveal itself. This work is the exact opposite of worldly effort, in which we strive to obtain concrete things and put ourselves into a state of strain. In the practice of Dharma, we must "strain without effort." This does not mean that we do nothing at all and simply remain as we are, because then we would continue to reproduce the same behavior patterns that have existed in us since beginningless time. We must make an effort to purify our ego-centered tendencies and become aware of our intentions.

We must also make an effort to meditate, otherwise no awareness, no insight will arise in us. But this effort should be free of ambition and of the wish to accomplish something. In a deliberate but relaxed way, we give all of our thinking and acting a wholesome orientation. Merely having the wish to become awakened is not sufficient. But we should also not strain after it, full of tension and impatience. The crucial thing is to change our attitude of mind – everything else follows naturally.

Hope and Fear

When we become proficient in accepting the movements of our mind in a relaxed manner that is free of judgment, even when these movements are strong and lively, greater clarity and transparency will arise in our mind. To have strong thoughts and feelings is actually a good thing – provided we deal with them in the right way. If we feel uneasy when emotions come up, then evidently we are still attached to a desire for a quiet mind.

Because of this attachment, we are easily tempted to want to have a pleasant meditation, a meditation without thoughts, problems and disturbances. We desire quiet and believe that when thoughts no longer arise, our mind will feel well. As soon as this wish is stirring, we can be sure that ego-clinging dominates: our longing for personal well-being pushes itself to the fore. This attitude is called hope – hope that something good will happen to us. It blocks the mind and prevents it from being truly free.

Even in the presence of an ego-centered attitude, meditation can lead to a certain stability of the mind, although it may be very limited. We may even believe that we have "awakened" because we have attained a state that is free of disturbance by noisy thoughts. Happy and self-satisfied, we settle into it, saying to ourselves: "Others can wait, I don't care about them now. The important thing is that I finally have attained my much-longed-for happiness." In that way, we make ourselves comfortable in this warmth and doze in cozy contentment, like a bear in hibernation.

If, on the other hand, we simply let go, then we do not hinder the power of the mind, and thoughts will liberate themselves spontaneously, of their own accord. Thoughts are mind, nothing other than mind. Thus, it makes no difference whether we are calm or excited. We should not separate thoughts and mind artificially. Since every thought that appears in the mind is nothing other than mind itself, we need not feel that we are the owners of these thoughts. We take note of them without wanting to insert ourselves into their play, and we let them go in a carefree manner. No tension arises in our mind then, and we create no problems.

However, if we interfere with the natural movement of the mind, everything becomes difficult. Then we act as though we wanted to protect our mind from its own thoughts. We search for a happiness without thoughts. But our thoughts cannot be sent away; they forever arise anew – and so everything becomes very complicated and painful. If we do not fight against this but give up our desire to control and we let go deeply, then there are no longer any difficulties. Then even painful experiences are no longer any problem.

By necessity, to possess a body is tied up with suffering. Birth is suffering, and it leads to further suffering, the suffering of old age, sickness and death. Our bodily existence entails experiencing sensory impressions in an uninterrupted succession, in which we involuntarily distinguish between pleasant and unpleasant feelings and always seek the happiness of pleasant feelings.

Being thus subjected to the continuous influence of sensory impressions and judgments, we have a chronic thirst for happiness. This search for what is pleasant will continue as long as we distinguish between pleasant and unpleasant experiences. However, any happiness experienced through the senses never lasts – because of our attachments it always ends in suffering.

*Basically, it is the longing for
happiness that leads to suffering.*

The more we long for happiness and strive seeking it, the more strained
our mind becomes. As long as we strive for a goal, for certain experiences or for a state of enlightenment that we consider to be separate
from us, our mind cannot be happy and relaxed.

We are attached to our thoughts and experiences and either try to
change them or protect ourselves from them or find something special in them. As a consequence, we find no peace. Our mind is restless and suffers ceaselessly. Therefore, in our meditation, we should
set our mind completely free and give up our search for happiness
and well-being. We should cease trying to accomplish anything and
hoping that something good will happen to us. When we do this, our
mind will stop tensing up.

To have fervent hopes of reaching a goal, to strive for experiences or to want to attain the much-longed-for prize of realization creates nothing but problems. Expectations that something special will
happen to us give rise to great strain in body and mind. They may indeed lead to something happening, i. e., the free flow of our energies
will be blocked, and we will experience strange states of mind that
we take to be valid meditation experiences. We allow ourselves to become fascinated with these states, develop attachment to them and
hope for more of them. Attachment causes strain – and strain necessarily creates experiences. But these experiences are not the path to
freedom; they are only the source of still more strain.

*Caught in hope and fear, we worry so
much about attaining realization, and
it is precisely this that prevents it.*

In true meditation we are free of concerns. When we ask ourselves whether we are capable of or good enough to attain realization, then this shows that we have not understood the instructions about the nature of mind. The mind is the dharmakaya, the truth body. We should simply remind ourselves: "My mind is dharmakaya, the lama's mind is dharmakaya, there is no difference between the mind of the lama and my mind. The dharmakaya pervades everything. Therefore, there is no cause for hope or fear, since everything is already there." We only need to relax and have faith in the power of the blessings of the Three Jewels and the lama, faith that the true nature of things will reveal itself in its full simplicity when we are open and relaxed.

It is easy to understand that true meditation should be beyond hope and fear. However, this should not lead to our wanting to get rid of these emotions or revolting against them, because then again we would be trying to accomplish something and avoid something else.

Thoughts as Friends in Meditation

Some practitioners of meditation only care about attaining personal peace. To gain that peace, they attempt to stop all movement of thought in the mind. They believe that thoughts come from the "outside" and try to fend off these intruders from the "inside," i. e., from the place where their feeling of 'I' resides. They act like someone who sits in their house, happy and contented, then notices someone passing by on the outside and suddenly assumes, for no reason at all, that this person is dangerous and wants to come in and disturb them. To prevent this, they jump up in a hurry and try to barricade all the windows and doors. Similarly, some meditators consider thoughts to be a danger, and the moment one arises, they want to refuse it entry, throw it out, get rid of it. But meditation is not an attempt to have no thoughts – the point is not to cling to the thoughts that arise.

To strive for calm, peace and contentment is not true meditation but indicates that we are afraid of the projections of our own mind. Under the influence of ignorance, we try to cut ourselves off from reality and seek rest for our beloved 'I'. In meditation, this leads to laziness and indifference, as in this motionless peace there is no urgency to carry out wholesome deeds and avoid unwholesome ones – we end up in a kind of mindlessness and waste our time. If the ideal of meditation consisted in attaining a state free of the movement of thought, then we ought to bow to a table, since it has never had any thoughts. According to that criterion, the table would be the perfect meditator who always rests in meditative absorption. But certainly this is not so.

The goal of meditation is not to become like a table but to realize the awareness of a buddha, i. e., total presence!

In view of the obvious problems that arise for us from our mental entanglements, we may wish to remove these problems without further ado by suppressing all thinking. In this undertaking of banishing thoughts from our mind, something that is virtually impossible to do anyway, one thought attempts to suppress all others. With great effort, we can indeed set up such a dictatorship that prohibits all movement of thought by cutting off each thought as it arises. But this could be dangerous for our mental health and certainly is not our goal.

The point is not to stop individual thoughts but to avoid maintaining chains of thoughts. When our mind ceases reacting to a thought that arises, it will recognize the thought as a movement of itself. Recognizing itself in the movement, it remains relaxed and finds rest.

Thoughts are not the problem, only clinging to them is.

We must not reject thoughts but be watchful with regard to conceptual thoughts that arise virtually automatically in the wake of a perception. According to the master Gampopa, the main disciple of Milarepa, in his time many meditators believed that it was a fault to have thoughts. Hence, they tried to repress all mental movement and concentrated so strongly that they fell into a state without consciousness, akin to swooning. This is the wrong way to meditate.

Rather, the point is to recognize that all thoughts are simply mind. Their true nature is identical to the nature of mind. Similar to the waves of the ocean, thoughts are the natural movement of the mind. Each wave has its own shape and size, but the water of the individual wave is the same as that of the ocean itself. We cannot separate the waves from the ocean. If we do this and consider "waves" and "ocean," as well as "thoughts" and "mind," to be separate things, then we make a distinction that does not correspond to reality.

In our meditation, we should look directly at the thoughts that arise. Then we will see that they possess neither color nor form – nothing that would confirm their existence. Recognizing their real nature, our mind enters into its original dimension: emptiness without boundaries, open like the sky – and as spontaneously as the thought has arisen, so it dissolves again naturally.

When we do not become fascinated by our thoughts but look at them directly, then all of our thoughts become opportunities for recognizing the simultaneously creative and empty nature of the mind.

In this recognition, thoughts dissolve like snowflakes that fall on a hot stone. A meditator with such a realization is capable of letting their mind rest in the free and unceasing play of arising and passing appearances. Since seeing the arising and vanishing of thoughts is the basis for our recognition of the highest reality, we should welcome them with as much gratitude as we feel for our teacher.

Once our mind is relatively stable and has detached itself from clinging to thoughts, then the more thoughts arise, the better it is. Gampopa said: "The meditation of someone who values thoughts will never suffer from hunger. The more firewood, the bigger the fire. The more thoughts, the more radiant the dharmakaya!" To believe that we could see the nature of mind while at the same time prohibiting the arising of thoughts is as absurd as hoping to see the sun while we remain in the darkness of a cave.

To allow thoughts to appear without hindrance and to disappear again naturally is the key to the "non-conceptuality" (often translated as "non-thought"), of which the traditional instructions speak. Here, to be free of thinking means that our thoughts do not elicit any reactions.

Non-conceptuality is a free, naturally aware state of mind in which thoughts appear without our clinging to them, so that no "thinking" occurs, i. e., no thought processes in the ordinary sense of the term.

In non-conceptual presence thoughts continue to occur, but we do not regard them as intruders that disturb us. They do not set off waves of hope and fear, or thinking about the past, present and future. In their true nature, the coming and going thoughts are the play of ultimate reality, illusory appearances in the openness of space. To be aware of this frees us from clinging. We might ask: "Who is it who recognizes the unreality of thoughts? After all, there must be someone who thinks and makes this discovery!" But when we look at the one who recognizes the nature of thoughts, we will again discover neither form nor color, etc. Thus we will see that there is no 'I', or subject, that experiences this recognition.

Thoughts are like the lama – they show us true reality.

For all these reasons, we should regard our thoughts as friends. They manifest, even though they are empty in essence, and they point to the multifariously manifesting and at the same time empty nature of the mind. This "empty" mind is creative and full of qualities, but its qualities are not different from its essential emptiness. The emptiness is the underlying dimension whose spontaneous creativity manifests as thoughts. Because of that, thoughts are not different from the ultimate nature of mind. There is not the "pure and perfect," empty nature of the mind on the one hand, and "impure and disturbing" thoughts on the other.

Moreover, with regard to their fundamental nature, among thoughts there are none that are purer than others. We do not need to sort them into good ones and bad ones, so as to keep only those that are pure and perfect. That would constitute an attachment to the idea of a concrete reality of thoughts.

When we look, we will see that all thoughts possess the same empty nature and are therefore of "one taste." All of them are equally the expression of the self-revealing creativity of one and the same empty mind. We need do nothing except look directly at them. When we recognize their true nature, our mind is liberated. This is called the "simultaneous arising and self-liberation" of thoughts. And Gendun Rinpoche continues:[8]

In the stream of meditation,
with time there remains no difference
between consciousness and the one

---

8   When he taught, Gendun Rinpoche frequently spoke in an almost poetic way. This passage is an instance of his breaking out into one of these spontaneous "vajra songs."

who is conscious.
Thinker and thought are equally
the play of the mind.

The separation between perceiver and perceived,
between subject and object, drops away.
Doer and deed
no longer are different –
everything happens in the expanse of awareness.

Mind is aware of itself
and rests in its natural state,
without seer and seen.
That is non-seeing;
that is natural consciousness.

Mind is aware,
but a subject is no longer present.
That is truly becoming conscious –
a perfect, lasting certainty.

Advice on Meditation Experiences

On the path of meditation, and in particular when we practice intensively, we encounter a multiplicity of experiences. According to their different tendencies and capacities, practitioners' meditation experiences may vary. But of whatever kind and intensity these experiences may be, they all have in common that they manifest in the expanse of timeless awareness. Experiences are always mind and do not possess any reality separate from it.

Meditation experiences are necessary for realization to be brought forth, and at times we may have rather strange or bizarre meditation experiences. This merely indicates that impurities are rising to the surface from the depths of our consciousness. We have to experience them in order to be able to free ourselves from them. When we do not allow ourselves to fall under their spell and we neither hold on to them with fascination nor reject them with fear, then they simply arise and dissolve again. This process frees us from obscurations that we were not even aware of before. With the arising and passing of these experiences, our obscurations also dissolve.

Meditation experiences bring to light obscurations that need to be dissolved, so that we may realize the purity that is inherent in the mind.

There are many different kinds of such experiences. At times, we may have the impression that we have many more thoughts than we did before, especially if we have just started to meditate. But this impression is false: through our meditation, we are developing a clearer and more awake consciousness and we perceive the movements of our mind more acutely. If we do not meditate, our mind ordinarily is as if dazed and is not aware at all of the incessant stream of thoughts. Hence, our impression of having many more thoughts when we meditate is not a fault but rather a good sign.

At times, we may feel sky-high and regard ourselves as great yogis who are able to master everything, as though we were the Buddha himself. We think that we have everything under control – it all seems to be so easy and excellent. At other times, we may have the impression that we do not even know any longer how to meditate correctly. The more we try, the less we seem able to accomplish – we are in a state of great confusion. Whatever we do only brings us suffering and generates harmful emotions. We feel utterly dejected and believe that nobody could possibly be more unhappy than we are.

It is as though we have sunk into the deepest abyss of samsara, into which not even the slightest glimmer of hope penetrates. We do not even have any desire to meditate anymore; it is as if our motivation has been totally destroyed. Or we may have a feeling of inner blankness, and we wonder whether we are even meditating at all. We do not know anything, cannot think of anything, have no reference points, and we say to ourselves: "I've already been practicing for so long now, but without any results – nothing has really changed." We are thoroughly discouraged and reluctant to practice, and we think: "It makes no sense to practice, everything is going wrong." And the more we think about ourselves, our practice and our teacher, the more upset we get.

At other times, we are full of inspiration and feel very happy about our practice. Nothing appears more wonderful to us than to practice Dharma. We feel great devotion to our lama and say to ourselves: "I don't want to lose any more time; I only want to practice. I've resolved truly and firmly to practice the Dharma now and nothing but the Dharma, yes indeed!" Our lama appears so magnificent and compassionate to us, and our practice is so wonderful that we want to spend our entire lives only doing Dharma practice.

Or we may say to ourselves: "I want to become a great master, a lama of great renown," and then again: "Oh no, I should meditate in strict seclusion, not be in contact with anyone, best live in a dark cave," and again at some other time: "No, this really isn't for me, I'd rather get married and build a big business." At times, we daydream about how we will teach the Dharma to others and receive great recognition for our practice. And then again, we may reprimand ourselves: "It's crazy for me to think in this way; this is just my monstrous pride!"

Everybody is probably familiar with these kinds of thoughts and inner debates and knows how much one can suffer from them. They are among the normal experiences that everyone has. Such thoughts and moods appear spontaneously and we cannot prevent them, and when we attach no importance to them and leave them as they are, they dissolve again all by themselves. The emergence of such experiences is natural and necessary but like all experiences they are merely of a fleeting nature.

Experiences are not the goal of our practice. The only thing that should be in our mind is natural awareness.

When experiences arise in our meditation, they are the natural result of the practice – they are just as natural as the blossoming of flowers in a summer meadow. To understand this helps us not to take experiences seriously. But we must go one step further and look into the experiences themselves. Then we recognize that they do not really exist. They are nothing but empty projections of our mind.

Our holding on to these experiences is a projection, too, and so is our noticing of this attachment. Everything has the same fundamental property of being nothing but the expression of our mind. Therefore, we should neither regard "dark" experiences as bad and suppress them nor regard "light" experiences as good and cultivate them.

It is said that experiences in meditation are like the morning mist that veils a mountain. When the mist disperses, it gives way to the light of the sun and the splendor of the mountain is revealed. In the same way, when such meditation experiences dissolve, they result in a stable and firm realization. Our mind forever expresses itself dynamically, and we must allow that to happen and in no way hinder the movement of thoughts and the emergence of any kind of experience.

*Whatever thoughts or experiences arise in our
mind, we simply continue with our practice.*

Pleasant experiences are not the sign of a "good" meditation, and
we should not attempt to prolong them or strive to re-experience
them, because fascination, pride and hope would then stir up our
mind unnecessarily and cause us to lose our stability. In the same
vein, we should not think that unpleasant experiences are the sign
of a "bad" meditation, or that we have way too many thoughts to
be able to make real progress, because then we would fall into the
clutches of anxiety and worry. If we assess our experiences positively or negatively, we become their prisoners and then our experiences become hindrances.

We should meditate in a completely unconcerned manner, free
from hope and fear. It is sufficient for us to recognize that all states
of mind are mind. Calmness is mind, and movement is also mind. It
would be wrong to judge a quiet mind to be "good" and an agitat-
ed mind to be "bad." If we cannot help thinking in this way, then we
should look directly at the thoughts "good" and "bad." When we do
that, we will see that such judgments again are merely projections of
our mind. We could also look directly at the one who comments on
these experiences and try to find the thinker. The recognition that
there is no thinker frees us from both the thinker and the thought –
and that is the moment of realization.

To look directly at the one who hopes that a pleasant feeling will
endure or who fears that his meditation is not correct, is the antidote
to hope and fear. Who is this someone who thinks that his meditation is good or bad? Does he have a form, is he located at a particular place, does he possess substance or color? What is his true nature?
We attempt to find something that we can pin down as the thinker.

We search for it everywhere, but we see nothing. In this not-seeing anything – a seeing without seeing something – we then rest.

In this way, we work with everything that appears in the mind. We will recognize then that judgments, as well as the judging mind, do not possess any self-nature. And in that way we "see" the nature of mind. This non-seeing seeing is the expression of the naturally empty luminosity of the mind, the knowing quality through which the mind is aware of itself. To rest in this without distraction is the highest wisdom.

As our understanding grows, experiences no longer influence our meditation, because we do not go astray in either attachment or aversion but open ourselves to the non-duality of mind and meditation. Meditation then no longer requires any effort – there is nothing to do or attain. Whenever we lose our motivation, we should remind ourselves of this and never have any doubt about our capacity to do *nothing*!

In addition to letting go of hope and fear generated with regard to ourselves, we should also free ourselves from expectations and fears that come from comparing ourselves with other practitioners, e.g., hoping that our practice is better than theirs or fearing that it might be worse. All emotions that arise from expectations and fears lead to disturbances in meditation. Rather than becoming envious, we should be glad when we see others practicing the Dharma well or better than we do. We should hold them up as shining examples. This will dissolve our jealousy and inspire us to actually practice the Dharma.

As we have already seen, on this path to deep recollection, the point is not to produce special states of mind or, in a search for experiences of clarity and joy, prevent the movements of the mind. That is a mistake frequently made in meditation. Practitioners who fall prey to it try to restrain the movements of their mind by concentrating harder and harder, until their subtle energies are stuck in the heart area, as if they were gagged. Their bodily posture also reflects this: they are crouched around their heart area, with shoulders pulled forward, head slightly lowered and chin drawn in, as though they want to create a frame in which they are able to keep a firm hold on their mind.

Of course, doing this is strenuous. These practitioners confuse meditative stability with absence of thoughts; they long for a mind free of thoughts. But their attempts to rein in the flow of thoughts only result in their mind tensing up. For the time being, they may have the impression that their mind is quieter and more stable. But this quiet is not a genuine one. It is full of effort, as they have to strain to maintain it, and as soon as this experience of apparent quiet wanes, they have to redouble their efforts to recreate it.

For the most part, it is ambition and bullheadedness that underlie such wrong effort in meditation. Some practitioners overtax themselves by assuming strenuous, stiff postures for long periods of time, postures that produce great tension and lead to a concentration of subtle energies in the upper part of the body, in particular the upper part of the face and head. They may even lead to headaches.

The nature of mind cannot be realized through strenuous effort. An unnatural, tense meditation can also lead to pain and energy blockages in the back, abdomen, upper torso and neck, with the result that we cannot sit quietly anymore and constantly have to shift some part of the body, in order to relieve the strain.

Another wrongheaded approach is to attempt to generate a state of meditation by tensely stretching the body upward and also directing the gaze upward, as though one wanted to collect all of one's energies underneath the top of the skull. This can become quite painful. Such a practitioner assumes that the correct meditation is a state in which their mind is completely gone, and they meditate stiffly, like a piece of wood, caught in the search for a mystical experience.

Every meditator runs the danger of making mistakes in applying the instructions. To avoid such mistakes, we should be aware that body and mind are connected by means of subtle energies that course in certain energy channels of the body. Movements of the mind are associated with movements of these subtle energies and they alter the state of the energy channels of the body. When our mind becomes tense, the channels in our body also tense up. And vice versa, a good bodily posture helps relax the channels and allows the subtle energies to flow freely.

Thus it is important, on the one hand, to have an open, flexible mind – not to hold on to, push away or force anything – and, on the other hand, to assume a physical posture that supports such a mental stance. Then the energy channels can open like flowers and the subtle energies can flow freely, and this in turn frees the mind. But when we put our mind under pressure, then our subtle energies no longer move freely and we experience difficulties: anger, dullness or unruliness may arise in our mind and all sorts of physical or mental problems may appear. Then our meditation is no longer natural – our mind cannot find its natural state.

Some practitioners regard meditation as a comfortable, somewhat diffuse mental state, a foggy kind of happiness, in which disruptive thoughts no longer occur and the mind wraps itself in a cozy cocoon of peace and quiet. They hold their head slightly tilted forward; it looks as though they want to block thoughts with their drawn in chin. This is an expression of great attachment – they want to doze gently.

As soon as they get to a point at which fewer thoughts emerge in their mind, many meditators develop the desire, be it conscious or unconscious, to rest in this pleasant state of quiet. But precisely for that reason, their mind then sinks into dullness. After some time, they may become aware of this dullness and begin to worry about it, which leads to increased thought activity. This may help them get out of the state of dullness but it may also churn up the mind which they then must balance again by applying the appropriate relaxation.

Only gradually, as they learn to let go of hope and fear, do they find their way to a balanced meditation.

Dullness arises because we hope for a clear, luminous state of mind. Once we understand this, we see to it that we let go of all hope and wanting. We cannot achieve true clarity through willpower. When we relax and leave our mind in its natural state, trusting its qualities, then clarity appears all by itself, as it is one of the fundamental properties of the mind. To want to attain it by force only brings about dullness.

When dullness does appear in our mind, we should regard it, just like all other experiences, as a mere movement of the mind that is not separate from the mind's fundamental nature. We should not let ourselves be "fogged in" by dullness but look through it, so to speak, to discover the space of clear and open awareness that is covered by it. In this way, we can use everything that emerges in the mind as a means to see the mind itself.

Some practitioners think that they know exactly what emptiness is. They are so convinced of its existence that they put emptiness in front of themselves, as an infinitely large projection that fills the entire expanse of space, as though they had a gigantic, empty bubble in front of themselves. Then they meditate on this artificially created emptiness and say to themselves: "Ah, this is emptiness; it is wonderful, everything is clear and empty!" Such thoughts are worth nothing. This supposed emptiness is a mere construct. But they expend much energy to maintain this artificial emptiness, and that may lead to great strain. This is how the "followers of materialistic emptiness" practice meditation; it is not meditation but mere diversion.

Others try to forcibly generate emptiness in their mind by denying the existence of all appearances and by "making the mind empty." These are the "followers of nihilistic emptiness," people who try to think away appearances. They say: "Everything is empty, nothing exists. Externally, there is nothing, and internally, there is nothing.

I who declare that there is nothing, do not exist either." They deny all manifestation. When they have managed with great effort to negate even the last thought in their meditation, then full of joy they think that what they have found is emptiness, that this is the nature of mind. But this has nothing to do with meditation; it is an intellectual game, devoid of any valid insight.

These faults appear when we lack confidence in the instructions and do not truly open ourselves to them. We pick from them what appeals to us and tinker with constructing our own idea of meditation. Because we lack the capacity for letting go that is grounded in trust, our efforts come to naught. Our mind becomes strained, frustrated and perhaps even angry, and real disturbances or venting of emotions may occur that produce great suffering. What all these faults have in common are the rigid ideas that underlie them and that deprive the mind of its freedom and its natural expression. Every meditator must make an effort to become conscious of the faults that they are falling victim to. Only when we clearly recognize our faults, are we able to free ourselves from them.

As long as there is still a separation into "me" and "my meditation," the meditation is artificial. In true meditation, the thinker dissolves in the recognition of their own true nature.

For example, when we think, "Finally, my mind is quiet, and I'm resting in my own true nature," then our mind is already no longer resting in its natural state but is analyzing and differentiating. The thought, "Ah, now I've understood what meditation is," too, only indicates that we have not understood anything.

There is no such commentary in true meditation, in which there is no separation into subject and object, no meditator and no observer. Awareness simply recognizes itself as empty, without boundaries and without center. The mind rests in openness, emptiness and self-recognition. True meditation is non-meditation. There is no "I know" in it and also no meditation. If we do not want to succumb to the fault of artificial meditation, above all we must truly listen when meditation is explained to us.

The true meaning of the instructions reveals itself to us when we listen to the meaning behind the words and open ourselves to their deeper sense.

In meditation the crucial point is to allow our mind to open and relax. But here in the West, children are very much trained in school to deal with words in an exact manner: this word means exactly this, that word means exactly that. They learn to make precise distinctions and not to mix up meanings. When they cannot handle words well, they are regarded as bad students. Often, they are under heavy pressure. When they cannot meet the high demands placed on them, they fear that something is not quite all right with them.

By contrast, nothing special was really demanded of children in the old days of Tibet. They simply were happy, as hardly any pressure was exerted on them. Later as students, when they received instructions, for example in Mahamudra, they did not cling to the words but kept their minds free and open. They took the words of instruction merely as aids to help them orient their meditation in a rough way. They did not put themselves under pressure.

But here in the West, most people are so tightly trained to make fine distinctions that they only hear the words and tend to cling to them: "This must be understood in *this* way, since it has been explained with *these* words – it cannot mean anything else." In their meditation, too, they may cling so much to the supposed reality of their experiences that they are barely open to other potentially more fruitful views.

Simple practitioners, above all, desire a harmonious mind. They have no interest in special experiences and complications. But here in the West, there appear to be many who regard inner harmony and balance as insufficient and always feel that something is missing. They think that only when extraordinary experiences arise are they really meditating. As we have already seen, quite a few people have a special liking for "emptiness" and try to make an experience out of it that they can practically grab with their hands. But that is entirely mistaken.

The instructions on emptiness should be understood as a remedy against our tendency to cling to supposed reality, and nothing else.

When someone believes that the world truly exists and that things exist truly and permanently, then the teacher attempts to correct this by explaining to them that things do not have any permanent existence and are "empty" of such an unchanging, lasting existence. This reference to emptiness is only a device used to protect the student against attachment. It should not lead to a new attachment. Emptiness as such does not exist. Like attachment to the reality of the world, attachment to emptiness is wrong. The latter is even more harmful, as it may lead to a nihilism that blurs all distinctions between wholesome and unwholesome actions. We say to ourselves: "Everything is equal, everything is empty, there is no cause for making distinctions." This is an extreme and dangerous view that could become a big obstacle.

However, the biggest obstacle on the path is lack of faith in the teachings and the teacher. It seems that we constantly need confirmation, assurances and entire discourses on the how and why of our practice. Many instructions appear to be necessary before we arrive at a simple faith regarding the nature of mind and are certain that the path outlined does in fact lead to its realization. Before we are willing to take our first step, our teacher has to convince us that our work, with absolute certainty, will be crowned with success, that our "investment" will pay off. We are constantly propelled by doubts to seek further explanations and confirmation. But realization cannot be attained through complicated explanations and analyses or through an artificial, calculating meditation.

> *The realization of the nature of mind*
> *can only be found in simplicity and in the*
> *direct contact of the mind with itself.*

Therefore, let us work on the quintessential thing: on confidence! When we apply the instructions with full confidence in all areas of our lives, then gradually our mind comes to rest, and through this we discover and confirm the veracity of the Dharma and of the advice of our teacher. The more our confidence and certainty grow, the more we find our way to simplicity. Our thinking becomes less complicated. This simplicity based on confidence cannot be found through extensive studies and reflections.

In this process of the natural calming of our mind, gradually everything artificial drops away from us. We drop our questions as to whether our instructions have been sufficient, whether there might be more profound ones, which aspects of meditation we should emphasize, and so on. If we have faith, then all these speculations that are only born of doubt will no longer find any fertile soil. We apply the instructions, as they were given, without wanting to improve them or picking whichever appear to us to be the easiest or most interesting. On the basis of our confidence, we find our way into the meditation in a completely natural manner, without spoiling its simplicity through artificiality or strenuous effort.

When we apply these simple instructions with full confidence, we are going for refuge in the right way. If we go for refuge in any way other than from the depths of our heart, we lack true faith and think that we must improve the Dharma. As a consequence, our personal preferences will distort the instructions. This applies in particular to the explanations on the nature of mind. Since they are so subtle and very susceptible to personal interpretation, they can easily be distorted.

If we lack confidence, we do not truly meet with the teaching and the master but remain trapped in personal views and ego-centered needs, and we may fight for our own point of view. When that happens, we find no relaxation, no letting go, but quite the reverse, i.e., enormous tension and fatigue. Our mind will be fascinated by its own ideas. But since it does not look at itself, it cannot realize its own nature, and all our effort in meditation will be in vain.

Thus the key to the realization of Mahamudra is to entrust ourselves fully to our teacher. Our trust and devotion to him enable us to receive his instructions without arrogance but with openness and help us apply them joyfully. Only in this way will we attain realization. Realization is the result of the blessings of the lama who points out to us the nature of mind, our faith in his instructions, and the diligence with which we meditate.

When blessings, confidence and joyful perseverance
come together, we are on the direct path to
realization that all buddhas have followed.

If, however, we are influenced by our personal preferences, then our path transforms into a time-consuming "path of detours." Therefore, we should receive the instructions on meditation with great respect and genuine openness, without presuming to criticize them rashly on the basis of a mere intellectual understanding. Our teacher helps us recognize whether our meditation is faulty and obscurations cloud our view. They should bring our errors to our attention and insist that we meditate correctly, even when they do not exactly make themselves popular by this. If the teacher merely seeks a pleasant relationship with the student, because they want to avoid burdens and bother, then this will not help the student make any progress. He or she will become more and more proud, more and more convinced that they are meditating correctly and never develop the true qualities of meditation.

When we are criticized by our teacher, we may think that the teacher ought rather to look at their own faults. But if we react in this way, we will never understand what the teacher is trying to show us and we cannot make progress in our meditation. On the other hand, when our teacher praises us, we may think that we have a really fabulous teacher, as they tell us exactly what we would like to hear. But in such a situation, we may never attain any fruition, as we do not get to see our faults and thus are not able to free ourselves of them or transform them into genuine qualities. We absolutely must entrust ourselves to a qualified teacher who is willing to point out our faults to us, without being afraid of negative reactions. Only then will our practice continue to develop.

> *When we drop all worries, our mind*
> *will spontaneously attain realization.*

Our mind will recognize itself by itself – clarity recognizes its own nature, its own emptiness. Beyond that, there is nothing to do. Only our fear of missing the goal blocks our path. Through faith our mind will relax and get to know itself more and more clearly. Its continual seeking will come to rest in the awareness of its own unimpeded dynamic nature.

Our mind resembles a mirror in which everything that appears is shown without any hindrance. Just as with a mirror, the pictures that appear in the mind have no tangible reality. Perceptions may arise in it in unlimited number; there can never be too many, and they can never be lacking in accuracy and clarity. Like a mirror, the mind holds on to nothing and always remains open to new things. This is the unimpeded and, at the same time, non-dispersed quality of the mind that reveals itself to us when we practice with deep confidence.

When we lack the confidence to allow our mind to be just as it is, fearing that it will scatter, then we basically reject the arising of thoughts and with it the natural luminosity of our mind. We only want its emptiness, without its dynamics and its manifold appearances; we wish to live only the ultimate aspect, without the relative. We would like to have the truth body only, without the enjoyment body and the emanation body.

Yet, as meditators we must learn to accept our mind in its totality, with all the qualities that are inherent in timeless awareness: emptiness, luminosity and manifestation – truth body, enjoyment body and emanation body. We cannot reduce the mind to only one of its aspects but must be aware of the fact that all three aspects are present simultaneously and that one aspect can never appear without the others.

Mental Calm and Intuitive Insight

As our meditation practice progresses, we develop an ever increasing capacity to dwell in effortless, relaxed recollection, regardless of what is appearing in our mind. At that point, meditation is happening all by itself. Our mind enters more deeply into the experience of inner quiet, and by and by our obscurations dissolve. Our mind becomes clearer and our attachment to meditative experiences lessens.

In deep relaxation, we allow the mind to rest in its natural state, not giving it any particular direction. By doing this, we attain ever more relaxed and liberated states of mind.

In the first stage of practicing mental calm, we become aware of the unceasing play of thoughts that appear in steady succession, continually arising and dissolving again. They rush past like a waterfall. Our holding on to thoughts has already decreased, but our mind has not really become quiet as yet. At this stage, the first meditative experiences of bliss, clarity and non-conceptuality make their appearance.

With further progress in our practice, the more subtle movements of the mind begin to fade away, too. Their flow is like a slow stream, and eventually they disappear almost entirely. We attain an experience of deep quiet. In this state of meditative stability, the second stage of mental calm, in which there is little movement of thought, our mind is already able to recognize itself.

If we continue to practice meditation in this way, then gradually all movement of thought comes to an end, and we attain a state of mental recollection that is a deep mental quiet. A deep silence pervades our mind in a natural way, in which even the spontaneous play of thoughts ceases. In this silence we rest undistractedly, without searching for something else and without really "meditating." Our mind remains without any movement of thought – like a waveless ocean in the radiant midday sun. Since it is distracted neither by thoughts nor by any meditation method, our mind simply rests in itself and is aware of itself. This self-awareness can only be found through meditation.

Our increasing capacity for relaxation, with its experiences of clarity, bliss and absence of analytical or conceptual processes, allows the mind to show its true qualities. This is mental calm. When we use this term, we do not refer to the kind of concentration practice in which we direct our mind to remain focused on an object without moving – that would only be a first approximation to mental calm. Rather, we are dealing here with a more profound practice of mental stability that is founded upon the recognition of the nature of mind.

Our mind now recognizes itself as essentially empty in its perceptions and, at the same time, as creative and dynamic – wisdom recognizes itself. A deep meditative recollection, *samadhi,* arises naturally. Samadhi does not refer to some mystical state of concentration, as one might think, but it refers to allowing our mind to rest deeply in itself, in the greatest possible openness, without following any projections. Our mind then recognizes itself in all appearances, without creating any duality. There is no longer any subject that projects the perception of objects. Our mind settles in itself in a natural way, beyond any duality. That is what is called mental calm, in the deeper sense.

Our mind is no longer fascinated by thoughts but contemplates its own true nature. No longer does it intentionally create thoughts, for the purpose of enjoying an internal dialog. Our inner chatter has come to rest, but we do not reject any thoughts that occur spontaneously now and then. Our mind recognizes in them its dynamic, creative aspect as well as its empty nature. And so our mind naturally finds its way to a steady, wakeful awareness in which no conceptual processes are maintained.

When our mind recognizes itself, a deep joy wells up in us, as the compulsions of attachment and aversion dissipate.

Our mind relaxes, it ceases to suffer, and it enters a state of deep joy. As our attachment to the supposed reality of the world of appearances dissolves, the experiences of bliss, non-conceptuality and total clarity of perception arise. These are the three marks of the realization of mental calm.

Initially, most often an experience of transparency, or "emptiness," appears. We have the impression that the world has lost its solid character and is without any real substance. In this state of calm, we experience the seemingly material reality of the world as less and less dense. The world appears unreal, like a dream or an illusion, luminous and transparent, without any solidity, and we understand that it is the creation of our mind. This experience arises quite naturally, and we should let it pass by as a mere movement of the mind, without grasping at it.

The transparent stillness of non-conceptuality is associated with an experience of joy because through it a limitless expanse opens up – our mind is totally quiet and our body totally relaxed. In a completely natural way, we rest in openness and deep joy. We experience great well-being and contentment and have the feeling that body and mind are not at all separate. The feeling of well-being itself is experienced as being empty and insubstantial.

At the same time, a quality manifests in our mind that we call clarity. By this we mean the dynamic, alive quality of the mind, a bright, wakeful awareness that is utterly clear, radiant and precise. Our mind perceives itself and all of its movements in a completely unclouded way. Every trace of fogginess, dullness or sleepiness has disappeared from it; there is not the slightest indication of any tiredness. This experience of an utterly precise awareness is associated with an experience of openness, of being immersed in a great expanse. All boundaries of our mind appear to have fallen away.

It is as though our mind animates everything around us, and this is also accompanied by a feeling of inner warmth, a deeply felt benevolence that is paired with joy. This state of joy and openness is free of any movement of thought, be it ever so subtle. We are totally quiet, and we feel as though our body were no longer present. The only thing that is left is our open mind which experiences bliss and warmth. When our state of recollection deepens even further, our perception of our body dissolves completely, and we have the impression that we could remain in meditation for as long as we wish.

In this undistracted dwelling in the experiences of bliss, clarity and non-conceptuality, there is no such thought as: "I am resting in meditation." No effort is required to maintain our state of recollection, because this utter stability is not artificial, as though we had put a lid on our mind, underneath which nothing is allowed to move. On the contrary, the old lids pop away, and we emerge from our customary confinement into a wide expanse in which nothing needs to be controlled but everything unfolds naturally.

As long as our mind generates thoughts, even if it allows them to pass by without attaching to them, we are not practicing genuine mental calm. We can only speak of mental calm when our mind naturally comes to rest in itself, free of all imaginings, in a still, relaxed, clear awareness that is aware of itself. The crucial difference between fruitless states of meditation and true meditation is the presence of this awake and relaxed self-awareness of the mind, because only in this state of recollection is it possible for our mind to change over from mere mental calm to intuitive insight into its own true nature.

It is important to know the difference between experience and realization. Bliss, clarity and non-conceptuality are only experiences and not yet realization. We should not hang on to them and try to cultivate them further but should leave them behind us, in order to attain realization. A characteristic of realization is that it is completely free of all attachment and of any judgment regarding whatever we experience in the moment.

When we let go of appearances in the moment of their emergence, we free ourselves of the many layers of attachment that restrict the freedom of our mind, like discarding clothes that are too tight. Our mind ceases to run after the objects that it used to grasp at. It comes to a state of rest and dwells in clarity, in the recognition of all phenomena as mind, as immaterial and ungraspable.

Our mind perceives itself as it is: creative and luminous, the source of all manifestation, and at the same time empty, without substance.

The deepening self-perception of our mind leads to a broader, all-encompassing state of calm, to the natural stability of a mind that is finding its way to its own true nature. By contrast, the ordinary practice of mental calm, in which, for example, we meditate on our breath, only brings about a superficial calming of the mind. True mental calm prevails when our mind perceives its own nature.

Our growing capacity for mental calm leads to the generation of intuitive insight. The clarity of our mind gradually increases and a dimension opens that is not the object of thought. The line separating the meditator and the meditation increasingly dissolves, until neither meditator nor meditation remain. This experience of the inseparability of the two leads into non-duality. As it becomes clearer and more transparent, our awareness separates itself from experiences and settles in a state of recollection of spontaneous non-duality, free from any perturbation due to dualistic patterns. It is here that the timeless awareness of penetrating, intuitive insight arises. There is no longer any separation of perceiver and perceived experiences. Meditation proceeds beyond duality. This is true realization, beyond all experiences such as those of bliss, clarity and non-conceptuality.

In non-dual perception, the mind recognizes its own nature which at the same time is the nature of the world of appearances.

The mind then sees without looking. No longer is there a person who knows. Intuitive insight refers to the condition in which the mind perceives itself without making a separation between seer and seen, subject and object. The observer has disappeared. In this "self-recognition" of the mind, there is nothing that is seen by someone. This first seeing of that which cannot be seen is realization, the first completely clear lighting up of recognition.

However, this recognition is not as yet complete – in the same way as we cannot claim that the narrow crescent of the moon that appears soon after a new moon is a full moon. It is undeniable that we have seen the nature of mind, but it still takes time to attain full realization. By analogy with the moon that takes fifteen days to become full, our mind has to go through ten bodhisattva stages until it recognizes fully and completely that it always has been the buddha mind.

In this transitional phase of developing intuitive insight, the meditator is like a little child who has no capacity as yet to develop great activity, even though it possesses the same limbs as an adult. We have no great ability as yet to actually apply our insight, but by developing our meditation further, our capacity for action will increase and we will be able to translate our realization of the nature of mind into concrete action for the benefit of all beings.

Through the continued meditation of intuitive insight our mind is purified and cleared. It gradually matures, and eventually we arrive at the direct insight that our spiritual master, our root lama, truly is a buddha. We achieve certainty about buddha nature, a confidence free of all doubt or reservation. We recognize that the nature of the Buddha, the nature of the lama and the nature of our own mind are one and the same and are completely inseparable. This is the sign that the timeless awareness of intuitive insight has been generated fully.

We should make an effort to maintain the open state of mind of meditation in our ordinary daily life and allow it to infuse all of our activities. For this it will help to again and again bring to mind the unreal, illusory nature of all experiences. Although the world appears to be very concrete, situations do not at all have the solid reality that we ordinarily ascribe to them. In our daily life, as in our meditation sessions, we should allow thoughts to arise without following them. They are like the image of the moon mirrored in the water: although they appear, they do not possess any true reality.

In this way, we gradually learn to use the events of our daily lives for making progress on the path to awakening. When we have problems or someone wants to harm us, we regard these situations or persons as manifestations of our lama that serve to teach us patience. All the suffering that we see around us provides us with an opportunity to develop compassion. We should not ignore it or reject it, but view it as a challenge to practice the qualities of awakening and work for the benefit of others. We should abandon our ordinary view of the world and direct our attention toward the deeper layers of reality that allow us to perceive this world as full of buddhas and bodhisattvas.

*Emaho! With amazement we perceive
that we live in a pure world!*

We did not suspect in the least what an abundance of qualities our daily life harbors. For a yogi, everything is a miracle. He or she delights in all things and is amazed by everything. We only have difficulties when we live with narrow, fixed views. When we become fixated on things, then there is no longer any room for movement, not even for breathing, but when we release ourselves from our fixed views, everything begins to flow and becomes easy. Nothing will be judged and pigeonholed – there is nothing that we need to meet with attachment or aversion. Everything is open, nothing is truly a hindrance, and everything will be joyfully used as a means for our liberation.

Further Explanation of Mahamudra

With our deepening practice of mental calm and intuitive insight, our meditation becomes non-meditation: our relaxed mind perceives all movements of thought as expressions of itself and recognizes in them its own emptiness and spontaneous creativity. Through this recognition, ignorance dissolves spontaneously and naturally.

By directly looking at itself, our mind cuts through its attachment to the world of appearances that, being in a state of ignorance, it had not previously recognized as a projection of itself. Through this it frees itself of its tendencies of grasping and rejecting, of its desire to possess and to destroy. All karma then dissolves naturally and without effort, as we recognize that the veils of ignorance possess no true reality.

At the beginning of our path, our obscurations still appear to us as something real that we need to be rid of. The more we progress in our practice and the more our mind recognizes itself, the more clearly we perceive that our obscurations are merely the play of the mind itself, and that they are of the same empty, clear and luminous nature as all other appearances. In the state of non-attachment, our obscurations dissolve by themselves. This is the spontaneous liberation of our mind through Mahamudra, the recognition of our mind's true nature.

Our mind then rests in itself, and in perfect equanimity perceives the equality of all appearances, the "one taste" of all phenomena. This gives rise to a feeling of joy that is deeper than any satisfaction through external things could ever be. All our attachments dissolve entirely naturally, without our having to fight them. At the beginning of our path, we regarded obscurations and emotions as problems that we wanted to eliminate. Now, as a consequence of the purification of the mind that is taking place, we discover the true nature of mind, which at the same time is also the nature of all of these temporary obscurations.

Even if these explanations seem clear and convincing to us, we must sit down and meditate, until our conviction becomes realization. Realization cannot be described, since in analyzing and describing we operate on the plane of duality, on which a subject looks at an object. Realization can only be experienced directly and personally. It brings complete certainty with it. We must meditate until we achieve a complete and boundless certainty in which our mind remains beyond all doubt, even though we are not able to describe this experience.

When we recognize the true nature of every thought, we shall recognize the arising and ceasing of thoughts as the display of the dharmakaya, the true nature of reality. This direct insight that quickly and directly leads to complete awakening, has been given different names. It is called the Great Seal (Mahamudra), the Great Perfection (Maha-ati), or the Way of the Middle (Madhyamaka). We also speak of this highest dimension as the Perfection of Wisdom (Prajnaparamita).

These different terms do not designate distinct things but point to one and the same reality, the same awakening. Even though different names are used to refer to different traditional paths, in their essence they are identical and do not exclude one another. Therefore, we should not create any artificial distinctions and cling to any of these terms or paths, identify with one of them and reject the others.

The practice of Mahamudra is founded on ground Mahamudra, follows path Mahamudra and leads to the realization of fruition Mahamudra. These three aspects of Mahamudra, ground, path and fruition, are inseparable and are the expression of a single, spontaneous reality, in which ultimately there are no such distinctions as ground, path and fruition. Mahamudra is buddhahood itself, the actualization of the truth body.

Occasionally, it is the *ground* of realization that is called Mahamudra, the Great Seal of the nature of all appearances. This refers to the spontaneous, unborn expanse of wisdom that since beginningless time dwells in and pervades all beings as the buddha nature. It is only because this ground is already present in us that it is possible for us to attain realization at all.

So that we may attain buddhahood, our practice follows the *path* of uncovering this buddha nature. This path is called Madhyamaka, the Path of the Great Middle, because it constitutes the complete unity of relative and ultimate reality, beyond all extreme views of existence and nonexistence. Without such a path that allows a continually increasing opening up to our buddha nature, the potential for buddhahood that lies in all of us would never fully unfold.

This path leads to the *fruition* of complete actualization of our buddha nature, which is called Maha-ati, the Great Perfection. This is the recognition that all phenomena in the universe, without any distinctions, have always already been perfect in their own true nature, because in their arising they have never been separated from ultimate purity. Also, the fruition is the full entrance into the awareness dimension of a buddha that has always been present in us as the ground. Thus, ground, path and fruition are one and the same reality that is merely presented from different viewpoints as different stages of realization.

*At the beginning, the buddha nature
resides in us like an undiscovered treasure, on
the path, it gradually reveals itself to us, and in
fruition, it manifests itself in us continuously.*

The term Mahamudra is often used as a synonym for the nature of mind and explained as denoting the three bodies of enlightenment. In this explanation the truth body corresponds to the fact that all appearances, outer and inner, sentient and non-sentient, just like our own mind, do not really exist and thus are empty by nature. The fact that this empty expanse of awareness is able to creatively generate appearances, corresponds to the enjoyment body. And the fact that these appearances are manifesting unceasingly in the most varied forms, corresponds to the emanation body.

Another explanation of Mahamudra follows the description of the five aspects of timeless awareness that are also called the *"five wisdoms."* From a non-dual perspective, all appearances are the expression of these five aspects of wisdom. To recognize appearances as empty and not to regard them as real – that is the *wisdom of the dharmadhatu*, the unchanging great expanse of all appearances. To be aware of the fact that although appearances are essentially empty, they nevertheless manifest spontaneously, clearly and distinctly – that is the *mirror-like wisdom*. To be aware of the fact that these aspects of emptiness and clarity form an inseparable unity – that is the *wisdom of equality*. To be aware of the fact that emptiness and clarity nonetheless are not identical but indeed are distinguishable aspects of the one reality – that is the *discriminating wisdom*. To be aware of the fact that all appearances manifest completely spontaneously and perfectly without having to be created – that is the *all-accomplishing wisdom*. These five wisdoms are five aspects of one and the same awakened awareness. When we let go of dualistic views, this expanse of Mahamudra awareness opens in which the various manifestations of the world of appearances are inseparably one.

Through Mahamudra meditation we free ourselves of all patterns that produce veils and obscurations in our mind. As soon as the mind is liberated from these tendencies, it is able to see the dharmakaya, its own primordial nature. To actualize the dharmakaya, or buddhahood, means that the mind recognizes itself as it truly is. For this to happen, we do not need to become a different person, or search for something outside of ourselves. We only need to look inwardly, at our own mind. Moreover, there is nothing to abandon externally, as there is no samsara external to us.

The samsara that we have to abandon is the
entirety of the self-centered patterns in our
own mind, our dualistic views – when this
is done, complete awakening is attained.

To enable us to dissolve our dualistic views, the *Vajrayana,* the "indestructible" vehicle of Buddhist practice, offers the method of meditating on a yidam, a luminous buddha body. We either visualize ourselves as the luminous form of a buddha, or we visualize it in the space in front of us. This kind of meditation gradually transforms our perception of ourselves and the world.

On the relative plane, what we regard as ourselves consists of the five aggregates *(skandhas)*: form, sensation, discrimination, mental formations and consciousness. Their interplay constitutes the totality of our physical and mental appearance. But through the filter of our dualistic view, we misconceive the true nature of these five aggregates. In order to recognize their true nature, we meditate on ourselves as a luminous buddha body. Through this our experience gradually changes. We begin to experience the five aggregates as the expression of the unity of the clarity (i. e., the dynamics) and the emptiness of our mind and to recognize in them the five aspects of timeless awareness that were described above. All the appearances that arise as the expression of the unceasing play of interdependent causation reveal themselves as empty projections of dynamic mind.

In our condition of ignorance, we believe in the reality of things, in the material existence of whatever our senses perceive. Our mind attributes a concrete reality to the five aggregates and identifies itself with them as 'I'. It neither perceives the aspect of emptiness nor the dynamic, clear aspect of appearances. To work with these strong obscurations is the aim of yidam practices. Step by step, they help us recognize that all physical manifestation – our body, our surroundings and all living beings – as well as the totality of the play of sensory impressions and consciousness, is really only the unfolding of the dynamic qualities of the nature of mind: clearly appearing, yet empty. We relax in this recognition, like a wave that relaxes into the ocean, as it recognizes that it has the same nature as the ocean.

How to Deal with Emotions in Meditation and Everyday Life

There is no fundamental difference between thoughts and emotions; both are nothing other than movements of the mind. Emotions are waves of thoughts that follow one another closely. They start with a single thought to which we attach great emotional importance and to which we then connect further thoughts, until these additional thoughts influence all our thinking, words and actions and veritably flood our mind.

Emotional entanglement is the result of ignorance: our mind does not recognize itself, and it becomes the victim of its attachments and allows itself to get swept away by emotions. Unable to free itself of them, it must fight to get or reject the objects that excite it so greatly. In doing this, it totally exhausts itself, when instead it could rest in itself in a relaxed way. Our mind could just let go of the emotions, in an awareness of their true nature.

In order to recognize the true nature of any emotion, we should look at it directly the moment it appears, in exactly the same way that we have described before for thoughts in general. Whenever an emotion churns up our mind, we look directly at it and try to find out whether it possesses a form, color or any other characteristic that would attest to its concrete existence. As a result of repeated attempts at such introspection, we recognize that emotions essentially cannot be grasped. They do not possess any concrete existence but are fleeting appearances in our mind, similar to a dream. An emotion is not "something" – there is nothing concrete that can be found. Our becoming aware of the fact that there is nothing to find leads to the direct recognition of the nature of the emotion. An emotion reveals itself to be an illusory appearance, and we recognize it to be an expression of our unceasingly creative timeless awareness.

Even though this practice of directly looking into the emotion is not an easy one initially, we should make a real effort to try to engage in it. With growing practice, we will recognize the five mental poisons – ignorance, desire, anger, pride and jealousy – in their true nature to be the five awakened wisdoms, the five aspects of timeless awareness.

In this way, the pure perception of the awakened ones will gradually unfold in us. Free of grasping and rejecting, we perceive the movements of the emotions simply as movements of our mind and not as disturbing emotions. We recognize that they are the expression of the natural dynamics of the wisdom nature of our mind. With this recognition, the emergence of an emotion is turned into a meditation on the nature of mind. Pure awareness prevails instead of confusion. Our view of the world opens into its pure, true dimension. Emotions, incidents, appearances that usually cloud or churn up our mind, now become instructions on the true nature of mind. This is the highest form of spiritual practice.

> *We begin with looking inward. Paying close attention, we recognize emotions without reacting to them and we allow them to dissolve.*

In this way, the recognition of the true nature of emotions will arise in us. We continue with this practice until we see how emotions dissolve directly the instant they appear. This is called the "self-liberation of emotions." It takes place in exactly the same way as the self-liberation of thoughts.

When we look directly into the innermost core of an emotion, the dynamically creative and empty nature of mind is seen, and this transforms the emotion into a force for liberation.

Then afflictive emotions are no longer a problem for us. In fact, the more of these difficult emotions arise the better. With increasing practice, with every stimulus, thought or emotion, we will succeed in remaining in the awareness of the true nature of mind, spontaneously and effortlessly, and therefore we will remain in equanimity. Then all of the thoughts and feelings that arise in our daily life serve as opportunities to free ourselves from karmic burdens and emotional obscurations, and the more of them arise the better.

In recognizing the true nature of our emotions, we free ourselves at the same time of all the suffering that afflictive emotions usually cause. Our suffering is caused by our belief in the reality of our experiences. As long as we believe that we *truly* have an emotion, we suffer. But when we recognize the illusory nature of the emotion, we free ourselves of the suffering that is caused by our taking the emotion for real and identifying with it.

If directly looking at the emotion turns out to be too difficult for us, then it may be helpful for us to consider the following. Our present emotion and the suffering that is associated with it are the consequence of previous actions and of the karmic forces that were produced by them. It is hopeless to try to push away the suffering and escape from it in that way. Such an attempt would only intensify the suffering. Instead, we should accept unpleasant situations as the natural ripening of the fruits of our previous actions and live through them consciously and with clarity.

This will produce in us the certainty that the dissolution of our ego-clinging is the only method that will put an end to our suffering. When we no longer act from an ego-centered position, then we do not create further karma, and we do not have to fear further suffering in the future. Thus, for us to accept difficult situations is a source of deep understanding.

We should make an effort in our daily lives, just as in our meditation, not to get stuck in judgments of "right" and "wrong," as this ego-centered outlook will only bring us into constant conflict with others. When we let go of our fixed views, we cease manipulating others. We no longer feel the need to force our own opinions onto others; we do not insist anymore on our own viewpoints. We understand that our deeply ingrained dualistic perception that divides the world into 'I' and "others" is a source of suffering, for ourselves and for others.

Once we have discovered that there is no 'I' that has to be nurtured or defended in relation to others, all possibilities of conflict are done away with.

The root of all conflict is our belief that we are right, that we know how things ought to be, and that others are wrong. All conflicts are rooted in this erroneous view, be they between individuals or entire nations. Therefore, to develop tolerance is an important part of our Dharma practice. Everywhere, we meet people who do not share our ethical outlook and our view of the world, who think and live differently and who we think are mistaken. However, there is no need for this assumption to elicit anger, aversion or intolerance in us – we do not need to regard ourselves as the custodians of what is right and proper in this world.

When we see that others are in fact wrong and carry out unwholesome actions that cause suffering for themselves and others, then this should elicit compassion and stimulate some creativity in us, so that we can find intelligent ways of helping them. We could say to ourselves: "This person, like so many others, acts under the influence of ignorance. They are prisoners of their ignorance and their habitual patterns of behavior, and they have very little room for choice and freedom of action."

When we adopt such a viewpoint, the situation becomes an instruction for us on the nature of conditioned existence and the fact that it is full of suffering. We ask ourselves how we can possibly help, and we seek ways of assisting this person. Even if at the moment our actual possibilities of helping them are limited, we resolve to continue to practice intensively, so that we will be able to offer effective help as soon as possible. In this way, we cultivate tolerance, lovingkindness and compassion.

When Dharma practitioners become narrow-minded and dogmatic and begin to believe that they belong to an elite that has a monopoly on wisdom, then their practice has become clouded by pride and jealousy and no longer has anything to do with real Dharma. If we want to correct such a grave aberration, we must become aware of our own pride and attempt to develop openness. Every day and in every situation, we should try hard to cultivate this openness and presence of mind. That constitutes true discipline, and through it our practice will deepen day by day. If we do not notice our pride, we will become more and more tense and prone to feelings of anger in our interactions with others. This anger may even be directed against our own teacher and against the practice of Dharma. That would be of the greatest danger for a practitioner.

There is also the pride of those who carry themselves in a humble manner, behave nicely, never say a nasty word, never fight or argue, never do anything wrong and are always friendly toward everyone.

They may appear to be humble and restrained, but often they harbor great pride. It shows itself in thoughts such as: "Oh, I'm not proud, it's the others who are proud and believe that they are always right." In this way, they conceal much envy and ill-will. This kind of pride is worse than others, as it may not even be recognized as pride.

There are many other kinds of pride. Some people think with condescension: "I will have nothing to do with people at such a low level!" Others say: "Sure, you are right, you are the best, just do what you like!", and they are actually too proud even to bother to get involved with others. Yet others, during the group meditation, carry themselves in an exceptionally holy and pure way that is very impressive and beautiful to behold. Everyone is proud in one way or another.

Pride is subtle and can be present in any attitude. If we examine ourselves, we will find it, and we will gradually be able to free ourselves of it. We will feel lighter then, will be easier to deal with and will have fewer negative feelings toward others. This is an indication that we have recognized our pride and that it is being dissolved. When we admit to ourselves that it is present, we develop an awareness of it, and that awareness dissolves the negativity. Only when we are able to see our own faults, can we dissolve them and become a bodhisattva who is free of negative feelings.

In order to uncover the qualities of a bodhisattva in ourselves, we have to engage in continuous inner work in which we will meet with many challenges. We have to face up to all the tendencies that are still hidden in us and that we have not yet worked on, and that can be painful. But we will not be able to get around this – buddhahood will not one day gently reveal itself to us all on its own.

Thanks to the kindness and compassion of our teacher and the Three Jewels, to some degree we have already become aware of our own ignorance and negativity, and some of our ignorance has already dissolved. This gives us confidence in the teachings and the teacher – the first sign that some degree of insight has developed. It is as though we have just awakened from sleep and opened our eyes a tiny bit. We do not see clearly as yet, but we are aware of the fact that we are beginning to see something that we have not seen before. This is the beginning of the bodhisattva path.

Bodhisattvas are keenly interested in others and are deeply affected when others suffer. From the depths of their hearts, they wish others to be full of happiness and free of suffering. When others experience happiness, they too are deeply happy, as others' happiness is their sole concern. Wherever such benevolence is found, any kind of jealousy, competition, pride, anger and envy simply disappear.

Bodhisattvas have no desire to be better or happier than others. In their hearts there is no place left for jealousy, and so they experience true inner peace, lasting joy, and a deep mental stability. Free of personal interests, they no longer cling to objects that they formerly chased after. Recognizing these objects as projections of the mind, they find inner peace. This peace springs from their concern for others – this is what we call mental calmness. Being free from attachment, a deep happiness arises in them, and their minds turn toward other beings, with the sole wish that others may be happy and free themselves from all suffering.

The more we turn toward others, the more we ourselves are filled with happiness and joy.

Phenomena

All phenomena,
the outer world and all its inhabitants,
are appearances of our own mind.

Appearances are mind,
appearing and yet empty,
empty and yet appearing.

Appearances are inseparable from emptiness,
deceptive like a dream or an illusion.
They are nothing and yet they appear –
like the moon on water.

To recognize this
completely liberates us
from our deep entanglement
in dualistic grasping and fixation.

Free of artificiality, relaxed and loose,
open to that freshness
that is the very nature
of self-aware consciousness.

Aside from this,
there is nothing to contemplate or meditate on.

Don't think,
don't meditate,
don't do anything.
Simply remain undistracted.
I beg you –
meditate naturally and let go!

Gendun Rinpoche

Preparing for Death

*The practice of Dharma gains its real
meaning in the preparation for death. It is
then that its full value becomes evident.*

Because we have practiced during our lifetime, we will have no fear
when the process of our dying begins. We will be rooted in faith
and know which attitude is helpful in this process and which is not.
We will reap the fruits of a life that was dedicated to the practice of
Dharma. If, however, we begin our practice only at the last minute,
its wholesome effects will not materialize in time. The consequences of our unwholesome actions will follow us into the process of dying like a shadow and lead to experiences of great suffering. Therefore, we should apply the instructions without delay and dissolve the
burden of our harmful actions while there is still time.

Perhaps we say to ourselves that it is better if we do not think too
much about death since we cannot avert it anyway, and the thought
of it may only scare or depress us. But it is not wise to repress the
thought of death. Only when we surrender to the reality of death, to
its inevitability and unpredictability, are we able to prepare ourselves
for it and look it in the eye calmly and with a clear mind.

Our death may happen at any time, be it through an accident, a sudden illness, spoiled food – virtually anything may become the cause of death for us. We cannot know when our time will come. And however we may try, we cannot prevent the arrival of death – just as little as we can stop the course of the sun. All riches and all power will not be able to help us in the least in the face of death. We will have to leave everything behind. If we have spent our entire lives accumulating things, trying to win friends, build up power and achieve fame, then that means that we have exclusively followed our ego-centered inclinations and become deeply entangled in them emotionally.

At our death, we will no longer have the opportunity to free ourselves from these conditionings. All the effort we have spent trying to extract happiness for ourselves from this life will only have resulted in a great mountain of negative karma, as all our actions were motivated by self-centeredness. At our death, the force of these unwholesome deeds will hurl us into one of the three realms of existence characterized by suffering, i. e., the hell realms, the realm of the hungry ghosts and the animal realm. In these realms great suffering prevails that is much more intense than that of the human realm.

If we are insufficiently motivated for spiritual practice, then this indicates that we have not thought enough about impermanence and death. We may not wish to think about the consequences of a life that was wasted with meaningless activities; thus we simply assert that it is unnecessary to prepare ourselves for death and the time thereafter. We are attached to worldly life and its pleasures and regard our present well-being as the most important thing. But eventually we will have to face up to the consequences of our actions, and then it will be too late to change anything.

When we surrender to the reality of death, much will become clear to us that previously was hidden from our view. We will see not only that death does definitely come but also that its arrival is totally unpredictable. It could come at any moment. We have no time to lose.

We should begin our preparation immediately and refrain from all actions that lead to painful rebirths. Meditating on the all-determining power of karma that decides how we will fare in the future is a powerful incentive for us to engage in wholesome actions, devote ourselves to the Dharma and stop losing any more time on our path to awakening.

The consequences of the many unwholesome actions that we have undertaken constitute the greatest danger in death. We must learn at once how we can dissolve these seeds of suffering with the aid of the Dharma and instead plant seeds of happiness. Only the Dharma, the path of dissolution of all self-centeredness, has this power. Therefore, we should apply the methods of the Dharma immediately. During the process of dying and thereafter, when we desperately seek protection, the only effective help will come from Buddha, Dharma and Sangha.

We would be wrong to think that it will suffice for us to open ourselves to the Three Jewels at the last moment. We must practice making wishing prayers and going for refuge in the Three Jewels and the lama over the entire course of our lives, so that this attitude becomes deeply rooted and completely natural at our death. When we are unprepared for it, dying is a painful process, and we might not react to it in as calm and collected a manner as we would wish, as it is not easy to let go of everything and walk into the unknown. It will be too late to learn anything new – our good habits will have to support us then.

When we devote our lives to the practice of Dharma, we learn to transform difficult circumstances into the path to awakening, purify our karma and free ourselves from the ballast of the past. The practice of Dharma also frees us from our deeply rooted tendency to make the same mistakes again and again and continually create new suffering. Gradually, it enables us to stand by others in their suffering and help them dissolve their karma. Through the power of our commitment to practice and through the purity of our motivation, we will be able to inspire more and more beings to walk the path of liberation. In this way, our practice indeed effects the benefit of all beings.

> *When* we are well prepared through our
> Dharma practice, death is an extraordinary
> opportunity to deepen our insight.

Very advanced practitioners are able to attain buddhahood during their death, by recognizing that their mind is the truth body. Somewhat less advanced practitioners, who by engaging in yidam practices have learned to see all appearances as the varied expressions of the mind of the Buddha, are able to attain liberation during death by realizing the enjoyment body.

If we are not quite such well qualified practitioners but have developed an open, relaxed mind and deep trust in the lama, then we will not feel threatened by the illusory appearances of the after-death state but will recognize in them the true nature of all appearances, i. e., emptiness. Since we have practiced devotion and openness toward the lama and also practiced making wishing prayers, we will be able to blend our mind with the mind of the lama. Through this, all the appearances in the after-death state, which are nothing other than the manifestations of our karmic tendencies, will be purified immediately as they arise. They dissolve when we recognize their true nature and we will attain complete liberation.

For all these reasons, it is vital that now, while we are still alive, we turn toward the study and practice of the Dharma and develop openness and trust in the master and the teachings. Material things and friends are of no help at our death. Only the power developed through our practice, and our confidence and capacity to open ourselves to the blessings of the Three Jewels and the lama, can protect us then.

Therefore, from now on, we should use all situations, particularly those that are difficult and painful, to develop trust and devotion to the Three Jewels and the lama. Situations in which we are suffering or are attacked or encounter difficult problems are the best training ground for us. We should not resort to worldly means of solving them but instead open ourselves to the blessings of the Dharma.

The more accustomed we become to going for refuge, the more it will also help us in our sleep, during heavy dreams, and during our death. Through the prayers that we direct to the sources of refuge in our waking state, we establish a habit that enables us to naturally go for refuge during our dreams as well. When we do this, our fears immediately dissolve and our dream takes a different turn. Moreover, our spontaneous taking refuge during the dream indicates that going for refuge has become a reliable, virtually automatic reaction that will support us also in the process of dying. Through the power of habit that we have developed during our lifetime of practice we will remember the refuge, and with it the Dharma, at our death and thereafter, and we will be able to find our way out of all fear and confusion.

Through our turning to the refuge, we will recognize the experiences of the dying process as projections of our mind and not mistake them for forces that act on us from the outside.

If we want to be certain that we will attain liberation at our death, in addition to faith and devotion we must develop a direct understanding of the true nature of all appearances. Therefore, we should unceasingly meditate on the fact that the entire world – all beings and phenomena – is without reality, like a dream, the illusory display of the mind. When we truly understand the illusory nature of all appearances of happiness and suffering, we will no longer attribute a concrete reality to our experiences and we will also recognize the projections during the process of dying as illusory. As terrifying as they may be, we will understand that they are merely images in the mirror of our mind. This understanding develops as we open ourselves to the blessings of the lama and the Three Jewels. Again and again, we come back to these key points of our practice: faith, openness and devotion.

If in our lifetime we have not learned to live our experiences as though we were living in a dream and to recognize the dream state itself to be an illusion, then it will be difficult for us to attain liberation at the time of death or in the after-death state. Since appearances and our tendencies manifest in the same way after death as they do now, without the benefit of Dharma practice we will regard our experiences then as being just as real as they appear to us now. Thus, in order to be well prepared for death, we should right now practice recognizing the unreality of all appearances.

The Tibetan word "bardo" is commonly used to designate the after-death phase, but actually bardo quite generally means "in-between state." At present, we are in a bardo, too, i. e., the in-between state between birth and death. The only difference between this bardo and the after-death bardo is that our experiences after our death will be more intense than now. Whatever we have experienced in former lives, whatever we experience in the present bardo, and whatever we will experience in the after-death bardo, is the result of the ripening of karmic seeds – the forces of our actions – that we have created in countless lifetimes. All these different bardo experiences follow the same laws: they arise from karmic causes and conditions.

Therefore, the best preparation for the after-death bardo is to learn to live in the bardo of the present moment, with the aid of our Dharma practice. From the perspective of the Dharma, our death is merely a change in the content of what we perceive. The appearances of our present world cease, and they make room for other perceptions. There is no real break: our mind continues to be what it is in its true nature and to perceive with the same tendencies. The frame of reference of our perceptions changes but fundamentally the same process continues – the reactions of our mind remain the same as before. In truth, death, as much as life, is an illusion, a transient in-between state, a bardo. Contrary to what we may perhaps assume, with our death everything does not simply come to an end.

> *Death is the continuation of life: a change of scene in the continuous process of change.*

Our perceptions after death are the continuing manifestation of our ripening karmic potential. This karma continues to be experienced by our mind and senses. Our sensory perceptions continue, even though for the time being we only possess a mental body and not a material body. And just as in our present life, we react with attachment or aversion and all the other emotions, depending on whether our karma produces peaceful or frightening experiences.

Our death can be compared with a move. We live in a house in which we have developed certain habits, and one day the conditions expire for us to continue to live there. We die, pick up our "karmic suitcases" and move somewhere else, to live in a different situation and environment. But even though we find ourselves in a new, unknown world, we continue to be accompanied by our old habits. The teachings of the Dharma help us orient ourselves in this new situation, because in this life we have already developed habits that will help us along in unknown lands.

At death our present frame of reference dissolves. Death is the end of our familiar world. If, during our lifetime, we have believed in the reality of this conditioned world, then our death will plunge us into total confusion. We will no longer be able to cope, as all familiar reference points, all the mirrors that formerly gave us the feeling that we exist, are missing. We discover that we are all alone. The illusion that we are surrounded by others, that we are somebody and that we are doing important things, collapses at death. And if we have not used our lifetime to develop deep confidence in the refuge and thereby in our mind, we will feel uprooted and lost.

*What remains of us at our death is our mind,
our view of things and whatever confidence,
experience and realization we succeeded
in generating in our stream of being.*

At our death, everything depends on whether we have truly learned to go for refuge – refuge in the lama, who at the same time is the true dimension of our mind. In the process of dying, when our surroundings dissolve and the outer lama can no longer be reached, we ought to be able, free of any doubt, to go for refuge in the true nature of the lama. Through such a taking of refuge, the true lama is available in ourselves.

At our death, our mind separates itself from everything material, from our body as well as from the world. It is completely naked then, no longer bound to this body that restrains it but also protects it from an overly quick translation of impulses into action. Our empty, dynamic consciousness displays an astounding power when it is no longer anchored to a physical body: in this purely mental dimension every thought has an immediate effect. If an emotion arises, we instantly find ourselves in an environment that mirrors this emotion. Even though our basic mental processes now and after death are identical, we may have a hard time now imagining our state of mind then, as we have never in our ordinary lives experienced this naked consciousness that is not connected to a body.

In our ordinary state, we continually create conceptual obscurations that conceal the true nature of our mind and of the world. We never really consciously establish contact with our deeper nature –

unless we practice meditation. In the time after death, our mind is highly mobile and possesses many powers that it has not learned to control. In addition, it encounters totally unexpected and unknown situations. Unprepared as it is, it can hardly respond appropriately to these challenges. It is very unstable – anything can happen, and it easily loses its balance. Depending on which direction our thoughts take, we may find ourselves in states of the deepest happiness or the greatest suffering.

The Dharma teaches us methods that enable us to recognize the nature of mind. These profound instructions, such as the teachings of the Great Seal (Mahamudra), the Great Perfection (Maha-ati), the Perfection of Wisdom (Prajnaparamita), and the Way of the Middle (Madhyamaka), with their impressive names, exert a great attraction on spiritual seekers. But to understand these teachings through our own experience requires regular, persistent practice. Only by means of such practice can we penetrate to the heart of these approaches and not remain stuck in a merely intellectual understanding. To regard ourselves as practitioners of these teachings, without truly understanding their meaning, would be an expression of spiritual pride.

At our death, we need a method that we have a real mastery of – overestimating ourselves will not help us then.

So it behooves us to exercise modesty and rely on a simple and safe practice that lies within our reach and safely leads ignorant people like us to liberation. Particularly suited for this purpose is the practice of making wishing prayers for rebirth in the pure land of Amitabha, the Buddha of Limitless Light. This practice makes it possible for us, solely through our faith in Buddha Amitabha, at our death to gain entry into the pure lands of the realization of the nature of mind. When we attain rebirth in a pure land such as Amitabha's pure land of Dewachen, we are liberated from cyclic existence, encounter no more obstacles and are able to quickly advance toward complete awakening.

Of course, it is possible for us within this lifetime to realize Mahamudra, the insight into the true nature of mind, but such an aspiration requires total commitment. We would need to direct all our energy toward this goal and practice untiringly for the entire duration of our life, until we mastered the *development* and *completion stages* of the meditation.

At the moment, most of us probably lack the requisite time and energy. Our karmic conditions just are not ripe for it – and perhaps we are also a bit too lazy! As was said above, for all those who are either too lazy or too busy to be able to practice intensively, but who have a deep longing for liberation from the suffering of cyclic existence, there is the practice of making wishing prayers for rebirth in Amitabha's pure land of bliss. This practice is simple and requires little time but it brings great results.

Of all the awakened realms of consciousness that are called pure lands, the pure land of Amitabha is the easiest to reach. During the entirety of his path to attaining buddhahood, Amitabha made wishing prayers beseeching the buddhas to make it possible for ordinary beings who during their lifetime had not yet understood the nature of mind to reach a land of realization. In the course of their spiritual development, every bodhisattva makes wishing prayers for their future activity. Amitabha saw that many pure lands are difficult to reach for ordinary beings, since entry into them presupposes that one has already attained a certain degree of realization of the nature of mind during one's lifetime.

He prayed that with his attainment of buddhahood a spiritual environment would come into being that would be accessible to all – solely as the result of the sincere wish to be reborn in this pure land and of unshaken faith in him. When he became a fully awakened buddha, through the power of his realization his wishing prayers were fulfilled and Dewachen manifested, a pure land that is open to all who have sufficient faith in him.

In order to reach Dewachen, we need great faith in Buddha Amitabha, and we must have no doubt that it is possible for us to be reborn there.

To be reborn in Dewachen, it is greatly useful to make wishing prayers daily, asking that we reach this pure land immediately after our death, without having to take birth again in cyclic existence. When we make these wishing prayers with great devotion over the entire course of our lives, we practice entrusting ourselves to Amitabha. Particularly helpful for this also is the meditation on Avalokiteshvara, the Bodhisattva of Great Compassion, as it is he who will open the door for us to this pure awareness dimension and lead us to Buddha Amitabha, his lama.

When we combine the Avalokiteshvara practice with the making of wishing prayers, a deep longing will arise in us to reach Dewachen. Of course, the practice also includes our making an effort to avoid all unwholesome deeds and to do as much as possible that is beneficial. When we thus orient our lives entirely toward liberation and awakening, we detach ourselves gradually from the concerns of this world and at the time of our death will be ready to leave the world of attachments behind us. When we have dissolved any desire to be reborn in cyclic existence, we will reach Dewachen directly after our death. We can be certain that this is within the reach of any one of us.

In order to be able to make this great transition and be filled with faith while we are undergoing it, we must have a clear understanding of what to practice during the process of dying. When the moment of our death approaches, we first offer our body, speech and mind as well as all wholesome actions that we have carried out in the course of our lives for the benefit of all beings. As completely as possible, we dedicate everything that is good to them and wish them the fulfillment of all of their wishes. May they be happy, may their minds open up, and may their open, happy minds swiftly lead them to buddhahood!

Then we arouse the strong, pure wish to be reborn in the presence of Buddha Amitabha, immediately after our death. To support this aspiration, we visualize Amitabha as a luminous form, located above our head or in the space before us. We imagine that he is inseparable from our root lama who has accompanied us our entire life and with whom we have developed a strong connection. We have already turned to him in many difficult situations, and now we can connect to the openness, faith and devotion that have arisen in us in this way. We clearly visualize our lama as Buddha Amitabha and develop confidence in his presence, until we feel with certainty that he is actually there.

Full of devotion and joy, we mentally offer him everything that we have regarded as belonging to us in this life: our possessions, our home, the different members of our family, our friends, our native country – in short, everything to which perhaps we are still attached, all the way up to our body. All of this we entrust to Amitabha; it no longer belongs to us. We offer it without any reservations or calculation, without expecting anything in return. We offer everything that we have to leave behind anyway. In this way, we free ourselves from the very last attachments that still bind us to this world.

Every remaining attachment to this life that is ending, be it ever so small, will be an impediment to our liberation in the moment of death.

Our attachments and the many afflictive emotions springing from them are the greatest obstacle to our rebirth in Dewachen. For this reason, we should internally part with everything now and offer it to lama Amitabha and to the benefit of all beings. When we do this, we generate a strong positive force that will help us on the path. Free of all cares and attachments, we can then fully turn to the buddhas Amitabha and Avalokiteshvara. In this deep letting go, our mind opens and it already begins to become permeated with the bliss of Dewachen.

Then, when our mind leaves our body, the transition takes place in a single instant and in a completely natural way. We leave our customary plane of existence behind us and assume a mental rebirth in the Pure Land of Bliss. By contrast, if we continue to cling to our possessions and to the pleasures of this life, then before and after our death we will encounter many obstacles, as we will be tormented by the fear of losing the objects of our attachment. And that is a source of great suffering.

After our death, we still perceive our body and our former surroundings for a while. It may disturb us greatly to have to witness the fact that the things to which we were attached now belong to others, possibly even to those who harmed us the most or whom we hated the most. We may have to witness how our relatives greedily pounce on our possessions and quarrel over them. Seeing that may touch off great dismay and anger in us, which in turn will directly catapult us into realms of existence characterized by great suffering. Because of this, it is very important that before our death we detach ourselves from all our relatives, friends and possessions and also offer our body to the Buddha, so that our mind is not influenced by whatever happens with and around our corpse after our death.

Once we have let go completely of this life and this world, we concentrate on Amitabha and on our wish to be reborn in his pure land, and we maintain this state of consciousness until our last breath. If we are completely focused on this goal, then in a natural way when we die our consciousness will go to Buddha Amitabha in Dewachen.

For this to happen, it is not even necessary to know the practice of *phowa,* a method of meditation for the directed transference of our consciousness into other realms. A deep faith in the power of our wishing prayers to Amitabha and the longing of our totally focused mind are sufficient.

With such faith and power of inner orientation, our consciousness will leave our body naturally through the crown of our head and we will be instantaneously reborn in a lotus flower in the Pure Land of Bliss. If we have developed a truly deep faith, then the lotus flower will open at once and we will be able to enter into this pure land of awakened awareness.

The lotus flower in which we are reborn signifies a mind filled with faith. If we have great faith, the lotus flower will be wide open. If our faith is fickle and we are lacking devotion, the petals of the flower surrounding us will remain closed, at least for the time being. This is by no means unpleasant, as we have everything we need. We have the opportunity to listen to all of Buddha Amitabha's teachings but we can see neither him nor our surroundings in Dewachen. Only when full faith has arisen in us will the lotus open.

A rebirth in Dewachen through mere instantaneous manifestation may seem to us like a miracle, but it really is just the consequence of our wishing prayers, in conjunction with the compassion and power of blessings of Buddha Amitabha. Such a rebirth in Dewachen is within our reach, provided we desire it fervently.

The description of the Pure Land of Bliss and its qualities comes from Buddha Shakyamuni himself. When we dwell in this land, we do not possess a body of flesh and blood. Rather, we have a luminous mental body that is an expression of our buddha nature. We do not pass through stages of development from infancy to adulthood – our luminous body is instantaneously perfect like that of a buddha. There is no distinction between men and women – the gender polarity is dissolved. Since there is no birth in the usual sense, we are also not subject to the processes of aging, sickness and death.

We live in this beautiful land, together with Amitabha and many bodhisattvas. We have no worries and need not work – all our wishes are spontaneously fulfilled, and we lack nothing. Everything has the nature of light, including the trees and plants. Our food – presuming that we want to consume any – is pure wisdom nectar. We need no protection from dangers or from the weather, so houses are superfluous. We have no fixed abode, can stay anywhere and are free from attachment to material goods. It is a place of great happiness and profound peace.

In this pure land, everything is the expression of the activity of Buddha Amitabha. Unceasingly, countless emanations of Amitabha spontaneously effect the welfare of all beings. They manifest in the form of Guru Rinpoche, Avalokiteshvara, *Tara* and innumerable other helpers who pervade all worlds. In the heart of Amitabha, Guru Rinpoche dwells in a luminous sphere from which his countless emanations stream into all worlds and realms of existence.

From a luminous sphere in Amitabha's right hand an uninterrupted stream of emanations of Avalokiteshvara emerge who protect and guide all beings with enlightened compassion. From a luminous sphere in Amitabha's left hand countless forms of the female buddha Green Tara emanate who protect all beings from fear and dangers and free them from all suffering. In this way, Amitabha and his emanations are ceaselessly at work for the benefit and awakening of all beings.

In Dewachen it is evident to everyone what constitutes awakened activity. The Dharma is omnipresent. Whenever we wish to listen to Amitabha's teachings, his instructions quite naturally enter our ears. We understand everything that he explains and are able to remember it later in its entirety. In this way, we quickly develop into bodhisattvas and eventually into buddhas, without having to follow a long path filled with obstacles and suffering. Nothing distracts us and our mind easily enters into deep meditation. We are capable of carrying out any meditation we desire and attaining its full realization.

When we join the sentient beings living in Dewachen, we are no longer reborn in cyclic existence due to our karma.[9] We ourselves no longer experience any suffering, but we perceive the suffering of ordinary beings in other realms of existence and are able to send out emanations to help them. For example, we are aware of the state of bewilderment or fright of beings who are wandering in the after-death state and we are able to lead them safely into the pure land.

On the plane of consciousness that characterizes life in Dewachen, we move by means of our mind. With a single thought we instantaneously move to where we want to be. With our mental body, we are able to visit a multitude of other buddhafields in which we can receive instructions from other buddhas. The conditions for inner development are ideal in Dewachen, and we should therefore cultivate an ardent desire to go to Dewachen at the end of this life.

These instructions open the door for us to Dewachen – now it is up to us to apply them. But we should not assume that we will be reborn there merely by thinking: "Perhaps I should try out Dewachen; this description doesn't sound too bad." A rebirth in Dewachen is the fruit of a life that has been wholly oriented toward this goal with regular Avalokiteshvara practice and the recitation of countless wishing prayers. Only then will there be a sufficient buildup of faith in Amitabha, Avalokiteshvara and Dewachen, so that this rebirth can take place spontaneously and without hindrances.

When we learn to meet every situation openly and use it for the path, then the qualities of the Dharma will reveal themselves to us quickly. We will learn how we can free ourselves from suffering and

9 Our remaining karma manifests in the form of impressions and thoughts arising in our mind while we are in Dewachen, and we purify it by immediately applying our deepening understanding of the Dharma.

transform it into happiness. Particularly helpful for us, as well as for all other beings, will be the meditation on Avalokiteshvara, the Bodhisattva of Great Compassion, and the recitation of his mantra OM MANI PEME HUNG. Avalokiteshvara is the manifestation of an enlightened compassion that embraces all beings equally. Enlightened compassion is inseparable from wisdom, the awareness of emptiness. Avalokiteshvara *is* the awakened awareness that dwells in all beings, whose nature is the unity of compassion and emptiness. He is not a god but a mirror of our own true being, and as such he is not separate from us.

When we recite his mantra, loving kindness and compassion will grow in us in a natural way, and the experience of emptiness will gradually arise in us. Loving kindness and compassion lead us to the realization of the truth body, the empty nature of the mind and of all appearances. Therefore, it is very useful for us to do this practice regularly, and to do it with confidence and joy. We always finish the Avalokiteshvara practice with wishing prayers for rebirth in Dewachen. Steady practice of this will greatly ease our death.

Even if we have attained no realization and all of our concepts collapse in the face of our death, we will still be left with our connection to Avalokiteshvara. Our faith in him and the power of all the mantras of enlightened compassion that we have recited will help us then. When in the last moments before our death we are seized by fear, we will automatically turn to Avalokiteshvara, call on him for help and receive refuge from him. It will be a completely natural thing for us to call out for the compassion and blessings of all the buddhas, because we have steadily cultivated this faith in our practice.

Our calling out to Avalokiteshvara will not come from our intellect but from the depths of our heart. We will feel his presence, his compassion will fill us, our mind will open up, and we will feel that our mind has become inseparably one with Avalokiteshvara's mind. Since we are reciting his mantra, our speech will become his speech, and our body will become inseparably one with his body. We will experience that our body, speech and mind are the same as Avalokiteshvara's enlightened body, speech and mind.

Then we can breathe our last breath without fear, full of confidence and faith. But previous to this, we must practice a great deal. When we thoroughly familiarize ourselves with the Avalokiteshvara practice now and practice letting our mind rest in its primordial state and in compassion, then this will become a habit that will greatly help us at the moment of death.

When our death approaches, we should free ourselves from all fear and not anticipate an experience of suffering. With a joyful mind we should dedicate all of our good deeds and spiritual merit to the benefit of all beings and imagine that they attain the happiness of awakening. By doing this, our mind becomes filled with love and joy. If we are already well acquainted with the practice of exchanging self and other (tonglen) and have practiced it frequently, we can carry it out now, too, and amplify it further by reciting the mantra of Avalokiteshvara and imagining that we become Avalokiteshvara.

Finally, we remain for a while in complete naturalness, beyond all ideas of 'I' and others. We conclude this wholesome action with the wish that after our death our body, speech and mind may become the source of everything that is helpful and useful for all beings:

Whatever it is that beings
in all realms of existence strive for or need,
may I spontaneously assume all forms
that fulfill such a need.

May all beings partake of this with pleasure,
with complete freedom,
without any restrictions and dangers,
and may all their wishes be fulfilled.

May I always be able to effect
the benefit of all beings.

When our capacity to dedicate ourselves entirely to the welfare of all
beings is still limited, we can make wishing prayers asking that this
mental attitude and activity may expand more and more, so that we
will be of ever greater usefulness in the future and eventually be able
to lead others to liberation. When we practice in this way, we will
feel great joy in the moment of our death.

To die with such a wish in our mind will lead to a rebirth that will
be very helpful for our path to awakening. Because of our spontaneous
inclination to loving kindness and compassion for all beings, in our
future life we will quite naturally find conditions that are conducive
to the attainment of buddhahood. We will be endowed with many
qualities and capabilities needed to help others. The power of making wishing prayers at the moment of death is truly extraordinary.

Our mental state at the moment of death is of such critical importance because our final mental impulses of this life instantaneously
lead to the experience of a mental world that is a mirror of those impulses. At the moment when our consciousness leaves our body, it is
very unstable and easily influenced. When the last moments of our
life are marked by anger or fright, then these emotions imbue our
consciousness with the corresponding energies and we are in danger
of being reborn in lower realms of existence.

If, on the other hand, our mind is calm, full of confidence and free
of attachment to this life, then it is possible to orient it toward rebirth
in Dewachen and toward liberation. At least, there is a high probabil-
ity that we will be reborn in one of the higher realms of existence.

Because of this, close attention should also be paid to the atmo-
sphere that surrounds a dying person, be it ourselves or someone else.
They should be provided with as much external peace and security
as possible. But even more important than external peace is the gen-

eration of a pure, altruistic motivation in the caregivers as well as in the person who is dying.

Dying is often accompanied by suffering, fear and even panic. Many people experience confusion, tormenting thoughts and strong emotions such as anger, disappointment and hatred when they are dying. We must learn in good time how to deal with these states of mind so that they do not sweep us away during our death, because to die in a negative state of mind has a strong negative influence on our next life. Often, we are then reborn in unfavorable circumstances, for example in a body that is unsuitable for Dharma practice, a condition that would influence our mind and all of our actions negatively. Our tendency to perform unwholesome deeds would be further strengthened and our karmic burden would increase.

In order to avoid this, it is important that we start learning now to master our feelings, so that we can relax when we are dying. Otherwise, we will die like animals who impulsively follow their instincts and emotions without understanding what is happening. As human beings, we have the opportunity to die with full awareness of what is happening to us and with the knowledge of what we can do to use the situation for the purpose of our own liberation.

At the moment of death, it is very important for all involved to be calm, balanced and free of attachments. This is true, above all, for the dying person, but it also holds for those who assist them. With sensitivity and wisdom, we should use all means at our disposal to make it possible for the dying person to leave this world in a peaceful environment and with a calm mind. We should attempt to support them in developing a wholesome mental attitude, even when they are not familiar with the Buddha's teachings and do not recite the same prayers. The most important thing in dying is to assume the right mental attitude.

The dying person experiences intense emotions. They are in pain, are nervous and weak – what is happening to them disturbs them greatly. In order not to stir them up even more, we should be gentle and careful in our movements and words and assist them in whatever way we can. We should avoid saying or doing anything that might fill them with regret or make them angry, proud, envious or jealous – any emotion that could lead to a difficult death and a rebirth full of suffering.

To elicit such emotions in a dying person – be it only out of ignorance or clumsiness – not only has strong consequences for them but also leaves negative karmic traces in us. Therefore, we should not act or speak thoughtlessly but be very careful and act in a conciliatory and sympathetic manner. When we learn through regular practice to relax our mind in all situations and not to let ourselves go with emotions, then this will be very helpful also in assisting the dying.

After their death, we can make the deceased's journey easier if we do not cling to them but develop compassion and carry out many wholesome actions of body, speech and mind that we dedicate to their enlightenment. It is particularly helpful for them and for their relatives for us to carry out the practice of Avalokiteshvara, if possible with other practitioners, in which we can offer lights, flowers and the like on behalf of the deceased. It is irrelevant whether the deceased had a close connection with the Dharma or not – the Avalokiteshvara practice is universal and reaches all beings equally.

If we wish to find inner freedom, it is essential for us not to react automatically to every experience with attachment or aversion. If we do not cultivate mindfulness and loving kindness, we will not succeed in getting out of these automatic reaction patterns. Only when we are aware of what is happening in our mind, can we take the time to find out which response to any given situation is the most sensible.

Without mindfulness, we will be pulled away by our self-centered impulses and inevitably further strengthen the spiral of negative karma. The only solution available to us for stepping out of this vicious circle and avoiding painful rebirths is to develop a pure, altruistic aspiration and an attentive moment-to-moment awareness. That is the best preparation for our death.

When we have worked on ourselves in the right way, we will have nothing to fear at our death.

If we have developed faith in the Three Jewels and the qualities of awakening and have purified our unwholesome tendencies in some measure, we will not regard our death as the dreadful end of a life full of joys but as an opportunity to gather more experience that brings us closer to liberation and also helps us liberate other beings. Then dying is no longer a cause for panic but an occasion for genuine joy.

Whether we experience death as awful or as liberating depends on us, on our actions and our inner work. When we have not consciously worked on ourselves, we will be like a fish that has been thrown on the beach and flaps about in its death throes. Whatever has molded our mind over a long period of time will be what remains in our death. It is not difficult to die with dignity when we are well prepared for it through a lifetime of practice.

A little song on the perfectly pure nature, that slipped out of my mouth

The royal view is to leave behind
all ideas of subject and object.
The royal meditation is not to do anything,
not to meditate and not to be distracted.
The royal action is to be free of effort,
accepting and abandoning.[10]

Letting go of hope and fear,
the fruition is revealed.
Beyond all reference points
where there is no mind,
the nature of mind shines.

Without progressing through stages and paths,
the end of the path of all buddhas is reached.
Without meditating on objects of meditation,
unsurpassable buddhahood is attained.

Gendun Rinpoche

---

10 "Accepting and abandoning" refers here to our attitude toward wholesome and unwholesome actions. In the state of Mahamudra it is superfluous to deliberately adopt wholesome attitudes and consciously reject unwholesome attitudes because the completely open mind that is not centered on self naturally and spontaneously acts for the benefit of all beings.

Closing Words

We will truly understand the richness and goodness of the Dharma if we lead a life that is oriented toward furthering the well-being of others. Leading such a life will give us the means of freeing ourselves of all entanglements, ulterior motives and vested interests. It will bring light into our darkness and allow us to see clearly.

When we discover how the Dharma helps us liberate ourselves from emotions and all the suffering that comes with them, we begin to appreciate its preciousness. We then develop a very intimate relationship with the Dharma – this is the fruit of our going for refuge in it. We are freed from doubts and no longer ask ourselves: "What should I do? Am I on the right path or not?" We have become certain that we have understood the true meaning of the Dharma.

A great simplicity manifests in our lives, and we arrive at a bright, clear openness in our mind. Our limitations dissolve, our lives brighten, and in the light of the Dharma all events acquire a clear meaning. Our lives run smoothly, we are taken up with the Dharma, and we no longer have to strain to understand it. Our vacillation between confidence and doubt ceases; we live in openness and transparency. With the pure perception of the Dharma, our mind opens up: all encounters, all events become instructions, and our lives become simple.

In this simplicity, we do not need to talk big, we do not need to convince ourselves or others, and we do not have to think with great effort: things are self-evident. The truth of the Dharma, and its profundity, become evident in a natural way. The Dharma comes to us because our mind has opened up in the true taking of refuge. A deep, joyful power comes into being in our mind, and we truly comprehend the Dharma.

May great benefit result
from these instructions
for all beings, our mothers.

May they be freed from all suffering
and open themselves
to the joy beyond all words.

SARVA MANGALAM!
May all be auspicious!

Gendun Rinpoche is like Milarepa –
in this life he attained the state of Vajradhara.[11]

The 16th Gyalwa Karmapa[12]

---

11 The level of realization of Buddha Vajradhara (Dorje Chang) is the recognition of the highest truth free of all veils, as it was realized, for example, by the famous Tibetan yogi Milarepa.

12 Until his death in 1981, the 16th Gyalwa Karmapa, Rangjung Rigpe Dorje, was the head of the Karma Kagyu lineage of Tibetan Buddhism. He was Gendun Rinpoche's root lama and instructed him to teach in Europe.

Gendun Rinpoche:
His Life and Work

May these glimpses
into the life of an awakened master
inspire many on their path.

Only very rarely did Gendun Rinpoche tell stories from his life. Usually when someone asked him about his life, he would say something like this:

"I was born to my mother.
Then I became a child.
Then I became a man.
Then I grew old.
And now I'm here."
    (And he would laugh.)

"I don't have a life story.
I've only been drinking tea
and eating tsampa."

However, a few times he told us a little more. Also, Lama Garwang, who knew Gendun Rinpoche in Tibet, escaped to India with him and now lives in Holland, told us a few things about him.

His Childhood

Gendun Rinpoche was born in 1918, in the Tibetan year of the Earth Horse, near Singka Dzong, the "fortress of clarity," a mountain that rises to 15,000 feet, in the province of Nangchen in the Kham region of eastern Tibet. The inhabitants of Kham are renowned in Tibet for their courage and honesty. Many of them have entered the way of the yogis and dedicated themselves intensively to meditation practice.

Gendun Rinpoche's birthplace, Chochodar, is located near the mountain called the "White Rock" of Khyodrag which rises above the valley of Puritang. The mountain is revered by Tibetans as a holy place. The famous yogi Sangye Yerpa is supposed to have been born there under extraordinary circumstances. Legend has it that a yak cow raised the yogi with her milk. Later on he meditated in the "Lion's Fortress," one of the many caves near the top of this mountain and attained full enlightenment. On a rock face there, one can still see the impression of a *dharma wheel* that appeared spontaneously in the stone and that attests to his realization.

Gendun Rinpoche's parents were neither rich nor poor. His father, Mongje Dhargye, was a stonemason who chiseled prayer formulas (mantras) in wood and stone, including gigantic mantras that he inscribed on rock walls. Gendun Rinpoche's mother's name was Gadoma.

From his earliest childhood, Lama Gendun had a deep longing for the way of the yogis. In the summer months when his family led their animals to the mountain pastures, they all lived together in a large tent. Rinpoche's favorite pastime as a little boy was to build himself a hideaway from tree branches and leaves, some distance away from the camp. Then he would sit in it in meditation posture and proclaim: "I'm a hermit." He would build himself a seat from soil, fill a vase with water, add various substances to it, sit down on his improvised throne and proceed to give empowerments while reciting prayers.

Of this part of his life, Rinpoche recounted: "Even though I had not yet received any religious education, my mind already longed greatly for the holy Dharma. Even at the age of four, I wished I could find a lama and practice the Dharma. I recall crying through the night over the suffering of all sentient beings and over my lack of ability to help them. I prayed intensively to meet a spiritual master. I observed the life of my parents, who were simple and upright people, and I noticed that all their time was taken up with the worldly concerns of this life. I said to myself: 'All worldly activities are useless and without lasting benefit. What is their use at the time of death? An ordinary life doesn't produce anything good. It can only lead to suffering.'

"I thought deeply about the suffering of the beings in the hell realms and the realm of the hungry ghosts and understood that their circumstances were the result of their having been preoccupied exclusively with worldly affairs in previous lives. I felt great pity and deep compassion for their misery and feared that my parents, too, would face a similar fate at their death. Through these intensive reflections, my mind forever turned away from worldly affairs.

"My father tried hard to teach me his craft but all his efforts were in vain. I was unable to learn to work with his tools with any measure of skill. My parents were worried about my future. Finally they yielded to my repeated pleas to find a master from whom I could learn the holy Dharma. They decided to bring me to the nearby monastery of Khyodrag ("rock of weariness") where I was able to obtain a spiritual education and everything I needed for my life. In this name, the word "rock" *(drag)* signifies strength and refers to the great joy that is generated from a deep confidence in the teachings."

First Years in the Monastery: 1925–1939

At the age of barely seven, as a little novice monk (although without vows), Rinpoche began his training at the monastery of Khyodrag in the Bharam Kagyu lineage. He lived very simply and in everything followed the rules of the monastic community. Soon he became a model for others because of his unconditional willingness to help them and share everything with them. But he had little interest in the traditional activities of the monks that consisted of reading and reciting texts, making offering cakes (tormas), performing ritual dances and engaging in a variety of formal studies. In contrast to the other monks, above all he wanted to meditate. In order to learn this, he spent his early years at the feet of some of the great masters of the monastery. In particular, he deeply yearned for the practice of the Vajrayana, with its profound methods of spiritual realization.

About this period of his training Rinpoche said: "Between the ages of seven and thirteen, I dedicated most of my time to the study of Dharma texts. After that, I started to put what I had learned into practice through meditation. I did my first retreat in complete seclusion in a house when I was thirteen years old but it only lasted a month. My next three retreats lasted several months each. My second retreat was in a cave on a mountain slope, the third in an underground cave and the fourth in a cone-shaped wooden hut.

"I was fifteen or sixteen years old when the 16th Gyalwa Karmapa, the head of the Karma Kagyu lineage, visited our monastery. He was still a small child and was accompanied by the previous Situ Rinpoche Pema Wangchug. The Karmapa stayed with us for three days and granted us a "black crown ceremony," a transfer of blessings unique to the Karmapa lineage. He performed it with the small black crown since the large crown was still too heavy for him. He also gave us an Avalokiteshvara empowerment, an introduction to our buddha nature through the practice of Avalokiteshvara, the bodhisattva of compassion. At that time I realized that the Karmapa was my real root guru.

"At the age of seventeen, I received lay ordination and then took the novice and full vows of a monk. Ordinarily, one has to be at least twenty-one years old to receive the full ordination of a monk but my parents each 'lent' me two years, and so I was able to take the vows much earlier."

Rinpoche was asked: "During these years as a young man, did you experience many obstacles and distractions in your meditation?" Rinpoche: "No, because I had received instructions that had made me understand that everything is a manifestation of mind." "Did you encounter many obstacles later in the course of your practice?" "Not at all. Since I didn't attribute any great capabilities to myself, I allowed things to go their natural course and never ran into obstacles."

On one occasion, Rinpoche told his retreat students a few things about his monastery: "The history of our monastery began with a cook by the name of Bharam Dharma Wangchug who for a time had been the retreat cook of the great master Gampopa. After only three years, Gampopa told his cook that he had attained the same degree of realization as Gampopa himself and that he was now free to teach the Dharma wherever he liked. Thus Dharma Wangchug went away and started gathering students around him.

"This was the beginning of the Bharam Kagyu lineage to which my monastery belonged. It is one of the four Kagyu schools that goes back to one of Gampopa's immediate disciples. Because of his limitless devotion to Gampopa, the cook not only attained liberation himself but also the capacity to show the path of awakening to others." Later, the teacher of Trungmase, the first Trungpa Rinpoche, who founded Zurmang monastery, also belonged to this lineage.[13]

Rinpoche continued: "There is a collection of life stories of thirteen highly realized masters of our lineage who lived in my monastery and in surrounding caves. They were very famous because they could move through the air and live in caves that were not accessible to humans by foot. They were neither afraid of snow leopards and bears nor of the icy cold. Occasionally they came flying in collectively for special rituals in the monastery. One time, one of these lamas flew in more slowly than the others, and he apologized about this by saying that he had consumed a little too much barley soup in the morning! The rock that they started off from and where they left their footprints in the stone can still be seen today.

"The monks did not live permanently in our monastery. Most of the time it was pretty empty because only a few lamas remained there throughout the year. All the others practiced in caves and wooden huts in the mountains. As their only clothing they all wore the white cotton cloth of the yogis, even in winter. Only on special occasions, for important rituals, did they meet in the monastery. When they all congregated, there were about six to seven hundred monks, but ordinarily not even a hundred were present.

"There was the small original monastery, a substantially larger offshoot, and four centers for group retreats. In each of these retreat groups one could find one, two or three outstanding practitioners. One of these retreat centers was dedicated to the continuous recitation of the mantra OM MANI PEME HUNG of Avalokiteshvara; one served to maintain the practices of the Bharam Kagyu lineage; and one was dedicated to the practices of the Karma Kagyu lineage.

---

13   The most recent of these incarnations was Chögyam Trungpa Rinpoche who was in recent times one of the most influential Tibetan Buddhist teachers in North America.

"The differences between these two Kagyu lineages are minimal because both go back to students of Gampopa. They lie predominantly in differences in emphasis in the oral transmission and in a few rituals. The specialty of the Bharam Kagyu lineage were some instructions in Mahamudra (the practice of the nature of mind) and in the *Six Dharmas of Naropa* (the practice of the nature of mind in all situations), which the lamas had received in visions of *dakinis*, for example instructions on how thoughts can be recognized as the nature of things *(dharmata)*, how ignorance can be recognized as luminous clarity and how the meditation on a buddha aspect (yidam) can be connected with the practice of the illusory body. Also, there were special instructions on the transference of consciousness during death (phowa). But by and large there were no great differences. In the beginning, I practiced in the Bharam Kagyu lineage, and now I teach in the Karma Kagyu lineage, just like my root guru, the Karmapa."

Rinpoche once explained the significance of the multi-peaked hat that he always wore during empowerments, and he also spoke of some of the sacred objects of his monastery: "The shape of this hat goes back to *Maitripa,* the great Mahamudra yogi and teacher of Naropa and Marpa. Maitripa was an Indian prince, and this hat originally was one of the insignia of his family line. But through him it then became the symbol of his Mahamudra transmission. He passed his hat on to Marpa who gave it to Milarepa, as an acknowledgment of Milarepa's realization of the practice of the subtle energies and channels. Milarepa passed it on to Gampopa, as the most important Mahamudra lineage holder, and the latter passed it on to the Bharam Kagyu lineage, presumably via his cook Bharam Dharma Wangchug and Wangchug's main disciple, the yogi Dechen Repa.

"This yogi was very famous because occasionally he simply became invisible. At other times, some of his students could see him but others couldn't, and sometimes he turned into brilliant rainbow light. He was incredibly active and founded altogether eighteen monasteries.

It was through him that the hat wound up in our monastery where it was kept in a large, sealed chest. I was able to see it only once and touch it through its protective layer of white silk when it was brought to our retreat center. We each received a hat like this, as they were the insignia of all authorized lamas in our monastery.

"There were many more sacred objects in our monastery but presumably they were lost when it was destroyed. Among these was a dakini statue that had formed spontaneously from a lump of clay in Naropa's hand and then floated off his hand into the air. Also, there were relics of Nagarjuna that were brought by dakinis seen by the lamas in visions when they intensively practiced prayers to Manjushri.

"The monastery also kept objects from many realized masters from the local area. One example is a cup and other things that belonged to the head of a poor family who lived in the rocks on the other side of the river, together with his seven or eight children. Whenever beggars visited him, he took a small amount of roasted barley flour, multiplied it and gave it to them. When he died, he manifested the rainbow body, and so did his wife and children.

"When the finder of mind treasures *(tertön)* Chögyal Dorje accomplished an accumulation of one hundred thousand feast offerings, Guru Rinpoche appeared in the sky and dropped a statue in his lap that remained with us in the monastery. This tertön counted his accumulation of the ritual simply by making impressions in the rock with his fingers." (Rinpoche laughed.)

The Years of Retreat Practice in Khyodrag: 1939–1953

In 1939, when he was twenty-one, Lama Gendun entered the traditional group retreat of three years, three months and three days duration. The retreat center of his monastery was located in a mountain hollow with a wide view, slightly above the monastery. With unshakable trust and deep devotion he absorbed the transmissions of his lamas and allowed his mind to become completely blended with their awakened mind. He practiced the Six Dharmas of Naropa and mastered the practice of the subtle channels and winds.

From then on, just like the yogis of past generations, he only wore a simple cotton cloth, and due to his accomplishment of the yoga of inner heat *(tummo)*, he attained the ability to melt snow and ice. Already in this first three-year retreat, through his body heat he was able to melt the ice that had formed in his offering bowls overnight, at many degrees below freezing. There are reports that in the third winter of his retreat no snow remained on the roof of his cell or within a radius of three meters around his door.

Even in the deepest winter he lived without any fire in his cell, and according to the testimony of others radiated a steady amount of heat, on account of his meditative absorption. He experienced neither hunger nor thirst and consumed very little food. During this first retreat, he attained direct and definitive knowledge of subtle mental states and generated many deep meditation experiences.

Looking back, however, he told us: "At the conclusion of this retreat, I thought I had understood the nature of mind. Twenty years later, I saw that at that point in time I had understood absolutely nothing. After this three-year retreat, I spent another year in the retreat center practicing alone. Then I made a year-long pilgrimage during which I visited all the holy places in Tibet. That must have been in 1943/44. This journey also led me to Tsurphu, the main seat of the Karma Kagyu lineage. There I met the Karmapa again, and again participated in the black crown ceremony. From Central Tibet I traveled directly back to my homeland of East Tibet and spent a further seven years in retreat."

During his renewed retreat at Khyodrag monastery he practiced alone in strict seclusion. His door was always kept locked, and his cook guarded the key to his cell, which was just large enough to allow him to make prostrations and engage in yogic exercises. It had only a tiny window that was covered with paper. The cook used to place his food in front of his door without ever entering the cell. Rinpoche said that during this time he never took more food into his cell through the small opening at the bottom of the door than what he needed for just that day. Everything beyond that, as well as offerings that visitors occasionally brought for him, he left in front of his door so that the other monks could partake of it.

He recounted: "After seven and a half years, my root lama Khenpo Mingyur, a completely realized lama who lived in the monastery, told me that I could open the door, come out and do whatever I liked, since I had reached the point at which it is no longer necessary to remain in retreat. I did as I was told. As a result, many people came to see me and ask me questions about the Dharma. This caused me some difficulties, as I had not seen anyone in a long time. I found it difficult to be with so many people who asked me so many questions. I then spent another three years in retreat, again in the monastery, because I realized that I had to deepen my practice further if I really wanted to be of any help to others."

One day in 1953, after Gendun Rinpoche had spent altogether ten years in retreat in the monastery, Tulku Tendzin of Khyodrag, his other root lama, came to visit him. The lama asked that the door to his cell be opened and then said to him: "It is time for you now to come out of retreat. For you, all clinging to thoughts has liberated itself spontaneously. Your meditation has been completed; you have attained realization in your practice, and it is no longer useful for you to remain in seclusion. You have truly become a "holder of blessings," an inexhaustible fount of goodness. From now on, by living among people, you can work for the benefit of all beings. Your realization is irrevocable. You are like a rock of gold; you can be sure of that. From now on, act on your own discretion."

In spite of these words, Gendun Rinpoche continued to remain in retreat. Only after a second visit from Tulku Tendzin and upon the urging of Khenpo Mingyur did he follow their instructions and bring his formal retreat to a conclusion.

In the Mountains of Tibet: 1953–1960

Gendun Rinpoche continued his narrative: "Then the Karmapa visited us again in Nangchen. A great tent was erected, and many people came to see him. Almost all the members of our community, save the cooks, were present. Two of my friends from the group retreat traveled with me, and after our meeting with the Karmapa, we spent several years in the mountains meditating. At the end of this period I had many dreams and signs that told me to move on.

"Together with a monk from my monastery who had also practiced in retreat for a long time, I set out on a journey to Central Tibet. We started our journey without any idea of where we would go. After arriving in Central Tibet, we withdrew into a cave that at one time had been used by Guru Rinpoche (Padmasambhava) and spent a year practicing there. Then we undertook a pilgrimage to visit many holy places in Tibet and Nepal at which we made abundant offerings and recited many wishing prayers."

After this, Gendun Rinpoche traveled on alone and practiced as a yogi of the Mahamudra *Chö* tradition. As such he did not accept a roof over his head, not even in winter. At night he took off his boots and sat down on them, to protect himself from getting chilled by the snow underneath. He drew his legs against his body and crossed his arms over them. In this meditation posture he spent the night. After wandering like this for a year, he continued his practice in remote caves that had been blessed by the presence of great realized beings of the past, such as Padmasambhava and Milarepa. It was in them that Gendun Rinpoche attained the realization of a high bodhisattva.

Although it is difficult for an ordinary person to gauge the qualities of an awakened human being, the power of Lama Gendun's blessings, his goodness and the warm radiance of his compassion were immediately felt even then by almost everyone who met him. Among other things, he was renowned for his ability to bring nonhuman beings to the Dharma, in particular beings who traditionally are called "evildoers" because they cause various kinds of imbalance, physical and mental illnesses and external harmful influences and obstacles that humans may suffer from.

Once when he meditated in a cave in winter, a thief came and stole his entire provisions of roasted barley (tsampa), the only food that he had left for the rest of the winter. Rinpoche found himself completely free of anger in this situation. He said prayers for the thief and continued to practice undaunted, without having any food. Two weeks later, he found a sack of roasted barley flour in front of his cave that had been brought by an unknown donor.

Like Milarepa he wandered from one area to another, sometimes accompanied by other yogis. His travels took him through all of Tibet, all the way to Mount Kailash. In some caves he meditated for only a few months, in others much longer, in one cave even for several years. At Guru Rinpoche's meditation cave in Kongpo he practiced for six months.

When he was asked why he had meditated in caves for so many years, Gendun Rinpoche playfully cowered like a little sparrow about to be pounced upon by a bird of prey and replied: "Because I was greatly afraid of death and of everything that is in store for us if our karma is not purified. I was convinced that my negative karma was enormous and that it could well lead to my rebirth in the lower realms. I sought a way of freeing myself from this. I have done everything and still do today to liberate myself from the conditions that might plunge me into these realms of suffering. Life is short, and from birth onward the condition of our bodies deteriorates. First I was young, now I am old, have white hair, and my life is almost over. But I have always been conscious of how short this human life is and how important it is to use the potential that is inherent in the teachings of the Dharma to the greatest possible extent. We may think we'll live for a very long time but in reality there is little time left for us to do what we have to do."

Escape to India: 1960

In 1959, when all of Tibet was occupied militarily by the Chinese, Gendun Rinpoche was still living in seclusion in the mountains. He was 41 years old. One day, the female protector deity Achi Chökyi Drolma appeared to him and advised him to leave for the south, assuring him of her present and future protection.

Gendun Rinpoche recounted: "Even if I had read the prophecies of Guru Rinpoche, I would not have received any indication of the great changes that were about to come to Tibet and the world. One day though, I had a dream in which I heard a voice that said that soon the situation in Tibet would become critical and that I should prepare for departure. But I didn't pay any heed to it. A little later, I dreamed of a woman whose head was covered with green silk. She told me that I must leave the area. I asked her who she was and she said: 'I am the protectress of this place.' 'And when should I go?' 'You will know it yourself.' In this vision, I saw a hill in the south of Tibet, at the border with India. It was Pema Kö, a sacred site, where eight months later I did a retreat. I saw myself standing on the hill and from the sky a shaft of white light emerged that struck my heart."

Gendun Rinpoche did not set out immediately but spent several months more in intensive retreat in the mountains. But he finally decided to go back to East Tibet, together with his friends. "On our way home, we once more visited Tsurphu (in Central Tibet) and learned there that the Karmapa was already on his way to India and at that time was staying at Paltsen Jowo Ri. We immediately set out to join him there but on our way we were stopped by the Chinese and could not continue. At a place called Nye, we met with friends and relatives and practiced a *Dorje Drolö* ritual to fend off harmful influences. Finally, we learned that the Karmapa had safely arrived in India.

"In a valley called Lo, we retreated into a cave high up in the mountains where Rechungpa (one of the two main disciples of Milarepa) had meditated at one time, and practiced there. During a feast offering ritual we decided that we would try to escape. It was looking very bad though, as the Chinese had already cut off all escape routes. Time and again, we encountered Tibetans who had attempted to escape and failed and who reported that absolutely no route was open anymore.

"I prayed to Buddha, Dharma and Sangha for protection and help. I entreated them to guide me, as I was determined to escape. Other Tibetans attempted to dissuade me; they were convinced the Chinese would kill me along with the others. But I was certain that fleeing was the best thing to do and that the Three Jewels would protect us.

"While we were preparing to escape, two of my friends joined us from their retreats in the mountains, and thus we left Kham – on foot and begging. I took nothing with me other than my body. It was a time of great turmoil. The resistance fighters in Kham as well as the Chinese stopped everyone traveling – everyone was suspected of being a spy. Frequently, people were killed without having had a chance to explain themselves. Twice we were stopped by the Khampa resistance fighters but thanks to the protection of the Three Jewels we were recognized as monks and treated kindly. With some difficulties we approached the Indian border.

"In the border area there were many Chinese soldiers because the Dalai Lama and his entourage had just crossed the border. We noticed that the Chinese were guarding the widely used pass to India. In order to get over this pass, one had to walk through a gap with steep mountain slopes on one side and the wild stream of the Brahmaputra on the other. Because of that it was easy for the Chinese to control this route.

"Within three days they learned that we were in the woods and started searching for us. We left Rechungpa's cave to which we had at first withdrawn in order to meditate and hid in the forest at the end of a narrow valley. There we searched everywhere for a way to cross over to India. At the site of a great waterfall, we found a winding path that led out of the valley over a mighty mountain top in the right direction. But even this path was guarded day and night by Chinese soldiers who were ready to fire. We were so close to them that we could watch them and hear them talk. Some of them were eating and drinking tea, others guarded the path.

"We waited for nightfall to try to get past them. We singlemindedly prayed to the Three Jewels and meditated on emptiness so that we could render our bodies invisible. In that way we were able to escape from the Chinese troops, even though we walked practically right through their middle. They had flashlights, and we came so close to them that we could see their guns, steaming teacups and glowing cigarettes and smell their cigarette smoke.

"But it was as though they simply could not see us. When one is continually in a state of emptiness and Mahamudra, invisibility manifests immediately. No time is necessary to enter this state. We prayed to the Three Jewels and continued on, even though some of us trembled all over with fear. It took us two hours to get past the Chinese, and it was certainly due to the blessings of going for refuge that we were not seen. The Tibetans who accompanied me were overwhelmed by this miracle and were extremely grateful.

"Our march through the Himalayas in the south of Tibet took us three weeks. It was a wild area, and we didn't see a soul. Only when we finally approached the Indian border did we encounter a few Tibetan resistance fighters. One of them was ill; he was writhing in pain and begged us lamas for help. I said prayers for him, blessed him, and shortly afterward he recovered. The resistance fighters notified their next post that a "great lama" was on his way who should be assisted in every way possible, and with that all difficulties were surmounted.

"In India we were first put in the transit camp in Musamari where we stayed for three days. The Indian government then told us that we were detailed to work in road construction in Sikkim, together with three hundred Khampas. The men had a very hard time there, and they asked me, as a lama, to say prayers for them to the female bodhisattva Tara instead of working. In this way, I spent three weeks with these Khampas in Sikkim. I soon learned that the Karmapa had settled in the nearby monastery of Rumtek, his new main seat, so I went there with a friend.

"It was already evening when we arrived at the monastery and the monks were assembled in the temple performing a *puja*. Karmapa was also there, and he beckoned me over. Soup was being served to the monks and Karmapa ordered that I should be given some as well. The monk in charge told me that I should eat the soup outside but Karmapa invited me to stay and saw to it that I was given a bowl.

"After the puja, Karmapa went upstairs to his room. We wanted to talk with him and followed him but one of his monks held us back and said we should come back the next morning, as Karmapa never granted an audience in the evening. So we went downstairs again. But shortly thereafter one of his monks came running and said that Karmapa wanted to see the two visiting senior lamas and that we should come right away.

"When we got to his room, Karmapa blessed us with both hands. One of his attendants again wanted to send us away, but Karmapa invited us to stay. He said that we should live with him at Rumtek. If we could take care of ourselves (in these difficult times), we should do that, otherwise we could simply call on his monks any time; they would provide for us. In case they couldn't give us what we needed, we should let him know and he would direct his own kitchen accordingly. We could hardly believe what was happening!

"Of course, my friend and I were overjoyed to have met with Karmapa again and to have received his blessings. But we were casting about for what to do next. We did not actually want to live in the monastery. It is said that if one spends too much time close to one's lama, there is a danger that the bond of pure view (samaya) will be damaged. This had never happened to us, and we did not want it to now. At the same time, we didn't want to bother Karmapa with these personal concerns.

"But soon thereafter Karmapa summoned us again and told us that the next morning we should travel with a *khenpo* whom he had sent to Baktsa in North India. We could live there, in Kalimpong, in the house of a generous patron. There was a small problem though: the khenpo had an Indian passport with which he could freely travel to Baktsa. However, we only had our Sikkimese refugee papers and we needed a special permit for this trip. Karmapa immediately got in touch with the authorities in Sikkim and pleaded with them to provide us with the necessary papers right away, since he definitely wanted to send us along with the khenpo. Everything worked out all right, and the next day we were able to drive to Kalimpong."

The Years of Retreat Practice
in India and Bhutan: 1960–1975

And so it happened that through the benevolent mediation of the Karmapa Gendun Rinpoche was invited to live in the house of Mr. Jyoti, a Nepalese patron who lived in Kalimpong in northern West Bengal.

He recounted: "I lived there for eleven years, together with three other people, including Lama Purtse who later accompanied me to Europe. We performed pujas and meditated all the time. Strictly speaking, this was not a retreat but it did resemble one, as I never left the house. Mr. Jyoti had a large temple in this house in Kalimpong. He provided for me, and so I was able to practice all the time without having to pursue some other kind of work. I didn't have to go anywhere, not even to perform any rituals."

Every year Gendun Rinpoche traveled to the monastery of the Karmapa at Rumtek where he received many transmissions from him, including the central texts of the Kagyu tradition of Mahamudra and the Six Dharmas of Naropa which he knew already and had realized but now received again with additional explanations directly from the Karmapa. Through this, the Karmapa definitely became his root lama. It must have been during that time that the Karmapa bestowed on Lama Gendun his name and the title Rinpoche.

He continued: "When my patron, Mr. Jyoti, went away on a trip for many months, I left Kalimpong and went to Darjeeling, met some friends there and then spent a month in Sonada with Norla *(Kalu Rinpoche)*. Karmapa then called me there and told me that I should now go to Bhutan and attend to his temple there. I replied that I could not do that because I had already decided to do a three-year retreat with Norla.

"Karmapa said: 'No way!', and he sent Tsongpon Konchog with a jeep to drive me to Bhutan straight away. The mother of the queen of

Bhutan had just built a temple in her palace which she had entrusted to Karmapa. I had really wanted to continue practicing in retreat. Eventually the situation resolved itself through a stroke of good luck: I was able to meditate in retreat in the vicinity of the king's palace, and another person took on the responsibility of performing the necessary rituals in the temple.

"Then the king of Bhutan died and the Karmapa and Dudjom Rinpoche (the head of the *Nyingma* school) were invited to direct the funeral ceremonies for him. Among other rituals, a particular kind of Chö practice was required and both of these masters requested that I perform it. On the way to the Bhutanese capital Timphu I stayed for a while in Pagdru Tagtsang where we practiced the Guru Rinpoche feast offering "Sampa Lhündrup" one hundred thousand times. The queen mother had requested these rituals.

"At this time, the great Nyingma master Dilgo Khyentse Rinpoche was staying in Pagdru Kyichu. On his invitation I stayed with him for a week. Topga Rinpoche, the secretary of the Karmapa, had just built a house in Bhutan, and he asked me to perform various consecration rituals there. One day Dilgo Khyentse Rinpoche told me that I should go to Europe and that he could help me obtain a passport. I replied: 'I will never go to Europe,' and when Khyentse Rinpoche asked whether I was sure of this, I answered: 'Of course, that's my firm decision.' He just said: 'You don't want to go to Europe, but you certainly will be going anyway.' "

The Karmapa Sends Gendun Rinpoche to Europe

Gendun Rinpoche continued: "In 1974, Karmapa again visited Bhutan. He invited me for breakfast and told me that he would be traveling to the West that same year and would visit quite a few different countries. He wanted to find out whether people in the West would be receptive to the Buddha's teaching. He said: 'I will be traveling to America and to Europe. The people there live in affluence but they do not know the true Dharma, so they suffer greatly from emotions such as pride, jealousy, desire and hatred that churn up their minds. We should bring the Dharma to them, as only a true spiritual path will be able to free them from their suffering. If the conditions for the transmission of the teachings of the Great Vehicle (Mahayana) are encouraging, then it will be your task to disseminate them in the West. There is no point in you objecting to this, as I know the signs. I know that you are a lama who has brought his practice to its conclusion. The time has come for you to work for the benefit of all beings. Thank you for your consent.'

"I was speechless, unable to reply. I felt completely crushed by the prospect of such a task. Karmapa said to me: 'If developments there are positive, you must definitely go to the West. You should not raise any objections and argue that you'd rather stay here. I've already told the Secretary of the Interior of Bhutan that you need a passport, and he has initiated the appropriate steps. If I get the impression that the Dharma could take root in the West, I will then know whether America or France is better for you. You should then establish a Dharma Center and a monastery there. The decision has already been made, and it is futile for you to resist.'

"I just sat there, saying nothing, thinking, 'What can I say? I don't know anything.' Back with Topga Rinpoche, I told him that Karmapa had spoken to me about all sorts of things. Topgala asked what it had all been about, and I said: 'Karmapa said I should go to a place called Europe.' Topga Rinpoche said: 'That's not a joke; you're supposed to go to the West.' I replied: 'If that is so, I'll say no. I'll apologize to Karmapa and tell him I can't do it.' I had never taught, but had always practiced by myself. I thought of myself as stupid and ignorant. I asked Topga Rinpoche once more to take me to Karmapa so I could tell him that I declined this task. But Topga Rinpoche countered: 'There is nothing you can do; you have to obey the Karmapa.'

"I asked Topgala to lend me his car because I wanted to drive to see Karmapa right away to clarify things. But he only said: 'You won't be able to change anything. I myself have already approached Karmapa about this, and the Secretary of the Interior has also tried to dissuade him from the idea, but Karmapa absolutely insists that you go to the West. If you now go to him and beg him not to send you, it will only make him unhappy.'

"Two days later Karmapa again summoned me to him, and I was glad to have the opportunity to put forward my plea to remain in Bhutan. But he replied: 'You can't stay in Bhutan. I have already initiated everything necessary so that you get an exit permit and a visa.' I objected: 'But I'm neither a scholar nor a great lama,' but Karmapa replied: 'I am your lama, and you must comply. I know you well: you are the best person for this task.' 'I don't know how to teach the Dharma. I've always lived alone and find it difficult to explain the Dharma.' But Karmapa said: 'The time has come for you to act for the benefit of others. You have fulfilled your personal benefit. Don't talk about your own abilities but go to the West to pacify the minds of the beings there. Don't worry about any difficulties. Jigmela[14] will be there to help you.'

"Soon afterward he departed for the West. Upon his return, Karmapa sent his personal attendant to fetch me and bring me to Rumtek. We left immediately, and I went straight to see him. He said to me: 'I have been all over America and Europe, and I'm certain the Dharma will flourish there. As far as practice is concerned, it seems there will be more activity in Europe. I have already been given a piece of land in France. That's where you should go.' I replied: 'What should I do there? I'm not capable of anything. Why should I, of all people,

---

14 Jigme Rinpoche is the nephew of the 16th Karmapa and was one of his personal attendants.

go there?' Karmapa simply replied: 'Don't think like that. When you first came to Rumtek, I told you to stay. The reason was that I wanted to appoint you to be the master of the three-year retreats. But then the khenpo went to Baktsa, and suddenly I sent you with him. This, too, had a purpose: the karmic connection that you and I have is such that wherever I bring the Dharma, you are the first to go as my representative, like a pioneer. That's why I sent you off with the khenpo.

'And that's why you definitely must go to the West now. This is important and very auspicious, and you can't refuse. You simply have to go. In Europe you must give blessings and empowerments and explain the Dharma, the same thing that Kalu Rinpoche does. And you shouldn't make yourself out to be a humble, insignificant lama, and act as though you were a nobody. There is not the slightest difference between you and Kalu Rinpoche. So that you are completely confident, I will tell you about your past karma that enables you to do all this now. I can tell you who you were in previous lives, or if you wish, I can tell you this on a future occasion.'

"I replied that I certainly didn't need to know and that he shouldn't tell me anything. He put his hand on my head and said with a smile: 'A benefactor, Mr. Benson, has offered me part of his property in France. We should build a great center there from which the Dharma will radiate in all directions. Many people will then be able to gain access to the teachings of the Buddha, and that will be of great benefit for the people in the West. Therefore, you are to go to Europe. Don't worry, you possess the karma that is needed to accomplish this task. The time has come for you to put it into action. I am the Karmapa – if you have faith in the name of the Karmapa, then you should trust my words.' And Karmapa laughed.

"Then he continued: 'Once you're there, you should build a temple, a monastery and a retreat center and teach the Dharma. And you should transmit the Dharma not just in one small area or one country but spread it everywhere. Then many people will be able to establish a connection with it and develop confidence in the Dharma. You must go soon, as the time is ripe, and one must act at the right time. People have very strong emotions, and the situation could change quickly. That's why you must go now.

'The times will change and people will change. If the Dharma is not established everywhere, great suffering will arise, similar to the suffering that beings experience in the hell realms. If we succeed in taking the Dharma everywhere, this suffering will be far less intense. The practice of Dharma can lessen it and even dissolve it. With the Dharma we provide people with the possibility to understand their emotions, to discriminate between what is wholesome and what is unwholesome and to change their conduct in a wholesome direction. This would really benefit the world at large, and that's why I'm sending you to the West. It is infinitely important for everyone to do everything they can for the benefit of all beings and to truly help them. That's why it is essential that the Dharma is introduced everywhere.

'It will be very difficult for Tibet to regain independence. Even if that were to happen, we certainly cannot return. We will remain here in India. Also, a time will come when difficulties will arise for the *tulkus* (reincarnations of realized masters) and they will no longer have a place to live. If you go now, you will be able to create a place where their activity for the benefit of all beings can flourish. That is why you must build this monastery.

'Even though the Dharma will regain a foothold in Tibet and in some small measure one will be able to practice there again, it will never again be as it was in the past when people could fully concentrate on their Dharma practice. People will have to work and will only be able to practice on the side. Because of that, it will be very difficult to fully reestablish the Dharma in Tibet, and it will not be able to persist there for very long. In Bhutan the situation is fairly good but it is uncertain how stable it will be in the future. In Sikkim it is very good at the moment but Sikkim will soon lose its independence.

'As far as Rumtek is concerned, it will not remain as it is now. In the future, even our relics here might be in great danger. That is why I'm considering taking them to the West where the situation is more stable. There are many important relics here. It would be an exaggeration to say that half of the relics that we had in Tibet are now in Rumtek. But I've gathered the really important ones from everywhere, and I'm certain that a third of them are now here. I was able to rescue them from Tibet. Not a single precious relic was left in Tsurphu but they may soon be in real danger. I hope to keep them safe in the West, not here, and therefore you must build a suitable monastery. I want to give you some of the important relics now to take with you to the West.'

"I replied to Karmapa that for the time being it would be better to keep them in Rumtek. He then showed me many statues, including the most sacred ones, which radiated blessings, and repeated that I must take these relics with me to ensure that they were not lost.

"One night, Karmapa sent the monk Chögyal to fetch me. I said to him: 'Not now, before dawn. You can still see the stars in the sky. It is still night.' But Chögyal replied that Karmapa had instructed him to fetch me and that I should come with him right away. I refused once again but he insisted that he would wait until I came with him. So I went. Karmapa was sitting in a big chair on the terrace in front of his house. On the other side there was a similar chair and Karmapa said I should pull it over to sit with him. The chair was too heavy for me and Karmapa himself helped me move it over.

"He asked me to sit down. Then he blessed me by laying both his hands on my head and reciting a prayer to the teachers of the transmission lineage, to Vajradhara, Tilo, Naro, Marpa, Mila, and so on. Karmapa recited this prayer three times and then told me that he had given me the complete transmission and blessings of the lineage and that I had become a holder of his lineage. With further prayers he then addressed the *Dharma protectors,* dakinis and *viras* and told them that he had given me the transmission and that they should protect and support me. He recited this three times, too.

"I was overwhelmed. I thought, 'What is this great master saying?' and looked behind me to make sure nobody was watching. I felt extremely embarrassed that Karmapa had given the transmission to me, a simple lama, and that he was showering me with so much attention. Tears welled in my eyes, and I was trembling with excitement. It was a shock for me. I have hardly ever spoken of this event. Karmapa told me so many things at that time. Even now the memory of it brings tears to my eyes.

"Then Karmapa showed me all kinds of illustrations of different temples and monastery buildings, one after another, and told me that I should build something similar in Europe. We sat like this until dawn. Karmapa explained many details. Then tea was served. Later, when Karmapa visited Europe, I still had not managed to build a temple. But he told me not to worry or lose heart. I should first establish a retreat center, the rest would follow.

"Back then at Rumtek, Karmapa literally said the following: 'You should definitely build a retreat center, and you will manage to do that. Also, you should definitely build a temple and a Dharma Center, and you will succeed in this as well. You should ordain many monks and also establish a nunnery, and you will accomplish this, too.' Karmapa repeated this several times. At that time I thought to myself, 'I'm an old man, and Karmapa has given me so many responsibilities. How will I ever manage?' I simply wondered about it. I just could not imagine how it would be possible, so I did not promise to turn all these plans into reality.

"But Karmapa knew exactly what I was thinking and said: 'You will live longer than I. Even though I'm younger than you, I will die before you. And then you must stay to complete these tasks. I have transmitted to you all the blessings, powers and abilities that you need. Because of that, you will be able to accomplish all this. In any case, after my present incarnation and before you die, we will meet again. You will only die afterward; that much is certain. I have placed many responsibilities on you but please don't think you won't manage. If it wasn't your karma to accomplish all this, it would be impossible anyway. Believe me, the time is ripe, and you have the karma. It won't be difficult for you. If you have the least bit of faith in the fact that I am the Karmapa, you'll be able to do this. Trust me! I am the Karmapa!'

"And he continued, 'Your ability to accomplish this is not from this life; it comes from your previous lives. The two of us have been working together on behalf of the Dharma over many, many lifetimes. That's where your present karma comes from. You are like a pioneer for my work. It is your karma to go to the West now. Even if you wanted to attain Buddhahood now, it wouldn't be possible in your present life. The two of us will continue to work together for the Dharma for two more lifetimes. After that, you don't need to take another rebirth, and you will attain buddhahood. I will definitely manifest in this world as the Karmapa for another three or four lifetimes. Thereafter my activity will spread greatly, through many emanations, but without the name "Karmapa."

'The tasks I have entrusted you with will present you with no difficulties. Trust me. I am the Karmapa, not just anybody. I know that your activities in this sphere will manifest completely naturally, simply due to your karma. Also, you needn't worry in the slightest about who will take care of the centers in the future. Shamar Rinpoche[15] will be there to look after them.'

"Karmapa gave me numerous instructions, many more than I have recounted now. This is just a summary of them. Lama Jigmela knows all of these instructions. He was always with Karmapa. Just like Karmapa's other most important students, Jigmela was always in his pres-

15   Künzig Shamar Rinpoche is one of the lineage holders of the 16th Karmapa and a regent of the Karma Kagyu lineage.

ence. When Karmapa told me all this back then in Rumtek, I didn't think I would be able to accomplish it. After all, I was nobody, just an old man without any qualities. Because of that, I still didn't promise anything to Karmapa. I just sat there and listened.

"When I left Rumtek, I said to Karmapa: 'You once said the West is like the Pure Land of Bliss (Dewachen). So I'm just thinking that now I'm flying to a pure land.' But Karmapa replied: 'Don't say that. The West certainly can't be compared to Dewachen, even though life there is very pleasant. It is still nothing but a human realm.'

"Finally he said to me: 'You should always make your own decisions. You have my full personal support for that. You can always refer to me and say that you are acting on my behalf. I will pay attention to how it all works out for you and what you are doing. You can be certain of my wholehearted support. In addition, I will give you a letter of authority to take with you.' I told Karmapa that I didn't need such a thing but he said: 'No, there will be a time when you will need this personal statement, and it is better to take it with you now.' But I said: 'I don't need it. If you, as the Karmapa, say everything will work out fine, then I don't need any written authorization.'

"Later, difficulties did indeed arise in connection with building the temple and the retreat center. At that time, Jigme Rinpoche was traveling with Karmapa in America and told him about these problems in France. As a result, Karmapa drafted a letter in which he said that everything should be done according to the wishes of Lama Gendun, and there should be no discussion about this. He wrote that he had given me his full blessings and that people should not have any doubts about my decisions. In this way, I obtained my letter of authorization after all, the letter that Karmapa had wanted to give me from the very beginning, and everything developed very well from then on. Whatever Karmapa says will come true.

"It might be that I have forgotten some of Karmapa's instructions. But as I said, Jigme Rinpoche knows them all. You can ask him. He was always with Karmapa, he lived in his rooms, ate with him, he was simply always with him, even when Karmapa traveled. I have known Jigmela since he was a child. He was present at all the important events. Only on the occasion when Karmapa gave me the transmission and fully blessed me was I alone with Karmapa. All prophecies that Karmapa makes come true. Some have been forgotten but they, too, will come about."

The Karmapa had instructed Gendun Rinpoche to accomplish the following objectives in Europe. These "five great wishes of the Karmapa" were the basis of Gendun Rinpoche's activities, and they still are the guidelines for the activities of his students:

- to create Dharma Centers so that the noble teachings of the Buddha become accessible to all who are interested in them
- to create retreat centers that offer the opportunity for deeper practice and realization to qualified students so that the profound teachings of the Kagyu lineage are preserved and qualified lamas can be trained who are able to pass on these teachings
- to establish a community of ordained men and women who completely dedicate their lives to the benefit of all beings through meditation, prayer and teaching
- to build a great temple that serves as a visible manifestation of the Three Jewels and as a place of practice for all
- to establish an Institute of Buddhist Studies with a library so that the Buddha's instructions can be preserved, thoroughly studied and translated into Western languages.

Gendun Rinpoche always thought of himself as the servant of these wishes of his teacher. His own person was completely unimportant to him. He simply saw himself as the extended arm of the Karmapa and wanted the lamas whom he trained to also see themselves as merely carrying out the activity of the Dharma in general and of the Karmapa in particular.

Gendun Rinpoche in Europe: 1975–1997

In August of 1975, Gendun Rinpoche arrived in France and settled in the Dordogne, a region in which several other Tibetan masters from the Kagyu and Nyingma traditions had also been given land. He was accompanied by the young Jigme Rinpoche, a nephew and close disciple of the Karmapa who as a tulku had received the complete Karma Kagyu transmissions from him, together with all the main lineage holders. The Karmapa had chosen this place in France to become his main seat in Europe.

At the time, Gendun Rinpoche described his task in the following words: "If we can establish a large center here, then many people will have the opportunity to hear the Dharma and receive instructions. They will benefit from this by learning how to investigate their own minds. Then they will realize that they act under the influence of emotions like pride, jealousy and hatred. They will be able to take a path on which they do not fall under the influence of these emotions. The short-term benefit of this will be that the afflictions of the Western world will be reduced. The long-term benefit will be that those who practice the Dharma will avoid the suffering of the three lower realms. So this is my task now: to work to build such a center."

The property that had been given to the Karmapa by Mr. Benson consisted of an old, partially dilapidated farmhouse with stables and many acres of land. As time went on, more and more helpers appeared who at first lived in trailers on the property. Gendun Rinpoche instructed them on a daily basis. In the morning, they were allowed into his room in order to engage in the preliminary practices of Mahamudra in his presence.

With time, this first group of helpers restored half the main house. That sufficed for the time being. However, furnishings and appliances were still missing; for an entire year there was no stove, refrigerator or heating. Then a temple was set up in the upper story. It offered a bit more space than the first meditation room. Gendun Rinpoche was in a better position to give teachings there, and everyone was able to perform the morning and evening meditation rituals together.

Shamar Rinpoche recounts: "In the beginning, Gendun Rinpoche and Jigme Rinpoche had to cook their meals in a pot that sat on three stones over an open fire. As far as possible, a former stable was set up as a room for teachings but the roof burned down and there was no money to repair it. Thanks to their patience and perseverance they stuck to it, and only because of that the center grew little by little. Some of the great masters of the Nyingma tradition lived nearby, and they told me how much they were touched by their enthusiasm.

"They found that both Gendun Rinpoche and Jigme Rinpoche possessed the extraordinary quality of following only the wishes of their spiritual superior, the Karmapa. People with such devotion and without any self-interest are rare and can barely be found today. Thanks to their stability and continuity the center grew, and new houses were built to receive and accommodate visitors. I first visited in 1980, and even though I was told that the center had already developed significantly, I found the conditions very challenging. I hardly dared imagine how difficult it must have been before."

In 1977, during the Karmapa's second journey to the West, the donation of the property was finalized. The Karmapa blessed the site of the future monastery and gave the center its final name of Dhagpo Kagyu Ling, "the seat of the lineage of oral transmission of Gampopa." This had been the name of the place in Tibet where the awakened yogi and monk Gampopa taught and from which the teachings of the Kagyu lineage were widely disseminated.

During this second visit, the Karmapa gave all the instructions that were needed for the future. For an entire week, he performed the *Chakrasamvara* practice and then consecrated the entire place with the blessings of this mandala. From then on more and more visitors arrived who were beginning to understand what the Dharma is all about.

From then until his death in 1997, Gendun Rinpoche dedicated himself untiringly to the task that the Karmapa had entrusted him with: to transmit the authentic Dharma to the people in the West. He reserved not a single moment for personal interests; not even once did he travel back to his native country or invite friends or relatives to visit him. All his activities were in the service of the people here in Europe, and his love and deep compassion and the example he set inspired many to enter his path with trust and devotion.

As the Karmapa had predicted, "Dhagpo" grew to be a large center at which the Dharma unfolded powerfully, principally through the presence of Lama Gendun. Filled with devotion and great respect for him, practitioners from all over Europe flocked to it to strengthen their practice and establish a deep bond with the Three Jewels through the power of his blessings.

In the first years of his activity Gendun Rinpoche accepted many invitations to teach the Dharma. He taught in many of the countries of Western Europe, mostly in France and Germany, but also in Greece (to which he traveled seven times), England, Belgium, Austria, Italy, and other places.

On November 5, 1981, the 16th Gyalwa Karmapa died, long before Gendun Rinpoche, just as he himself had predicted. The activity of the Dhagpo mandala continued to spread after his death. Many great masters of the Kagyu lineage taught in Dhagpo. Gendun Rinpoche himself constantly gave teachings, empowerments and text transmissions. He taught the most important cycles and foundational texts thoroughly and numerous times, such as Gampopa's "Jewel

Ornament of Liberation," the Ninth Karmapa's "Ocean of Definitive Meaning," commentaries on mind training (lojong) such as Jamgon Kongtrul's "Great Path of Awakening," Togme Zangpo's "Thirty-Seven Bodhisattva Practices," and Gampopa's "Precious Garland."

He gave refuge to many people (i. e., introduced them to the path of awakening) and explained unceasingly how to tread this path through faith, devotion and compassion. On special occasions he gave the bodhisattva vows, mostly within the context of courses lasting several days. Soon his students started practicing the Mahamudra preliminaries, and they were all looked after by him personally.

It would be difficult to enumerate all the teachings and transmissions that Gendun Rinpoche gave. He simply gave everything that is necessary and helpful for a person to advance on the path of the Dharma. Among other things, he transmitted the complete instructions for the path of Mahamudra, for the guru yogas of Milarepa, Gampopa and the Karmapas, explanations of the practice of the Buddha of Limitless Light (Amitabha) and of the Pure Land of Bliss (Dewachen), the rituals of the Swift Liberator (Green Tara) and the Bodhisattva of Compassion (Avalokiteshvara), the complete practice of Cutting Through Ego-Clinging (Chö), the vajra songs of Saraha, Tilopa, and other great masters, and the practice of Medicine Buddha. Again and again, he gave direct instructions on how to deal with the emotions, on the meditation of mental calm and intuitive insight, on how to generate the understanding of the nature of mind, on the relationship between teacher and student and on the unceasing cultivation of compassion.

With the help of Lama Purtse, who had accompanied him since his days in India, he oversaw the daily rituals of Tara, *Mahakala,* and Avalokiteshvara as well as the monthly and yearly practices in accordance with the Tibetan calendar. Parallel to this, the center was being expanded steadily: guest rooms, living rooms, the temple, the kitchen and dining room, the lama house and the workshops all had to be constructed. In the early years, there was even some agricultural work on the extensive grounds. By the year 1981, the first seven Dharma groups in French cities had been founded. Today there are forty groups, all visited regularly by Dhagpo lamas.

The Retreat Center and Monastery Dhagpo Kundrol Ling

In 1980, about twenty of Gendun Rinpoche's students approached him with the wish to dedicate themselves more intensively to meditation practice under his direction and to receive from him the full transmission of the Kagyu lineage. Gendun Rinpoche agreed, and they set out to search for a suitable place for a three-year retreat. Shamar Rinpoche agreed to be the retreat's patron.

They inspected many houses but there was always some problem, and the project was not realized until 1983, when the well-known Tibet expert and filmmaker Arnaud Desjardins offered to sell the lamas a former school camp in the Auvergne. The property was located in Le Bost, a tiny, quiet village in the northern foothills of the Massif Central. The Karmapa had already performed the black crown ceremony twice in this house and on one of those occasions had told Gendun Rinpoche that Mr. Desjardins would be very helpful to them at some point in the future. The building was well suited to accommodate all the prospective retreatants and provide communal meditation rooms; so it was acquired immediately, together with a small park and a pond.

Thus in 1984, Rinpoche founded the three-year retreat center Kundrol Ling, "the place where everything is liberated." It offered Western practitioners with a serious commitment to the Dharma the opportunity to practice the profound teachings of the Vajrayana under conditions optimal for the transmission. The context of intensive group practice is well suited to the transmission and practice of the teachings that introduce the student to the nature of mind and ultimately enable them to reach buddhahood. The traditional form for this transmission within the Kagyu lineage is the group retreat of three years, three months and three days. This involves four daily meditation sessions of two to three hours each, some two hours of study and the group practice of Mahakala.

Gendun Rinpoche said the following about the three-year retreat: "The purpose of this kind of retreat is to enable us to help others and to attain the true aim of our lives, full awakening. When we carry out a three-year retreat we stop postponing this aim and create an opportunity for ourselves to attain it in this lifetime. This retreat is a great help for finding the way into deep meditation, for dissolving the self-centered tendencies that we have accumulated over eons and for realizing Mahamudra.

"For the duration of the retreat, all participants live like monks and nuns; they take the chastity vows and follow the same basic rules, and they also wear robes. Because of this, they are like a single organism. In the communal meditation everyone receives the benefit of the meditation of the entire group. Even if one does not attain awakening right away through the three years of practice – although that is entirely possible – every participant changes in a wholesome direction and is greatly supported on their path.

"Candidates for the retreat should already be familiar with the fundamentals of the Dharma through a certain amount of study and practice. They should also be able to read Tibetan and be familiar with the simpler rituals of the Vajrayana. This retreat is not something for children. Body and mind should be healthy and resilient. The only correct motivation for it is the wish to help all beings – it is not a matter of just wanting to become a lama."

He continued: "The duration of three years, three months and three days matches a natural cycle of body and mind during which our karmic energies can be completely transformed. If the practitioners completely renounce their worldly attachments, they will be able to clearly perceive all their karmic patterns in their minds during this length of time and transform them into wisdom."

During Gendun Rinpoche's lifetime, in agreement with Shamar Rinpoche, the first year of the three-year retreat comprised ten days of practice of the protector Vajrakilaya, then five months of Mahamudra preliminaries *(ngöndro)*, followed by a month of training the mind in compassion (lojong) and six months of meditation on four masters of the Kagyu transmission lineage (Milarepa, Gampopa, Karma Pakshi, and Mikyo Dorje), accompanied by the meditations of mental calm (shamatha) and intuitive insight (vipashyana). The second year was dedicated to the intensive practice of a particular buddha aspect, the yidam *Vajravarahi*, and this was followed in the third year by the Mahamudra practices of the Six Dharmas of Naropa *(tummo*, illusory body, dream, clear light, *phowa*, and *bardo)*, a month of Chö practice and two months of meditation on the female bodhisattva White Tara.[16]

Following the establishment of the retreat centers, Rinpoche spent a great deal of his time with the retreatants and increasingly curtailed his traveling. For years he had prepared the fourteen men and five women of the first retreat group, and he now gave them all the transmissions and explanations in person. Virtually every day he visited them during the midday break, advised them about their meditation experiences and clarified all their questions. He looked after each individual person. In the afternoons, as preparation for each new practice cycle, he elucidated the practice texts and commentaries line by line and explained the methods and deeper purpose of the practice.

---

16 Since 2008, according to the wishes of the 17th Karmapa Thaye Dorje, the first retreat is now a three-year foundation retreat that focuses on the above-mentioned practices previously done in the first year, but it also finishes with Chö and White Tara.

It is difficult for the outsider to imagine how much time and energy such spiritual care requires. But Rinpoche was very clear about his priorities. He knew that the availability of the authentic Dharma in the West depended crucially on the degree to which Western practitioners themselves were able to penetrate to the core of the practice. So he concentrated completely on this task and spent a large part of his time in the retreat centers. His efforts have borne fruit; his example lives on in his students. Since then, more than three hundred practitioners have followed the example of this first retreat group who paved the way for them.

Rinpoche knew exactly what was going on in the mind of each of his students. He was able to describe to them in detail the thoughts they had had in various situations, regardless of whether he had been present or not, and also to explain their meditation experiences well. To everyone he could give precise advice on how to dissolve any obstacles that presented themselves and how to accomplish the next step in the practice.

On top of this, he had an incomparable ability to change any situation into pure joy – through his love, his humor, his lack of attachment. Because of that, difficulties hardly ever took root in his students for any length of time. Untiringly, he showed his students the way to let go into simplicity and freed them from the jungle of ego-clinging. In many situations, a simple laugh from him sufficed to clear the way again.

Thierry Charbonneaux, the secretary of the retreat center in its first few years, recounted: "In January 1984, I had the good fortune to arrive here with the first group of future retreatants. It was quite an adventure. We found that this unknown house in the Auvergne that we had just acquired was completely empty. For the next three months, until the beginning of the retreat, we camped out. First, we had to set up the two small temples and erect the fence required for the retreat. Gendun Rinpoche himself lent us 50,000 francs – everything he owned at the time. Effectively it was a gift, since we weren't able to give him much of it back.

"During the retreat, we ran out of money and went to Rinpoche: 'What should we do, Rinpoche, we've already spent almost all the money set aside for the coming month?' He said: 'Take the little money that's left and build a stupa with it.' We were mightily surprised – instead of showing us how we could find money, he showed us how we could spend more of it. He explained: 'When you're short of money, the cause is that you haven't been generous enough.' So we started with the construction. From the moment the stupa was completed, new donations started coming in – hardly just by chance. People had seen the picture of our stupa in our circular, felt inspired by it and came to our help. Our situation improved."

In 1986, another group of men and women had started a three-year retreat in Germany in which German and English were the languages of instruction. It took place in the retreat center at Halscheid that Gendun Rinpoche had newly acquired. He divided his time now between the French and German retreat groups and responsibilities in the public center of Dhagpo Kagyu Ling. He hardly traveled to other places anymore. An exception was Kamalashila, the main German center of the Karma Kagyu lineage near Mechernich, where he taught whenever he visited the German retreat group.

In 1987, twelve participants from the first group of male retreatants in France decided to embark on a second three-year retreat, and many took monk's vows for this. The program of this second retreat consisted of four yidam practices (Vajrakilaya, Chakrasamvara, Mahakala, and Jinasagara). The essential goal was to truly become one with the mind of awakening and to use the powerful methods of the Vajrayana to dissolve the attachment to self. Along with this, the daily practice of the Six Dharmas of Naropa was continued and deepened. Hence, over a period of six and a half years the participants in these two three-year retreats learned the same meditation practices that Tibetans learned in a single three-year retreat.[17]

Thierry continued: "During this second retreat from 1987 to 1990, a student of Gendun Rinpoche gave him a house with a piece of land in Laussedat, only two miles from Le Bost, with the desire that the community use it for the purposes of the Dharma. Rinpoche decided to accommodate the women there for the third retreat cycle. The men would remain in Le Bost. Around this time, Rinpoche met an affluent patron in Germany who offered him his support and during a visit to Le Bost made a very generous donation.

"In this way began a much larger project than we had ever dreamed possible. We purchased the old farm next to the retreat center along with the surrounding properties, where today you will find the monastery, the temple and its beautiful park. The old farm has been converted and serves to accommodate lay practitioners who help with the projects of the monastic community.

"Gendun Rinpoche explained to us that the idea was not to build in order to attract people and fill the houses; but rather, to build because so many people were waiting to come here, and Rinpoche would not otherwise be able to take them all in. For him, a clear need or wish had first to be present – the necessity always preceded any work project. And since these wishes were truly positive, he said, money would not be a problem. Everything that was needed materially would be found sooner or later, in harmony with our basic wholesome attitude – this attitude was what counted.

"Everything here in this center arose in this way. It was never Rinpoche's objective to erect as many buildings as possible. He always said: 'You are not construction workers. The real house that you're building is inside yourselves. And you aren't really building for your-

_____

17 In 2008, this set of two successive three-year retreats was extended to a total of four by the 17ᵗʰ Karmapa, so that still more time could be provided for the necessary inner process of ripening and for essential studies.

selves at all but for all the future generations that will come here. We live in a time of degeneration in which suffering is increasing continually – that's why it's more important than ever that there is a place in which the Dharma is firmly anchored. These structures are really not for ourselves. We can meditate anywhere, including outdoors. But there has to be a place on earth where everyone knows that the Dharma, the path that ends all suffering, is taught, a place where people can go and find an entry into the Dharma.' "

More and more people wanted to carry out the three-year retreat under Gendun Rinpoche's direction, so in 1989 he decided to expand the retreat center in the Auvergne to offer facilities for eight groups of eleven to fifteen participants – four each for men and women. This included the German and English speaking participants who now joined the retreats in the Auvergne. The retreat equipment of the German center in Halscheid was brought to France, and the large house was converted to a public meditation center.

In the spring of 1990, the next generation of retreatants gathered in the Auvergne, along with many other helpers, to build all the new rooms needed and the group temple. Rinpoche visited the construction site every day to inspire all the workers through his visible presence. He investigated every work site with genuine interest and personally checked the progress of the work. Everything was done in-house, from the foundations to the roofing and plastering. Hardly anyone had any knowledge of construction work, and much new experience was accumulated.

At the same time, this communal work was a good preparation for the retreat because the participants got to know and appreciate each other, and they also had an opportunity to smooth out some of their rough edges. In February of 1991, forty women and fifty-eight men began a three-year retreat. It was the third cycle. From this time on, Gendun Rinpoche lived permanently in the Auvergne, in the immediate vicinity of the retreatants. Only two or three times a year did he still travel to teach in the big public courses in the Dordogne. His daily life was very simple, well-ordered and humble. He rose early and practiced in his room the entire day. About an hour before lunch he received visitors, some of whom had traveled very far to see him, gave them advice and blessed them. He did not leave his meditation seat and always continued with his prayers and meditations for the benefit of all beings, even when he was listening to those seeking advice.

He didn't have to listen for very long to know what was on his visitor's mind. Often he didn't even wait for the translation before giving his answer. Moreover, he frequently surprised the questioner with answers that referred to areas of their lives and their emotions they had not mentioned at all but that harbored a much more fundamental problem.

In the language of the Dharma one would say that he knew the karma of every person he encountered, and therefore could dispense advice skillfully tailored to the individual abilities of the questioner. In all this, he was fully aware that everyone he encountered had the potential of a buddha in them and on their deepest level already was a buddha, even though there was still so much work left to do for them to manifest this on the relative level.

He was not afraid of pointing out his students' faults to them in various ways. He would first speak in a general way of emotional entanglements and faulty views that he had noticed, to see whether his students had sufficient insight to apply his remarks to themselves. When that was not enough, he would often imitate their behavior and facial expressions in a playful way, thereby holding up a mirror to them. When that still did not suffice, he could also be very direct, without ever being hurtful. One could always feel the loving, supportive touch of the master that turned even a piece of advice that would otherwise be hard to swallow into something that was experienced as a gift. If time permitted, he enjoyed taking a little walk after lunch – most of the time to the stupa, which he circumambulated with quick steps while saying many mantras. He was always happy when the lamas came to talk with him about their practice or seek advice about how to manage all the tasks that he had entrusted them with.

His conduct was in every respect exemplary and his discipline flawless. He also possessed a great measure of joyful spontaneity, and he never felt disturbed or bothered, not even in inopportune situations. There was room for everything and everyone in his presence. To everyone he gave the same personal attention and love. In order to care for the large number of retreatants, he now had to give the instructions a total of four times: to the women and the men, and with French and English translations.

In all these years, Lama Gendun never traveled to India or Tibet. His sole purpose was to establish the Dharma sufficiently firmly in the West so that his students would be able to transmit it to future generations on their own. In 1994, he transferred the responsibility for the public Dharma centers, the two monasteries and the ten retreat centers to several of his students individually and to the monastic community as a whole, and during the last three years of his life he increasingly withdrew from active involvement in projects and decisions.

He checked to see to what extent his students were able to manage on their own and extended his help where they still needed it. Thus he accustomed his students to their future tasks and prepared them for the time when he would no longer be able to stand by them directly in word and deed. In this way, everyone was encouraged to grow into their future responsibilities and learn to stand on their own two feet.

As a result, starting in 1994, several Western lamas assumed the responsibility of guiding the fourth cycle of three-year retreats largely on their own. Gendun Rinpoche initially visited the retreatants at monthly intervals and then every three months, explaining the essential points of the respective practices and answering their questions about their practice. Also, whenever it was necessary, he showed how one could skillfully deal with difficult situations and inner blockages in retreat.

It was Lama Gendun's wish that his students always act as a community. For example, the lamas were directed to look after all the regional Dharma groups collectively, alternating their visits. This was done to prevent students from becoming attached to an individual lama and the sangha thereby becoming fragmented. It also ensured that individual lamas had the opportunity to withdraw repeatedly for months or even years of practice without the spiritual care of the students suffering.

The creation of a harmonious community of monks and nuns was particularly close to Lama Gendun's heart. Most of these would be Dharma teachers whose responsibility was to preserve and transmit the teachings. He said: "We know that the awakening of all beings depends on their wholesome actions, and we must therefore generate an attitude that produces such actions. Instructions must be given that are practiced and lived out in the community, so that this unselfish attitude is generated, and that realization then transmitted. To accomplish this task, the community should organize itself in the form of a monastery."

The Dharma Center Dhagpo Kagyu Ling

Dhagpo Kagyu Ling, the public center in the Dordogne, continued to grow steadily. Every summer, many visitors came to listen to Gendun Rinpoche's precious instructions and to live in the luminous presence of his awakened mind. His presence and his words were so powerful that in listening to him the right understanding of the Dharma arose spontaneously. Everything was crystal-clear. There were even a few listeners who in his presence realized the nature of mind, even though they were hearing these teachings for the first time, at least in this life. A simplicity emanated from him that was permeated with wisdom. All the complications caused by ego-clinging had been dissolved in him – the only thing that counted was the welfare of others.

"Dhagpo" has now become the main European seat of the 17th Gyalwa Karmapa, Thaye Dorje, and it continues to be overseen by Jigme Rinpoche, together with the Western lamas. Throughout the year, introductory courses are offered on the Dharma, and there are many opportunities for study, contemplation and meditation on the Buddha's teachings. In addition, there are regular teachings by great masters of the Kagyu lineage.

For several years now, a summer university has been in session which is offered by khenpos of the lineage, and in several cycles of studies various foundational philosophical texts of Mahayana Buddhism are being taught. In addition, a library is being built whose purpose is to make available to students the greatest possible number of rare books from the spiritual heritage of Tibet (and other Buddhist countries) that are in danger of being lost. Thus, the five wishes of the 16th Gyalwa Karmapa have now been realized in the form of multifaceted activities that benefit a wide range of people.

In addition, Gendun Rinpoche inspired the creation of Dharma centers in many places, including retreat centers especially geared toward laypeople[18] as well as a large network of regional Dharma groups in which meditation sessions take place regularly and the Dhagpo lamas teach in alternation.

---

18   These places include Dhagpo Dedrol Ling (Marfond) and Dhagpo Dhargye Ling in the Dordogne, France; Kundrol Phuntsok Ling in Jägerndorf, Bavaria, and Shedrub Phuntsok Ling in Möhra, Thuringia, both in Germany; and Rigdrol Ling in the mountains near Thessaloniki, Greece.

The final months with Gendun Rinpoche

From April to July 1997, Gendun Rinpoche received the eighteen-year-old Tenying Rinpoche, the reincarnated lineage holder of the Bharam Kagyu Tradition from his monastery in Tibet. Every day he taught him Mahamudra and transmitted the instructions to him that traditionally are given at the beginning of the three-year retreat.

In spite of being a bit exhausted from this intensive teaching activity, he thought it important in August 1997 to share a week with his many students in Dhagpo. It turned out to be his last time with them. He gave the initiation of the female buddha of long life Drupa'i Gyalmo (queen of realization) and on that occasion said in jest: "For someone who is old a long life initiation is particularly important."

In September 1997, Gyatrul Rinpoche came for a short visit and received instructions from him. Gendun Rinpoche was still somewhat weak and was careful to treat himself gently. During this time he talked a lot about what activities should be developed in the monasteries and retreat centers in the future. Although he foresaw some difficulties for the centers, he had confidence in the future, based on signs in his meditation.

On the occasion of the conclusion of the three-year retreats on October 22, 1997, more than a thousand visitors and friends came to the Auvergne. Most of the students who had participated in the preceding retreat cycles under Gendun Rinpoche's direction were present. In the days preceding the event, he had felt very well and had personally attended to many details, in particular those concerning the ceremonies about to take place in the large Karmapa Temple for the first time.

Everyone was to receive his blessing individually, and he wanted everyone to have a meal together in the temple after the ceremony, so that this first gathering of the entire sangha in the temple would be an auspicious event. It was a very festive occasion. In the days preceding the conclusion of the retreats, Lama Gendun had auspicious dreams on three successive nights in which the retreatants offered him many prostrations, long life prayers, gifts and good wishes and also showed their devotion to him in other ways.

After their traditional circumambulation of the retreat sites with symbolic offerings in front of the stupas as a sign of their gratitude, the one hundred and four retreatants were welcomed with a short ceremony in the monasteries of the monks and the nuns, respectively. Gendun Rinpoche then received them in the new Karmapa Temple where one thousand Buddha statues had been placed in their alcoves. The retreatants collectively made a mandala offering of the universe and then received Gendun Rinpoche's blessings.

Gendun Rinpoche appeared extremely happy, smiling and radiating his wonderful benevolence – everything that he saw before him had been accomplished in accordance with the wishes of the 16th Gyalwa Karmapa. During the blessing itself Lama Gendun was extraordinarily solemn and in deep concentration, as though he knew that this would be his last meeting with his students. However, during the blessing he showed no signs of tiredness, and in the days following the end of the retreats he received visitors for talks and blessings, just as he always had.

Nine days later, during the night of Friday, Oct. 31, 1997, Gendun Rinpoche left his body, after twenty-two years of tireless activity in Europe. For two and a half days he remained in thugdam, the meditation in the nature of mind that is practiced by great meditators at the time of their death. During this time, the area of his heart remained warm and his face appeared young and radiant. He bore the blissful expression of someone who is in deep samadhi. He appeared forty years younger, and viewing him evoked a deep feeling of happiness.

On the first day after his death, a sweetish fragrance resembling that of saffron began to spread from his body into his room and then became so strong that it was noticeable in the adjacent temple. A spirit of joy began to spread throughout the entire mandala. It is almost a miracle that none of his students, with all their different degrees of personal development and maturity, felt left alone or abandoned. To his students this was evidence of his continued presence, his still perceptible all-pervading goodness and the extraordinary degree of his realization. Fortunately, Gendun Rinpoche had prepared his students for this moment for years. Frequently, he had spoken to them about his death in the following way: "Don't worry but keep a joyful mind. Don't be attached to the physical presence of the lama but meditate on the lama from whom you are never separated."

His body was preserved for forty-nine days in the traditional manner so that his students, many of whom had traveled far, would have the opportunity to practice near it. Every day during this period, group meditations took place in the temples. One week each was dedicated to the meditations of Vajrayogini, Vajrasattva, Chö, Chakrasamvara, Amitabha, and Jinasagara. These rituals were performed for the sake of the continuation of an awakened activity like his in this world.

It was a unique and powerful time in which a special blessing was perceptible – a time of inner purification during which further seeds of awakening were sown in his students. Many visitors arrived to show reverence to his kudung (the mortal shell of an awakened being) and meditate near him while a small group of students performed many recitations of the "zangchö mönlam" (the Samantabhadra wishing prayer of excellent bodhisattva activity) and practiced guru yoga.

On December 18, 1997, the ritual cremation of the embalmed body took place under the direction of Künzig Shamar Rinpoche and in the presence of the community of practitioners. Rinpoche's body was surrendered to the flames in a specially built cremation stupa in the forecourt of the temple. During the cremation, three separate fire offering ceremonies took place around the stupa, with simultaneous offerings to the blazing wisdom fire.

His Legacy

Rinpoche's work is being continued by the community of lamas under the direction of the 17th Gyalwa Karmapa. When one considers everything that was accomplished through the activity of Gendun Rinpoche in only twenty-two years, there is cause for great joy. Regarding the future, Gendun Rinpoche several times said that the continuation of his work would depend on two conditions: that his students continued with their practice, alternating between periods of activity and retreat, and that the community remained united.

In 1998, in spite of the recent death of Gendun Rinpoche, one hundred and eight men and women started the fifth three-year retreat cycle. A dozen practitioners who had already completed two three-year retreats also decided to undertake further retreats of twelve years and longer.

Today, in the year 2010, aside from sixty participants in the ninth cycle of the three-year retreat, the community consists of forty monks and nuns, most of whom have completed two three-year retreats and now continue their practice in the monastery, alternating between activity and meditation. They continue to develop their understanding of the teachings through study and meditation. Visitors, too, have the opportunity to practice under retreat conditions and be helped by the resident Dharma teachers. Thus, in the sixteen years since the monastery came into existence, many visitors have come to it for courses and short periods of intensive practice.

In addition, the Dhagpo lamas teach in regional Dharma groups in various countries, giving public instructions and advising interested parties about their individual practice. They are also available to guide the practitioners who participate in the various Dharma Centers.

Today, at Dhagpo Kundrol Ling, the sites for the women (in Laussedat) and for the men (in Le Bost) each consist of a monastery complex and four three-year retreat centers, a long-term retreat center and a public temple, as well as accommodation for visitors, volunteer workers and short-term retreatants, along with rooms for the administration, and in each of these complexes stands a blessed stupa that symbolizes the awakened mind of all sentient beings.

At the heart of this mandala, with a view of the volcanic mountain chain of the Puy-de-Dome, rises the great Karmapa Temple that was consecrated in October 1997 by Gendun Rinpoche and that serves as a venue for large events and for ceremonies and meditation courses. In it one can find a 15 foot tall Buddha statue, surrounded by one thousand smaller Buddhas, all of which were created at the center by the disciples. The walls and ceiling are painted with beautiful frescoes. Next to the temple, a small hermitage with twenty rooms is available to visitors.

Gendun Rinpoche's unusual quality was his simple presence which was completely open and accessible. He never gave the impression of wanting to be someone special but liked to conduct himself like an ordinary lama. Anyone could approach him without any difficulties. He stayed close to the place of his main activity all the time, so he could pass on the teachings to his European students on a daily basis. Commonly, realized beings develop so much external activity that they are not nearly so accessible in everyday life. But Gendun Rinpoche expressed his love by being ever available and close to his students, and because of this he had a great impact on his community of practitioners.

The 16th Gyalwa Karmapa said this about him: "Gendun Rinpoche is like Milarepa. In this life, he has attained the level of Vajradhara (the realization of the highest truth, free from veils). In his next incarnation, Lama Gendun's power will be inconceivable."

Künzig Shamar Rinpoche described him as follows: "Gendun Rinpoche was a yogi. He should properly be called a Great Meditator, as he had committed himself to the path of meditation since early childhood and never gave up his commitment until he reached enlightenment. This is how to obtain enlightenment: by fulfilling the commitments that one has entered into. It is not easy to be like him!

"He meditated his entire life, and this led him to the highest realization and to all his extraordinary abilities. All of us valued him highly as a lineage holder of Mahamudra and the Six Dharmas of Naropa and as one of the few lamas who could still give these transmissions. He truly was one of the great *siddhas* of the Karma Kagyu lineage. When it is said that he was like Milarepa, what is meant by this is that one should pray to him as one prays to Milarepa. In that sense they are equal. It also means that Rinpoche attained the highest level of perfection of Mahamudra.

"To bring the Dharma to the West, it was necessary to send an awakened master with stable realization, and so the Karmapa chose Gendun Rinpoche. Actually, the latter only wished to live in simplicity on the streets of India like a beggar. That's what Gendun Rinpoche told the Karmapa when the Karmapa requested him to go to Europe. He added that since the Karmapa was a living buddha, he would think about his request, because if he accepted the Karmapa's wish, he would never break his promise and disappoint him – thus he needed time to think about it. However, the Karmapa insisted that Gendun Rinpoche accept his wish. Lama Gendun then said: 'You are a living buddha, and you know the benefit that will accrue from this for a great number of sentient beings. If I have the opportunity to serve you, this will mean that I have the opportunity to effect the benefit of many beings. Therefore, I accept this task.'

"It is certain that the teachings were transmitted authentically through Gendun Rinpoche here in Europe and have remained completely pure. Thus, the essence of the Dharma has been preserved. As to the question of the succession of Gendun Rinpoche, it is obvious who will maintain and continue his activity. Gendun Rinpoche unfolded all of his activity on behalf of the Karmapa; he put only his wishes into action. He always said that the latter should again take charge when his work was completed. Naturally, therefore, his work will go on with the buddha Karmapa."

After the previous Karmapa passed away and when the succession was still unclear, Gendun Rinpoche once spoke to his students about the kind of faith they should develop in the Karmapa: "When you generate the strong wish and imagine the Karmapa in front of you, he will in fact sit on his throne in front of you. There is no doubt about it. Those who met the 16th Gyalwa Karmapa can rely on his blessings all the time, regardless of whether he is physically present or not. Karmapa's blessings go beyond his physical manifestation. Those who have never met him, can rely on the awakened mind of the Karmapa in a broader sense, too. I myself practice in this way.

"The Gyalwa Karmapa was my root lama. One can have no doubt about his blessings and the fact that he is ever present. We are never separate from the Karmapa. He is actually there when we pray to him. I myself do it in this way. You can be sure that his blessings will dissolve all problems and confusion. I view myself as a servant of the Karmapa and as his student. The Karmapa is always with me, all the time. I am not waiting for him; I have already found him."[19]

---

19 Many people have asked what made Gendun Rinpoche so certain in the stand he took in the discussion surrounding the recognition of two different Karmapas that erupted in 1992. His certainty came from repeated nightly visions in which he encountered the young reincarnation of the 16th Karmapa. He saw him so clearly that he was able to describe to his students his face, his general looks and even his hands. When he saw the first photos of the boy

Gendun Rinpoche said the following about his masters: "My actual lama is Vajradhara, the Dharmakaya Samantabhadra, and that is the path I have more or less followed. But it is true that I have received many transmissions from great masters of different traditions, masters with flawless, uninterrupted transmission lineages who convey untainted blessings. It makes no difference whether these were masters of the Kagyu or Nyingma lineage. The two lineages interpenetrate and enrich each other.

"Among the important lamas from whom I learned at different stages of my life, first of all there were the three lamas who were responsible for teaching in our monastery and a great hermit who lived in the vicinity of the monastery and from whom I received many instructions. Then I met the previous Situ Rinpoche Pema Wangchuk and the previous Jamgon Kongtrul Rinpoche Khyentse Öser, both of whom I regarded as my teachers.

"Finally I met the Gyalwa Karmapa, who was the master of them all. I entered into his blessings by regarding him as the master of all my previous masters. He accepted me as his student and entrusted me with many tasks, almost against my will. From among the best known Nyingma masters, the revered Dilgo Khyentse Rinpoche has given me many instructions, and I have also relied on Dudjom Rinpoche, the head of the Nyingma lineage, even though I met him much less frequently."

Shamar Rinpoche wrote the following about Gendun Rinpoche: "Lama Gendun of Khyodrag monastery is a truly spiritual human being who has totally dissolved all attachments and all desire for wealth, esteem and reputation. It is difficult today to find someone who is as capable as he is in meditation and Dharma activity and in giving every student the guidance that they need. This, as well as his ability of transmitting true blessings to his students, indicates his

---

Thaye Dorje, he did not have to look twice to be certain that this was the reincarnation of the 16th Karmapa.

spiritual realization. Such a Mahamudra yogi is hard to find; he can be compared to a precious wish-fulfilling jewel, the source of everything that one wishes for and needs."

In an interview from the 1970's, Gendun Rinpoche concluded his life story with the following words: "At first we are conceived in the womb of our mother. We are almost invisible then. Then we are born and grow up, become adults, and finally we grow old, as I am now. Our bodies become feeble, our teeth and hair fall out. Then we die. Our dead body decays and disappears. Nothing remains of it. My gray hair is my *mudra* of impermanence." Then he added: "We should water the flowers today, or else they will dry up and die, just like myself, an old man."

This short biography of Lama Gendun Rinpoche gives only an incomplete insight into the life and work of this master who in reality cannot be described. In his memory, the following verses with which he blessed thousands of people in personal meetings over the years are reproduced here.

May we never in all our lifetimes
be separated from the perfectly pure lama
but rejoice in the plenitude of his teachings,
perfect the qualities of the stages and paths
and quickly attain the realization of Vajradhara.

May the precious mind of awakening arise
in those in whom it has not yet arisen,
and may it not decline but steadily increase
in those in whom it has already arisen.

May all sentient beings turn their minds toward
                              the Dharma
and follow the noble teachings as a path.
May the path dispel our confusion,
and may confusion arise as timeless awareness.

Glossary

Skt.: Sanskrit; Tib.: Tibetan

afflictive emotion: Skt. klesha. Includes all mental states that arise due to clinging to a self and give rise to gross or subtle tensions in the mind. The five principal types of afflictive emotion are also called the "five poisons": pride, jealousy, desire, ignorance and hatred.

Amitabha (Skt.): The Buddha of Infinite Light. Amitabha is to be understood on two levels. In general he represents the inherently pure mind of all sentient beings and as such is synonymous with the *dharmakaya*. More particularly, the name Amitabha refers to a great bodhisattva who made vows on his path to reaching buddhahood that all beings endowed with deep trust in the mind of awakening would be able to enter into his pure land *Dewachen*. He is now called Buddha Amitabha.

Avalokiteshvara (Skt.): Tib. Chenrezi. The bodhisattva of great compassion; also the tantric deity or "buddha" who embodies awakened compassion.

bardo (Tib.): lit. "in-between state." Often used to refer to the after-death state, i. e., the intermediate state of existence between two successive lives. More broadly, bardo is also used to refer to several other transitional states, e. g., the set of six bardos: the bardos of the present life, meditation, dreaming, dying, dharmata, and becoming.

bodhicitta (Skt.): lit. "mind of awakening." A distinction is made between *ultimate bodhicitta* which is the direct insight into the true nature of things, the wisdom of emptiness, and *relative bodhicitta* which is the wish or intention to attain full awakening for the sake of all beings, so that one is able to lead them to that same awakening. This heartfelt wish is the central motivation on the bodhisattva path. Relative bodhicitta is itself further divided into aspiring and engaged bodhicitta (see the main text).

bodhisattva (Skt.): In its Tib. transl. lit. "hero of awakening." Someone who has the courage and makes the firm decision to work for the awakening of all sentient beings without exception and without being concerned with their own well-being.

buddha (Skt.): lit. "awakened one." A fully enlightened being, freed from all obscurations and fully endowed with all awakened qualities.

buddha nature: The potential for buddhahood present in every sentient being.

Chakrasamvara (Skt.): One of the principal yidams in the Karma Kagyu tradition.

Chö (Tib.): lit. "cutting through." The practice of cutting through ego-clinging, a meditation practice of offering the body in one's imagination as food for all beings in order to cut through the illusion of and attachment to a separately existing 'I' or self. Chö was introduced to Tibet by the Indian master Padampa Sangye (~1040–1117) and elaborated and widely propagated there by the renowned female practitioner Machig Labdron (1055–1149).

dakini (Skt.): In its Tib. transl. lit. "sky goer." A female embodiment of awakened energy that inspires and protects practitioners; also a type of tantric deity such as Vajrayogini.

development and **completion stages** of meditation: In the development stage of tantric meditation (Tib. kyerim), also called creation or generation stage, one works with the creative aspect of the mind, e. g., by carrying out visualizations of the mandala of a deity and generating an awareness of the illusory nature of all appearances, including oneself. In the completion stage of tantric meditation (Tib. dzogrim), one lets go of all mental images and allows the mind to merge with the non-dual dimension that underlies all appearances. In the Kagyu tradition these two phases are not practiced sequentially but as a unity.

Dewachen (Tib.): Skt. Sukhavati, lit. "great bliss." The Pure Land of Bliss, which is the field of activity of Buddha *Amitabha*.

Dharma (Skt.): The noble teachings of the Buddha as well as their practice; in a broader sense also the teachings of other authentic lineage holders. The term holds a large variety of meanings, such as truth, reality, law, custom, phenomena, quality, and others.

Dharma protector: A peaceful or wrathful, male or female embodiment of buddha activity who protects the teachings and practitioners from malevolent influences and removes obstacles on their path. On an inner level the protector stands for the practitioner's firm resolve never to waver from their bodhisattva vow.

Dharma wheel: A Buddhist symbol that consists of eight spokes, a hub and an outer rim. It symbolizes the Buddha's teaching of the Noble Eightfold Path whose source is the truth of the liberation from all suffering and which applies to all beings and all phenomena.

dharmakaya (Skt.): Truth body; one of the *three buddha bodies*. Synonymous with the non-conceptual, open nature of mind that is the very nature of awakening.

dharmata (Skt.): The absolute or ultimate nature of reality; the empty nature of all phenomena.

Dorje Drolö (Tib.): A wrathful yidam; one of the eight manifestations of *Guru Rinpoche* (Padmasambhava).

emanation body: See *nirmanakaya*.

empowerment: A ceremony during which the authorization to hear, study and engage in a specific *Vajrayana* practice is given by the master to the practitioner.

emptiness: Skt. shunyata. The absence of anything that could be grasped at by the dualistic mind, the absence of any self-entity or apprehended self.

enjoyment body: See *sambhogakaya*.

faith: Tib. depa (Wylie: dad-pa). Depa is also translated as confidence or trust. In Buddhism, faith is viewed as a mental factor that involves a clarity free from laziness, worry, desire, and doubt, and that acts as the basis for inciting intention toward wholesome action. Initially, a Buddhist practitioner develops a reasoned faith from observing the positive results of their practice. Eventually, they transcend the need for believing when they gain direct experience of things formerly only assumed. Specifically, in the Buddhist teachings, faith has three aspects: inspired faith (the inspiration coming from the Dharma and from those who practice it), aspiring faith (the longing or aspiration to follow the path of awakening), and confident faith (the conviction or certainty gained through deep, personal insight). Because of its usual religious connotation, some Buddhist teachers prefer not to use the term faith, although it best covers the above range of meanings.

five wisdoms: Five aspects of the timeless awareness of a buddha, associated with the five buddha families. These five aspects are: dharmadhatu wisdom, mirrorlike wisdom, wisdom of equality, discriminating wisdom, and allperfecting wisdom.

Gampopa (1079–1153): Great Tibetan yogi from whom originated the various lineages of the Kagyu school; foremost disciple of Milarepa. Among his principal disciples was the first Karmapa, Düsum Khyenpa. Originally Gampopa belonged to the *Kadampa School*.

Guru Rinpoche (Tib.): lit. "precious master." Common designation of Padmasambhava, an Indian tantric master who brought the Dharma from North India to Tibet in the 8th century CE and is revered as a great trailblazer of Buddhist teachings, in particular the *Vajrayana*.

illusory body: One of the *Six Dharmas of Naropa*.

intuitive insight (Tib. lhagtong, Skt. vipashyana): A form of meditation in which one directly in-

vestigates the nature of mind and phenomena. It starts with an analysis of the mind and its functioning and progressively leads to the realization of the absence of self in the individual and in all phenomena.

inner heat: See *tummo*.

Kadampa (Tib.): A school of Tibetan Buddhism that was founded by the Indian master Atisha (980–1052). It is known for its thorough practice of fundamental contemplations such as those of impermanence and karma, for its intensive mind training in compassion and for the practice of the foundations of the bodhisattva path. All extant schools of Tibetan Buddhism have been strongly influenced by the teachings of this school.

Kagyu (Tib.): One of the four main schools of Tibetan Buddhism: along with the Nyingma, Sakya and Gelug.

Kalu Rinpoche (1905–1989): A great Kagyu master who was one of the first lamas sent by the 16th Karmapa to Europe and North America to spread the Dharma; a contemporary of Gendun Rinpoche.

karma (Skt.): lit. "action." Our karma is the totality of forces and influences that have been set in motion by our previous actions. These karmic forces affect all our experiences, actions and views unceasingly. Karma is dynamic and can be altered through changes in our present thinking and acting.

Karmapa (Tib.): The title of the head of the Karma Kagyu lineage of Tibetan Buddhism. The Karmapas are the oldest lineage of reincarnated lamas, established by the first Karmapa Düsum Khyenpa (1110–1193) who was a disciple of Gampopa.

khenpo (Tib.): lit. "someone who knows," a professor. A title given to a monk who, after completing a ten year course in Buddhist philosophy and other studies, has attained a proven level of knowledge and received authorization to teach.

lama (Tib.): lit. "weighty," a teacher of spiritual weight. Title for a Dharma teacher in the Tibetan tradition who has been given authority to teach and guide practitioners. In old times the qualification of a lama included spiritual attainment.

lojong (Tib.): lit. "mind training." A genre of texts and practices, most importantly of bodhicitta, that originated from the *Kadampa* School. Among its most important authors are Atisha, Geshe Langri Tangpa, Geshe Chekawa, and bodhisattva Togme Zangpo.

Mahakala (Skt.): A Dharma protector and tantric deity; a daily group practice in Karma Kagyu retreats and monasteries.

Mahamudra (Skt.): lit. "great seal." The highest teaching, meditation practice, and meditative accomplishment in the Kagyu School;

often divided into ground, path, and fruition Mahamudra.

Mahayana (Skt.): The "Great Vehicle" of Buddhist teachings. Mahayana practitioners vow to remain engaged in cyclic existence until the very last being has been liberated from it. Figuratively speaking, their practice becomes a great vehicle which takes up all beings. The heart of their practice is the development of compassion and wisdom.

Maitripa (1007–1078): A highly accomplished Indian master; Mahamudra teacher of Naropa and Marpa.

mandala (Skt.): A symbolic, graphical representation of a deity's realm of activity, often in the form of a painting or in colored sand. Also, loosely used, the realm of activity of a particular Dharma teacher and their sangha.

Manjushri (Skt.): The bodhisattva and tantric deity who embodies the wisdom of all the buddhas.

mantra (Skt.): lit. "that which protects the mind." A short prayer formula in the form of Sanskrit syllables that focuses the mind of the practitioner on the qualities of the meditational deity and embodies it in the form of sound. An example is Avalokiteshvara's mantra OM MANI PEME HUNG.

Marpa (1012–1097): Tibetan master who brought the Buddhist teachings from India to Tibet; founder of the Kagyu school; disciple of Naropa and teacher of Milarepa.

mental calm (Tib. shine, Skt. shamatha): Also called "calm abiding" or "mental quiet." The practice of meditation in which the mind becomes clear and calms down until it remains settled with or without a reference point. Mental calm gives rise to the experiences of subtle joy, clarity and non-conceptuality. Mental calm and *intuitive insight* are mutually reinforcing.

merit: The positive energy generated by performing wholesome actions of body, speech and mind that is directed toward awakening; a dynamic power that enables the practitioner to move forward with the requisite energy and overcome obstacles. The accumulation and dedication of merit for the benefit of all sentient beings is one of the "three seals" of any authentic practice in Tibetan Buddhism which involves generating a pure motivation, performing the main practice, and concluding with the dedication.

Milarepa (1040–1123): A great Tibetan yogi and poet; chief disciple of Marpa and teacher of Gampopa.

mudra (Skt.): Usually a symbolic or ritual gesture performed with the hands and fingers, but also used to describe entire sets of practices.

Nagarjuna: Indian Buddhist master and philosopher (circa 2nd century CE).

Naropa (956–1041): Indian Buddhist yogi; disciple of Tilopa and main teacher of Marpa.

ngöndro (Tib.): The preliminary or foundational practices that precede the tantric practices of the *Vajrayana* and the practice of *Mahamudra*.

nirmanakaya (Skt.): Emanation body; one of the *three buddha bodies*. The term used for the physical manifestation of a buddha in this world and, in a deeper sense, for all manifestations in the mind.

nirvana (Skt.): Peace, the cessation of suffering; the opposite of *samsara*. It can refer to a range of states of liberation, from liberation from suffering and its causes all the way to the fully developed timeless awareness and freedom from all veils that characterizes a buddha.

Nyingma (Tib.): One of the four main schools of Tibetan Buddhism. It is the oldest school and was firmly established by Padmasambhava *(Guru Rinpoche)* in the 8th century C.E.

obscurations: Factors in our mind that veil direct awareness of the true nature of phenomena.

phowa (Tib.): The transference of consciousness at death; one of the *Six Dharmas of Naropa*.

puja (Skt.): lit. "offering." Name given to a wide variety of devotional and offering ceremonies practiced in all Buddhist traditions. In the *Vajrayana*, it often refers to the ritual practice of the liturgy of a deity, done alone or as a group.

realms of existence: According to awakened masters such as Gendun Rinpoche who are able to see them, aside from the human and animal realms, there are also other realms of existence of comparatively greater and lesser suffering. All these realms arise out of attachment to the illusion of an 'I'. The greatest degree of suffering is experienced in the hell realms in which beings are trapped in

their projections of paranoia, hatred, persecution, torture and incessant strife. Slightly less but still inconceivably great is the suffering of beings in the hungry ghost realm who due to their lack of generosity suffer from unquenchable thirst and hunger because they cannot take in any food out of revulsion or fear or because it would burn them internally. Animals, too, have to bear many kinds of intense suffering. The realms of lesser suffering and of comparative ease and happiness are those of the gods, the demigods and humans.

refuge, going for: Alternatively "taking refuge." The practice of seeking protection from *samsara* through the sources of refuge, i.e., the Three Jewels of Buddha (awakened mind), Dharma (the teachings of the path of awakening), and Sangha (the competent helpers on the path).

ringsel (Tib.): Relic pearls; small, commonly white pearls of a bone-like consistency that are sometimes found in the cremation ashes of great practitioners.

Rinpoche (Tib.): lit. "precious one." Honorific title that is frequently used to address or refer to great Tibetan lamas.

samadhi (Skt.): A general term for deep meditative absorption.

samaya (Skt.): The sacred links that are formed with the master, the tantric practice and the co-disciples in the Vajrayana; generally implemented in the form of vows and commitments.

sambhogakaya (Skt.): Enjoyment body; one of the *three buddha bodies*. The subtle, visionary manifestation of a buddha and, on another level, the dynamic, creative nature of mind.

samsara (Skt.): Transl. as "cyclic existence." Refers to the world of projections that arises because of clinging to a self. As a result of that clinging sentient beings are propelled by their ignorance, delusions and afflictive emotions and by the karmic force of their past actions to be reborn again and again in various realms of existence until they are liberated through awareness of the true nature of reality.

sangha (Skt.): The community of reliable guides toward awakening; one of the sources of refuge.

siddha (Skt.): Someone who has gained the full accomplishments of the practice of the Vajrayana; an outstanding adept.

Six Dharmas of Naropa: Also called the Six Yogas of Naropa. They comprise the practices of tummo, illusory body, dream, clear light, phowa, and bardo.

skandha (Skt.): lit. "aggregate, heap." The interplay of the five aggregates of form, sensation, discrimination, mental formations, and consciousness constitutes the totality of our physical and mental appearance. The continuous interaction of these five aggregates is erroneously taken to constitute an 'I' or 'self' by our dualistic mind, and identification with these aggregates is the actual cause of suffering.

stupa (Skt.): A structure containing Buddhist relics and used by Buddhists as a place of worship, e.g., through circumambulation.

Tara (Skt.): A female *bodhisattva* and *yidam* who manifests in multiple forms. The two most widely practiced forms are Green Tara who helps all beings in distress and fear and White Tara who confers compassion, healing, and long life. According to the tradition, Tara was born of the tears of *Avalokiteshvara* who despaired over the fact that beings continually fell back into their self-centered behavior patterns and the resulting suffering.

tertön (Tib.): A discoverer of sacred Buddhist treasures concealed in nature (e.g., ritual implements, texts) or in the mind (e.g., practice instructions).

Tilopa (988–1069): Indian mahasiddha; originator of the main Kagyu Mahamudra lineage; teacher of Naropa.

tonglen (Tib.): lit. "giving and taking." The most important *lojong* practice of exchanging self and others, using the in- and out-breath. A meditation practice in which one visualizes taking upon oneself the suffering of all beings and sending them all one's own happiness, wealth, good fortune and merit.

three buddha bodies: Three aspects or levels of manifestation of a buddha as well as three aspects of mind. The *dharmakaya* is the ultimate, empty nature of the awakened mind, the source of all Dharma teachings. The *sambhogakaya* is the dynamic aspect of mind that has the capacity to create manifold illusory appearances and that highly developed practitioners meet in visions and in deep meditation. The *nirmanakaya* is the buddha aspect that manifests in the world to help ordinary beings.

Three Jewels: Buddha, Dharma and Sangha; the sources of *refuge* in the *Mahayana*.

truth body: See *dharmakaya*.

tsampa (Tib.): The flour ground from roasted barley. It is often stirred into hot, buttered tea and constitutes the main staple food of the Tibetan diet.

tulku (Tib.): The reincarnation of an accomplished practitioner.

tummo (Tib.): The yoga of inner heat, based on bodhicitta; one of the practices of the *Six Dharmas of Naropa*.

Vajra (Skt.): An old Indian symbol: the thunderbolt with which the Hindu god Indra is said to be able to split a whole planet; symbol of indestructible strength. The frequently used translation as "diamond" is not completely fitting in this context.

Vajradhara (Skt.): Tib. Dorje Chang, lit. "holder of the vajra." The primordial buddha who represents the primordial, indestructible purity of our mind which is the ultimate source of all enlightened teaching.

Vajrakilaya (Skt.): A wrathful *yidam* and Dharma protector who embodies the awakened activity of all the buddhas, and in particular the power of overcoming obstacles on the path to awakening and purifying the spiritual degeneration of the present age.

Vajrasattva (Skt.): A *yidam* whose practice is widely used to purify negative karma and obscurations of body, speech and mind.

Vajrayana (Skt.): The "Indestructible Vehicle," also called the Path of Secret Mantra or Mantrayana. A form of Buddhist practice within the *Mahayana* that is based on a collection of texts called "tantras" which according to the tradition were taught by sambhogakaya buddhas. Tantric practice relies on renunciation, compassion, and devotion. It unveils the innate buddha nature through the transmission of blessings, prayers, visu-

alization, mantra recitation, and
yogic exercises.

Vajrayogini (Skt.): A *dakini* and
yidam in female form; one of the
most important meditational de-
ities in Tibetan Buddhism.

vira (Skt.): lit. "hero"; also called
a "daka" in Skt. The male coun-
terpart of the *dakini*; a being or
awakened energy that protects
and supports the dharma, its
teachers and practitioners.

yidam (Tib.): A meditational
deity who embodies a particular buddha aspect and on which
we meditate in the *development
stage* of the Vajrayana, principally using our visual imagination and *mantra* recitation, with
the purpose of uniting our mind
with all the aspects of awakened
mind that the yidam represents. A
yidam has the function to "bind
the mind" so that it can realize
its own true nature.

Contact Addresses

Dhagpo Kundrol Ling, France
Retreat monastery, long- and short-term retreats
Website: www.dhagpo-kundreul.org

Men:
Le Bost, F-63640 Biollet, FRANCE
Phone: (33) 0473 52 24 34
Fax: (33) 0473 52 24 36
Email: ktl@dhagpo-kagyu.org

Women:
Laussedat, F-63640 Saint Priest des Champs, FRANCE
Phone: (33) 0473 52 20 92
Fax: (33) 0473 52 21 93
Email: laussedat@dhagpo-kagyu.org

Dhagpo Kagyu Ling, France
International Dharma Center & Study Institute
Landrevie, F-24290 Saint-Léon sur Vézère, FRANCE
Phone: (33) 05 53 50 70 75
Fax: (33) 05 53 50 80 54
Email: dkl@dhagpo-kagyu.org
Website: www.dhagpo-kagyu.org

List of Vajra Songs

Picture Credits

Front cover: Gendun Rinpoche, 1995, Bettina Secker
Back cover: Gendun Rinpoche, 1997, Bernard Boulanger
Page 15:   Gendun Rinpoche, Bernard Boulanger
Page 91:   Gendun Rinpoche, 1996, Bettina Secker
Page 122:   Gendun Rinpoche with mala in his hand, 1975,
                Michel Dieuzaide
Page 196:   Gendun Rinpoche with his hand on his heart,
                Bernard Boulanger
Page 230:   Gendun Rinpoche with Maitripa initiation hat,
                1984, Bernard Boulanger
Page 241:   Gendun Rinpoche, hands in praying mudra,
                photographer unknown

Used with permission